Witches'
Spell-A-Day
Almanac

Holidays & Lore
Spells, Rituals & Meditations

ISBN: 978-0-7387-7204-2
Cover design by the Llewellyn Art Department
Interior art © 2018 Laura Tempest Zakroff: pages 9, 31,
49, 71, 91, 111, 131, 151, 175, 197, 219, 241
Spell icons throughout © 2011 Sherrie Thai
Astrological calculations compiled and programmed by Rique Pottenger,
based on the earlier work of Neil F. Michelsen.

Published by Llewellyn Worldwide LTD
2143 Wooddale Drive
Woodbury MN 55123

Printed in China

Contents

A Note on Magic and Spells

The spells in the *Witches' Spell-A-Day Almanac* evoke everyday magic designed to improve our lives and homes. You needn't be an expert on magic to follow these simple rites and spells; as you will see if you use these spells throughout the year, magic, once mastered, is easy to perform. The only advanced technique required of you is the art of visualization.

Visualization is an act of controlled imagination. If you can call up in your mind a picture of your best friend's face or a flag flapping in the breeze, you can visualize. In magic, visualizations are used to direct and control magical energies. Basically the spellcaster creates a visual image of the spell's desired goal, whether it be perfect health, a safe house, or a protected pet.

Visualization is the basis of all good spells, and as such it is a tool that should be properly used. Visualization must be real in the mind of the spellcaster so it allows him or her to raise, concentrate, and send forth energy to accomplish the spell.

Perhaps when visualizing you'll find that you're doing everything right, but you don't feel anything. This is common, for we haven't been trained to acknowledge—let alone utilize—our magical abilities. Keep practicing, however, for your spells can "take" even if you're not the most experienced natural magician.

You will notice also that many spells in this collection have a some-what light tone. They are seemingly fun and frivolous, filled with rhyme and colloquial speech. This is not to diminish the seriousness of the purpose, but rather to create a relaxed atmosphere for the practitioner. Lightness of spirit helps focus energy; rhyme and common language help the spellcaster remember the words and train the mind where it is need-ed. The intent of this magic is indeed very serious at times, and magic is never to be trifled with.

Even when your spells are effective, magic won't usually sparkle before your very eyes. The test of magic's success is time, not immediate eye-popping results. But you can feel magic's energy for yourself by rubbing your palms together briskly for ten seconds, then holding them a few inches apart. Sense the energy passing through them, the warm tingle in your palms. This is the power raised and used in magic. It comes from within and is perfectly natural.

Among the features of the *Witches' Spell-A-Day Almanac* are an easy-to-use "book of days" format; new spells specifically tailored for each day of the year (and its particular magical, astrological, and historical energies); and additional tips and lore for various days throughout the year—including color correspondences based on planetary influences, obscure and forgotten holidays and festivals, and an incense of the day to help you waft magical energies from the ether into your space. Moon signs, phases, and voids are also included to help you find the perfect time for your rituals and spells. (All times in this book are Eastern Standard Time or Eastern Daylight Time.)

Enjoy your days and have a magical year!

Spell-A-Day Icons

 New Moon

 Meditation, Divination

 Abundance

 Money, Prosperity

 Altar

 Protection

 Balance

 Relationship

 Clearing, Cleaning

 Success

 Garden

 Travel, Communication

 Grab Bag

 Air Element

 Health, Healing

 Earth Element

 Home

 Fire Element

 Heart, Love

 Spirit Element

Water Element

2025 Spells at a Glance by Date and Category*

	Health, Healing	Protection	Success	Heart, Love	Clearing, Cleaning	Balance	Meditation, Divination
Jan.	2, 23, 28	7, 22	4, 16, 18	5, 31	8, 19	11, 14	6, 15, 21
Feb.	6, 13, 18, 21, 25		2, 4, 15, 20, 22	3, 14	26	16, 24	1, 8
March	3, 9, 31	15, 27	17, 30	26	5, 16, 19, 22		1, 4, 8, 12, 24
April	4	15	8, 21		11, 19, 23, 26	22	10, 13, 14, 18, 24
May	14, 28	16, 18, 19, 24	23	2, 15	4	5, 21	6, 7, 9, 11, 25
June	13	6, 12		1, 8	10		2, 15, 18, 26
July	9, 12, 22	11, 19, 20, 27	5, 15	31	8, 16, 28		1, 18, 21, 29
Aug.	16	22, 28, 30	10, 20, 25, 26	19	15		6, 13, 31
Sept.	6, 13, 18	8	15, 16, 27, 28		12, 30	17, 22, 23	4
Oct.		4, 14, 15, 20, 24, 30	18	26	23, 25	1, 5, 19	2, 3, 17, 31
Nov.		13	6, 26	24			1, 12, 14
Dec.	6, 15, 18	3, 7, 29, 30	1, 16	12	8, 10, 24, 28	11, 13, 27	14, 31

*List is not comprehensive.

2025

Year of Spells

January

Happy New Year! The calendar year has begun and even though we may be in the depths of winter (in the Northern Hemisphere) or the height of summer (in the Southern Hemisphere), we stand at the threshold of fifty-two weeks filled with promise. Legend has it that this month is named to honor the Roman god Janus, a god of new beginnings and doorways, but it is also associated with Juno, the primary goddess of the Roman pantheon. Juno was said to be the protectress of the Roman Empire, and Janus (whose twin faces look to both the past and the future simultaneously) encourages new endeavors, transitions, and change in all forms. Since this month marks the beginning of the whole year, we can plant the seeds for long-term goals at this time, carefully plotting the course of our future success.

In the United States, there are three important holidays occurring in January: New Year's Day, Martin Luther King Jr. Day, and Inauguration Day. Each of these days exemplifies powerful change and transition. The dawn of a new year heralds a fresh start, and whether snow-covered or bathed in summer heat, January offers renewed possibilities for all.

Michael Furie

 January 1
Wednesday

1st ♑

☽ v/c 1:02 am

☽ → ♒ 5:50 am

Color of the day: Brown
Incense of the day: Marjoram

New Year's Day – Kwanzaa ends

Bright Beginnings

Happy new year! Here is a simple candle spell to get your year off to a bright start.

You will need one white taper candle and ribbons or strings in an assortment of colors. Each piece should be long enough to wrap around the candle a few times.

On the morning of January 1st, assign a goal to each ribbon or string. The goals should align with the colors based on personal preference. Some suggestions are pink for love, blue for healing, or black for protection. Choose colors that make sense to you and write them down if need be. Wrap each ribbon or string around the candle one at a time while stating its purpose aloud. For example, for the pink string, say:

This year will bring me friendship.

When you're done, your candle will be wrapped in colors. Place this wrapped candle in a window or outdoors where it can absorb the hopeful energy of the first day of the year. Retrieve it after dark and remove the strings. Each day throughout January, safely light the candle for a little while to release its magic until it is gone.

Kate Freuler

NOTES:

 January 2
Thursday

1st ≈

☽ v/c 11:13 pm

Color of the day: Purple
Incense of the day: Clove

hanukkah ends

high Vibrations
Aura-Cleansing Spray

Winter still holds tight with icy fingers and frigid breath, but we can raise our vibrations in preparation for new goals and possibilities that come with a new year. Aura-cleansing spray is an easy, smokeless alternative to smoke cleansing. It can remove the negative gunk and low-vibrational energy that can accumulate over the winter holidays. You will need:

- A 4-ounce glass spray bottle
- 4½ tablespoons water
- 1½ tablespoons witch hazel
- 20–25 drops lavender essential oil (for calming energy)
- 20–25 drops cedar essential oil (for cleansing and courage)
- A small amethyst crystal

Add all ingredients to the spray bottle and shake to mix. *Optional:* Write words of intention on an adhesive label to stick on your bottle for added power. You might choose words like flourish, strength, thrive, abundance, courageous, resilient, or renew. Use the spray before meditation, high-tension social situations, spellwork, or any time your energy feels off. As you spritz, say something like this:

I am exactly where I need to be.

My vibe is clear and true.

I release all negativity.

My light is shining through.

Monica Crosson

NOTES:

 # January 3
Friday

1st ♒

☽ → ♓ 10:21 am

Color of the day: Rose
Incense of the day: Violet

An Abundance of Options

You'll need a jar or box and slips of colored paper. Consecrate the container by holding it as you intone:

I charge this vessel as a multiplier of options, all in accordance with the highest good, harming none.

Visualize it filling with divinely intelligent energy. This spell is incremental, so to begin, choose a situation and brainstorm ideas for changing it. Get creative, even if some ideas seem a little far-fetched. Choose your favorites and write them on individual slips of paper, adding them to the jar.

Repeat this process with new situations as they arise, adding more options to your vessel where they will energetically multiply. Whenever you feel stuck, shake the jar and draw a slip (return it to the jar when done). Even if you don't choose to use that particular idea, it can spark creative thinking, generating fresh options. You can burn some of the slips ritualistically (and safely!) to free up space as needed.

Melissa Tipton

 # January 4
Saturday

1st ♓

Color of the day: Black
Incense of the day: Magnolia

Dream Key Spell

The first month of the year is the perfect time to set new intentions about what you want to accomplish over the course of the next several months. Find a key—a new key, an old key, or even a skeleton key—and designate it as your key of the year. If you want to achieve a new dream, this key can be something you use all year long. You can wear the key around your neck, carry it in your pocket, or leave it in a special place on your altar. Keys are magical and will help open new doors to manifest success in the future. The key is a good reminder of your personal power and the ability to find the doors necessary to accomplish your goals. These words can help magnify your intention:

With this key, I will attract to me

The doors and opportunities for my dreams to manifest, so mote it be.

Sapphire Moonbeam

 ♥ **January 5**
Sunday

 👁 **January 6**
Monday

1st ♓

☽ v/c 9:30 am

☽ → ♈ 2:01 pm

Color of the day: Yellow
Incense of the day: Hyacinth

Courage in Love Spell

Use this spell to gain courage in opening your heart to love and pursuing your happiness. You'll need a piece of clear quartz or rose quartz, some cinnamon, some powdered ginger, and a small pouch or scrap of fabric. Take the materials outside under the moon and hold the quartz in your hand. Think of the quartz as your own heart, and feel the love you have to offer flowing out of your heart and into the crystal. Next, envision the loving experiences you wish to have and the feelings that will come with them. Sprinkle a generous amount of cinnamon and ginger onto the crystal. Place the crystal and spices in the small pouch, or wrap them in the piece of fabric, tying the corners together. Hold the bundle toward the moon as you state three times:

*Great moon above, I say yes to
love! I walk without doubt. I act
without fear. With unending
courage, I say yes to love here!*

Carry the bundle with you.

Melanie Marquis

1st ♈

2nd Quarter 6:56 pm

Color of the day: Silver
Incense of the day: Hyssop

An Epiphany Meditation

Today is the Christian holiday of Epiphany. Most Western Christian faiths observe this as the day that the Magi visited the baby Jesus. It also marks the day of Jesus's baptism. The word *epiphany* means a sudden understanding or insight into a matter. This would be a good day to meditate on issues facing you and how you may solve them.

Sit at your altar with pen and paper. Ground and center. Think about what's going on with you. Begin to make a list of these issues, even if it sounds ridiculous. Stop when you feel like it.

Go over the list. Do any solutions come to mind? Leave the list on your altar. Come back to it in a few days. Go over your list again. Cross out anything that's not important. If you want to, meditate again on important matters as you search for solutions.

Refer to your list from time to time. If you finish working through your list, discard it.

James Kambos

January 7
Tuesday

2nd ♈

☽ v/c 4:16 pm

☽ → ♉ 5:11 pm

Color of the day: White
Incense of the day: Ylang-ylang

Against a Slandering Enemy

To break ties with someone who is speaking lies about you, use this spell to burn yourself out of their memory. Perform this ritual when the Moon is in Aries—before it moves into Taurus at 5:11 p.m. EST. You will need:

- Five of Spades playing card (from a new deck)
- A black ink pen or marker
- Heatproof dish
- Matches or lighter

With a black pen or marker, write your full name (First, Middle, Last) across the central spade on the playing card. Beginning on the bottom left spade, connect the spades with a black line in a clockwise direction. Write the full name of your enemy outside this line, on each side of the card. Burn the playing card in a heatproof dish (preferably outside because of the smoke).

Recite this while burning:

Three rings of fire surround me. Burn away my name. As the ash is blown away by the wind, so let my name blow away out of your mind.

Take the remaining ash outside and toss it into the air.

Brandon Weston

Notes:

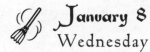

January 8
Wednesday

2nd ♉

Color of the day: Topaz
Incense of the day: Honeysuckle

Shake It Off

A very hectic time of the year has just passed. Even those who revel in resolutions may find baggage, anxiety, or other negativity still hanging around from the last couple of months. Go outside, even if it's cold, and find a spot where your feet touch ground or snow (not asphalt or concrete) and plant yourself firmly in position. Give yourself a good steady base and then begin shaking your hands, your arms, and roll your neck in all directions. Add in a chant of "revive my life." Twist at the waist as you give all these body parts a good shaking. Visualize residual negative energy flinging from your body, like a dog shakes off water. Keep your feet firmly planted, remaining grounded while you let fly any stagnant energy.

Visualize clean, crisp, renewed energy snaking up your body through your legs to cleanse and replace what was lost. Take several deep breaths, releasing through your mouth with a big *whooooosh* to finish letting it all go.

Kerri Connor

January 9
Thursday

2nd ♉

☽ v/c 5:50 pm

☽ → ♊ 8:07 pm

Color of the day: Crimson
Incense of the day: Apricot

Apricot Warmth

Today is National Apricot Day. Apricots are associated with warmth, hope, love, soothing, beauty, and wisdom. For this spell, gather these supplies:

- A blanket and pillows
- 1 white tealight candle in a cauldron
- Matches
- The Ace of Cups, Sun, and Nine of Pentacles Tarot cards
- A citrine stone
- An apricot-flavored drink
- Fresh or dried apricots

Create a cozy nest with pillows and blankets, with a safe space for the tealight. Place the tealight in the cauldron and light it, saying:

I bask in the apricot's warmth.

Set the Sun card on the ground in front of the tealight, the Ace of Cups to its left, and the Nine of Pentacles to its right. Place the citrine on the Sun card.

Eat and drink, visualizing the joy, creativity, and stability in the cards, enhanced by the apricot's power.

Let the candle burn down safely, or relight it over three days until it burns down. Carry the citrine with you until summer. Plant the apricot pit on Imbolc.

Cerridwen Iris Shea

NOTES:

January 10
Friday

2nd ♊

Color of the day: Pink
Incense of the day: Mint

National houseplant Appreciation Day

Today is National Houseplant Appreciation Day. Plants relate to the element of earth. Houseplants bring a little bit of nature indoors. There are many ways to observe this holiday. Talk to your houseplants. Prune overgrown plants and remove any dead leaves. Share snapshots of your plants online. For a winter mood booster, visit a greenhouse or other plant shop and spend time among luxurious plants. If you have room, buy yourself a new houseplant.

Now is also a good time to cast a spell for nurturing your plants. You'll need a green stone, such as aventurine or moss agate, big enough that it won't get lost on your plant shelf. Hold the stone and say:

Stone of earth and jewel of green,

Make my plants the strongest seen.

Let them thrive and let them grow

Ever green despite the snow.

Place the stone among the pots on your plant shelf. It will help keep them healthy and green.

Elizabeth Barrette

January 11
Saturday

2nd ♊

☽ v/c 7:03 pm
☽ → ♋ 11:24 pm

Color of the day: Brown
Incense of the day: Sage

Spell for Justice

Suspected witch Phyllis Money was acquitted on this day in 1694 in Westmoreland, Virginia. In her honor, perform a working for justice for yourself or for a worthy cause.

Crystals associated with fairness include sapphire, red jasper, blue lace agate, and iron pyrite. Herbs believed to bring about justice are basil, mint, sage, and juniper. Choose one of these stones and one of the herbs and place them in a small cloth charm bag made of blue fabric.

Light frankincense incense while visualizing a fair, right, just outcome for the situation. Write your desires for justice on a small piece of paper with red ink. Slip the written request into the little cloth pouch, and tie it closed with red thread as you voice your desire aloud. Carry this bag with you during events related to the situation and for a week afterward.

A.C. Fisher Aldag

▽ January 12
Sunday

2nd ♋

Color of the day: Gold
Incense of the day: Almond

Sunday Sweetness Spell

I love Sundays. It probably started when I was a kid and my family ate Sunday dinner with my grandparents. The richness of roast beef and Yorkshire pudding mingles in my memory with the knowledge of my grandparents' love. Today, let's do a Sunday sweetness spell.

It is your choice: you can choose either an activity that delights you or a special food treat—bonus points if it's sweet. Make time today to pause mindfully, take a few deep breaths, and savor the sweetness of that moment or of that edible treat. As you exhale, sigh:

Oh my, this is so sweet.

Feel the flush of pleasure flow to your body, mind, spirit, and emotions.

It's time now to think of where in your life you would most benefit from some added sweetness. Breathe and exhale sweet energy mindfully into that area, joyfully affirming:

Oh my, this is so sweet.

Dallas Jennifer Cobb

☾ January 13
Monday

2nd ♋

Full Moon 5:27 pm
☽ v/c 11:46 pm

Color of the day: White
Incense of the day: Rosemary

Create a Crystal Battery

Let's tap into the power of the new year and full moon today. We start the new year full of energy and hope for new prospects, so it would be nice if we could capture part of that energy for use later in the year. We can create a crystal "battery" that will store energy that we can use whenever we need it throughout the year.

You will need a crystal to charge. I would recommend a clear quartz, but any crystal that you feel connected to will work. You can sit outside, or if it is too cold, you can do this by a window under the light of the full moon. Take the crystal and sit with it in your hands. Take a deep breath and let it out. Repeat twice. Each time you exhale, feel the energy move from you into the crystal. As you complete the transfer, say:

*Store energy within, so I can
tap into it in order to begin.*

Charlynn Walls

 # January 14
Tuesday

3rd ♋

☽ → ♌ 4:12 am

Color of the day: Black
Incense of the day: Geranium

Disappointments and Gratitudes

We're in the depth of winter, with its long, dark nights and short days, and it's a perfect time to reflect on the light and dark within our own lives—the gratitudes and the disappointments.

You'll need a black candle, a white candle, a saucer, matches, a fireproof bowl, a pen, and two pieces of paper.

Write your disappointments on one piece of paper. What has not materialized as you had hoped? Who or what have you lost? What has caused you pain?

On the second piece, write your gratitudes. What are you thankful for? Name your strengths, gifts, and successes.

Set the black candle on the saucer and light it. Speak your disappointments aloud, then put that piece of paper into the bowl and set it aflame. As it burns, extinguish the candle, leaving the disappointments in ashes.

Light the white candle. Speak your gratitudes aloud, feeling the light and warmth as you do. Be grateful for the light's brilliance and for the light of your own life. Keep the second piece of paper on your altar, reading it often.

Susan Pesznecker

NOTES:

January 15
Wednesday

3rd ♌

☽ v/c 11:10 pm

Color of the day: Yellow
Incense of the day: Lilac

Create a Sacred Mask

We are just a couple of weeks into the new year—yay, we made it! Today's spell is about creating a sacred mask to help us embody our divinity throughout the rest of the year. This can be a mask that you like to wear for rituals, when celebrating sabbats, or just whenever you want to connect more deeply to your sacred self.

Get your favorite craft supplies, such as glitter, feathers, and beads, and a simple face mask from the craft store. Set up your sacred space and set your intention to bring creativity and divinity in so that you can make a beautiful mask (or multiple masks if you like) that represents your sacred self. Allow yourself to create without judgment or expectation. Just allow the magic to flow through you. When you are finished, give yourself a little fashion show and show off your fantastic magical creation!

Amanda Lynn

 # January 16
Thursday

3rd ♌

☽ → ♍ 11:46 am

Color of the day: Green
Incense of the day: Nutmeg

Obstacle Remover Spell

Have you ever peeled an orange to eat and discovered it had lots of seeds? Perhaps you find them inconvenient because they must be painstakingly picked out before you can enjoy the delicious fruit. Sometimes situations in life can be the same: you're on the way to a good thing, but there are annoying obstacles in the way. These obstacles could be miscommunication, schedule conflicts, or other small inconveniences. When you find yourself stumbling over roadblocks on the path toward your goal, try this orange seed spell to remove those bumps in the road.

Peel the orange and split it into segments. Use a knife, your fingers, or whatever suits you to remove all the seeds one by one. As you do so, contemplate the issues that stand in the way of your goal. Name them out loud if you like. Gather all the seeds in the palm of your hand while imagining the obstacles. Throw the seeds in the garbage or compost, symbolically casting away the issues. As you eat the remaining orange slices,

visualize your situation as you wish it to be, free of all the things that were holding you back.

Kate Freuler

NOTES:

January 17
Friday

3rd ♍

Color of the day: White
Incense of the day: Thyme

Potent Sigil Magic

Write down your intention as concisely as possible, then cross out all vowels and repeated consonants. On scratch paper, arrange the remaining letters into a symbol, making sure each letter touches at least one other letter. You can layer letters on top of each other, turn them upside down, etc. For a witchy boost, first transcribe them into a magical alphabet (do an online search for "magical scripts") and then arrange them into a symbol.

The sigil is done when you like the way it looks. Play around with designs until one feels alive and energetically zingy. *Tip:* Try rotating the paper. Sometimes a sigil will feel blah one way and suddenly light up when you flip it around. You can copy the sigil onto colored card stock using a gold or silver paint pen if you want to get fancy.

Activate your sigil by raising energy (chant, bring yourself to orgasm, dance, etc.) while staring at it, sending energy into the symbol. Place it on your altar, and let it work its magic!

Melissa Tipton

January 18
Saturday

3rd ♏

☽ v/c 9:01 pm

☽ → ♎ 10:33 pm

Color of the day: Indigo

Incense of the day: Sandalwood

Good Luck Broom Spell

January is a great time to add a broom above your entryway door to boost the luck and protection for your house and everyone in it for the year. Brooms help sweep away stagnant energy and dispel energy that is not welcome in your home. Add your own magical touch by making a broom with fallen branches and twigs from a nearby forest. If you buy a broom instead, a cinnamon-scented one is a good way to enhance your good fortune. If you don't have access to a cinnamon broom, you can always add your favorite essential oil scent or even fresh herbs/flower petals to the broom. When you walk across the threshold of your house, the pleasant scent will reinforce the intention and remind you of the protection and good luck broom. These words are a short blessing to say once the broom is placed above the entryway:

Now that I have this broom in place,

May it bring good luck and protection to my space.

Sapphire Moonbeam

 **January 19**
Sunday

3rd ♎

☉ → ♒ 3:00 pm

Color of the day: Orange

Incense of the day: Frankincense

A Pine Clearing Spell

Spiritually, pine has clearing and cleansing qualities. Use it at this time of year to clear your home of any negative energy. This spell will cleanse your space. You'll need one small evergreen branch of any kind.

Begin by opening all curtains or blinds on all windows. Go into each room and fan the evergreen branch toward each window and exterior door. Visualize any negative energy leaving. As you do this, say:

Dark energy, be gone to the north, east, west, and south.

Only light and joy remain in this house!

Breathe deeply. Discard the evergreen branch or compost it.

James Kambos

 January 20
Monday

3rd ♎

☽ v/c 11:34 pm

Color of the day: Ivory
Incense of the day: Lily

Martin Luther King Jr. Day –
Inauguration Day

I have a Dream

On this day we celebrate the life and legacy of Rev. Martin Luther King Jr. and inaugurate the 47th president of the United States. Using a fireproof dish or candleholders, light one green candle for healing and one blue one for peace. Recite and meditate on these words from Rev. King's "I Have a Dream" speech, delivered on Aug. 28, 1963, at the Lincoln Memorial:

> *Even though we face the difficulties of today and tomorrow, I still have a dream. It is a dream deeply rooted in the American dream. I have a dream that one day this nation will rise up and live out the true meaning of its creed: "We hold these truths to be self-evident, that all men are created equal."*

(Feel free to add in "women" or adjust your statement to "all humans are created equal.") When done, recite these words again as you blow out your candles, allowing your statements to be carried away through the air.

Kerri Connor

 January 21
Tuesday

3rd ♎

☽ → ♏ 11:20 am

4th Quarter 3:31 pm

Color of the day: Gray
Incense of the day: Bayberry

Clear Answer Candle Divination

Use this divination when you need a clear yes or no answer or guidance when deciding between two distinct options. Take a small taper-shaped purple or white spell candle and hold it in your hands as you think of your question. Place the candle in a holder on a firesafe dish. Use a marker or eyeliner pencil to make marks on the candleholder to demarcate two halves. Let each side represent one of the two choices you're facing, or use one side to represent the "yes" and the other side to represent the "no" answer. Light the candle and let it burn down completely. Observe the melted wax formations. On which side of the candleholder did most of the wax fall? Whichever side the wax favored indicates the answer to your question.

Melanie Marquis

January 22
Wednesday

4♓ ♏

Color of the day: Brown
Incense of the day: Lavender

A Protection Oil

Utilizing the protective qualities of Scorpio and Mars, this oil protects against all who might try to harm you magically. It's especially good against works of illusion or glamouring, as well as influences from the dead. You will need:

- Olive oil (or your preferred carrier oil)
- A bowl
- A sewing needle (unused), or you can use a long thorn, like those from the honey locust tree (*Gleditsia triacanthos*) or certain cacti
- Basil essential oil
- A bottle or canning jar

Pour the olive oil into the bowl. You can use as much as you'd like. Just make sure you have a bottle or jar to store it in.

Face the east and place the bowl in front of you on a tabletop. Take your needle or thorn in your right hand, and use it to stir the oil three times in a clockwise circle. Repeat these words each time you stir:

Armor on my body. From all evil curses. From all works of the dead. Be swords. Be spears.

Add a few drops of the basil essential oil to the bowl, then stir three more circles while repeating the charm another three times. When you're finished, bottle the oil. To use, rub some of the oil onto your hands and feet while reciting the charm three times.

Brandon Weston

NOTES:

January 23
Thursday

4ᵗ♏
☽ v/c 7:03 pm
☽ → ♐ 11:29 pm

Color of the day: Purple
Incense of the day: Myrrh

Graceful Imperfections

We have all made mistakes that have left us feeling inadequate in some way. They haunt us as we try to sleep, reminding us of our shortcomings and filling our heads with guilt. This spell reminds us to find the grace within us to wash away our imperfections and align with the energy of self-love.

You will need:

- A few dried rose petals

- A glass half-filled with tap water

- A piece of scrap paper

- A washable marker

Before you go to bed, drop the rose petals into the glass of tap water. Stir clockwise three times with the index finger of your power (dominant) hand to imbue it with loving energy.

Write guilty thoughts, minced words, or stumbled deeds on the scrap paper with the washable marker, and drop the paper into the glass. As you watch the words dissipate in the water, say:

I forgive and I forget because I love me.

With grace and love, I release guilt, shame, and inadequacies.
Monica Crosson

Notes:

January 24
Friday

4ᵗ♐

Color of the day: Coral
Incense of the day: Vanilla

A Compliment Goes a Long Way

National Compliment Day, which is celebrated today, is a great way to spread positive energy to yourself and others.

First, look in a mirror and stare deep into your own eyes. Take a deep breath and exhale. Take another deep breath and, as you exhale, say:

You are amazing.

Repeat that until you believe it.

As you go about your day, find reasons to give people compliments, be they family, coworkers, or strangers. It could be anything from "I love that color on you" to "You did a great job on that project" to "What a lovely cup of tea you made. Thank you!"

Do this without expecting anything in return. Revel in the joy of telling someone something good.

Before bedtime, look in the mirror again and say:

You are extraordinary.

Repeat it until you feel it.

Cerridwen Iris Shea

 January 25
Saturday

4ᵗ♐

Color of the day: Blue
Incense of the day: Pine

Robert Burns Supper

January 25 is celebrated by Scots people as the Robert Burns Supper, named for the man regarded as the national poet of Scotland. Friends gather to eat "neeps and taties" (turnips and potatoes) and toast Burns with glasses of whisky.

This is a wonderful time to enhance creativity for yourself and your friends. Carry stones that represent inspiration, such as aventurine, carnelian, labradorite, or amethyst. Call upon the poetic muses as each attendee tells a story, sings a song, or writes a short poem in Burns's honor.

A.C. Fisher Aldag

January 26
Sunday

4th ♐

☽ v/c 4:40 am

☽ → ♑ 8:43 am

Color of the day: Amber
Incense of the day: Heliotrope

Home Blessing Spray

Smoke ceremonies to bless and cleanse the home are very popular nowadays, but what if you don't like all that smoke? If you have sensitive lungs or just don't enjoy the smell, an easy alternative is to create your own room spray with water and a few essential oils.

This spray is meant as a general positive energy booster. It can be used to uplift the mood in your home and keep your house smelling fresh.

Gather these materials:

- A small spray bottle (available at dollar stores)
- Water to fill the bottle
- 3 drops pine oil
- 3 drops sage oil
- 3 drops peppermint oil
- 1 small tumbled quartz crystal

Place the water, oils, and crystal in the spray bottle and cap tightly.

Take the bottle to a warm, sunny spot and hold it up so the rays are touching it. Say:

Blessings and happiness, safe and sound, my home is a place where good vibes abound.

Spray around the house as needed. Don't spray directly onto furniture or textiles, as it may stain.

Kate Freuler

NOTES:

 # January 27
Monday

4th ♑

Color of the day: Lavender
Incense of the day: Neroli

Altar Dressing

Winter is a good time to take care of your altar. Periodically you should take everything off of it, clean up, and give it some attention. Start by removing any altar tools like candles, bowls, crystals, or wands. If you have one or more drawers for storing tools and supplies, then empty that too. Clean each of those items with a suitable cleaner or just wipe them down with a soft cloth. Take off the old altar cloth, then wash it or hang it to air out. Clean the altar table or shelf with appropriate furniture polish. Then say:

> Altar clean and altar clear,
>
> Hold the spells that I hold dear.
>
> By the moon and by the sun,
>
> You support all I have done.

Now put on a clean altar cloth. Return your altar tools and supplies to their usual places. If possible, include a vase with a bouquet of fresh flowers. Your altar is now ready for use again.

Elizabeth Barrette

January 28
Tuesday

4th ♑
☽ v/c 10:48 am
☽ → ♒ 2:31 pm

Color of the day: Maroon
Incense of the day: Ginger

Tea for Imbolc

With Imbolc coming in just a few days, I like to use this time to start doing a ritual cleansing of my body and spirit. To do this, I drink herbal teas. Today's herbal tea is made of two ingredients associated with the goddess Brigid: rosemary and dandelion root. Not only are they helpful in detoxifying the body, but they also promote the purification of the spirit. If you don't grow these herbs normally, a good option is to get these items at your local market. You can get the rosemary in the produce section, and can most likely find dandelion root herbal tea bags. Gather your herbs and let them steep in boiled water for 10 to 15 minutes. While they steep, recite the following chant:

> Herbs of Imbolc, blessed tea,
>
> I drink you in for purity.
>
> I call you in this magic hour,
>
> Heal me with your cleansing power.
>
> By sacred water and sacred flame,
>
> Nourish me in Brigid's name.

Slowly drink your tea and feel the healing powers of Brigid and Imbolc come to you. Enjoy!

Amanda Lynn

NOTES:

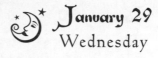 **January 29**
Wednesday

4th ♒

New Moon 7:36 am

Color of the day: White
Incense of the day: Bay laurel

Lunar New Year (Snake)

The Circular Energy of Generosity and Abundance

Today marks the Lunar New Year of the Wood Snake, traditionally a day to practice abundance magic. The Cantonese greeting of "Kung hei fat choy" loosely means "Wishing you success and prosperity."

When my daughter was small, we went to new year celebrations in Toronto's Chinatown. Elders often gave my daughter delicate red and gold envelopes with folded money inside. Such delight on her face when she opened it!

The Wiccan Rede teaches that what we send out returns to us threefold, so let's cast a new moon Generosity and Abundance Spell, knowing that what we give, we receive, and what we send out always comes back. Let's initiate the circular energy of generosity and abundance.

Fold cash into a few envelopes. Decorate and charge them with red and gold. Give them away to people with the greeting "Kung hei fat choy," setting the circular energy in motion.

Dallas Jennifer Cobb

January 30
Thursday

1st ♒

☽ v/c 6:29 am

☽ → ♓ 5:52 pm

Color of the day: Turquoise
Incense of the day: Jasmine

hearth Blessing

The hearth is the center of your home. It may be a fireplace, a woodstove, a central furnace, or even your kitchen range. Wherever it is, it deserves a blessing.

Begin by cleaning your hearth—a gesture of care and respect. Perhaps your fireplace or woodstove needs the chimney or flue swept and cleaned, and the floor in front of it swept or polished. A furnace may need its filter changed or vents vacuumed out, while your range might need to be cleaned and polished. Some of these are safety measures as well.

As you work, speak words of thanks to the hearth for its gifts of service and protection.

Next, offer a blessing to your hearth. Purify it by flicking salt water in each corner as you say:

Sacred fire, center of warmth,

Service given consistently,

Serving me through sun and storm,

Blessing made, so mote it be.

Susan Pesznecker

January 31
Friday

1st ♓

Color of the day: Pink
Incense of the day: Rose

Drawing in Love

Friday is the day of the week for tapping into the power associated with Venus and love. In order not to negatively affect someone else's free will, you can simply cast a spell to draw potential love to yourself.

For this spell, you will need a small sachet in which to place a few herbs and a piece of paper. You can make the sachet from leftover fabric, or you can purchase a drawstring bag. On a piece of paper, write down all the qualities you are looking for in a romantic partner. Fold the paper and place it in the sachet, then add herbs that symbolize love. Some choices may come from your pantry, including cinnamon, rosemary, and basil.

After adding all the herbs you want to include, say:

I draw to myself the love to me that is predisposed

As I draw the strings of this bag closed.

Place the bag near where you sleep until you have a new love in your life.

Charlynn Walls

February

The word *February* is based on the Latin *februa* and refers to the Roman festival of purification of the same name. This festival later became integrated with February's infamous Lupercalia. Since ancient times, February has been observed as a month of cleansing, cleaning, purification, and preparation for the warm months ahead. We see the Celtic Imbolg (Candlemas) celebrated in February to perpetuate the summoning of solar light. In many parts of the world at this time, the promise of sunlight seems bleak, even imaginary. The world around us is slowly awakening from its wintery slumber, and some semblance of excitement begins to grow in the hearts of those attuned to the seasonal tides.

Daylight hours are short in February, so this time of year can sometimes feel depressive. We must actively cultivate our inner light through regular exercise, solid sleep, meditation, yoga, ritual, studying, artwork, and planning ahead for the year. When performing magickal work this month, remember that your energy levels may be lower than usual and you must summon your own inner light to strengthen and illuminate your efforts. Do whatever it takes to stay on top of your game, keep energized, cultivate happiness, and embrace February's cleansing rebirth!

Raven Digitalis

February 1
Saturday

1st ♓

☽ v/c 5:06 pm

☽ → ♈ 8:10 pm

Color of the day: Gray
Incense of the day: Patchouli

Amethyst Sorting for Clarity

Before Imbolc stirs, I like to work with amethyst to sort worries. You will need an amethyst for this spell. Sit where you will not be disturbed for twenty minutes.

Close your eyes and let your thoughts whirl. Give your monkey mind freedom to roam over stresses and worries.

Count to ten.

Pick up the amethyst. Place it in one palm, and cup the other palm over it.

Breathe, visualizing a set of cubbyholes, with the amethyst glowing, brightening, as the chaos settles down. Those pesky concerns climb into their own slots, compartmentalizing themselves.

Sit quietly until the twenty minutes are up, then place your hands on the ground and drain away excess energy. Keep the amethyst in a safe place.

Your worries and stresses are now organized. When you are ready to deal with each one individually, hold the amethyst and let its light lead you to clarity as you work on the issue.

Cerridwen Iris Shea

February 2
Sunday

1st ♈

Color of the day: Orange
Incense of the day: Marigold

Imbolc – Groundhog Day

Self-Mastery Spell

My favorite movie is *Groundhog Day*. It is an encapsulated version of my own life. I repeat things over and over until I achieve some mastery and am finally able to change the outcome of the scenario. Today, use Groundhog Day energy to empower your own spell of self-mastery. Make a quick list:

- What habits support and sustain your well-being?
- Who are your "people," with whom you feel safe, supported, and accepted?
- What do you need to do daily to feel well?

Knowing what and who uplift us can enable us to turn to them versus reaching for something that lowers our energy. Be like Bill Murray and set out to bring mastery to your life. Know what your supports are. Choose, in the moment, to be honest, kind, friendly, and helpful. With practice and of course repetition, we make magic of self-mastery.

Dallas Jennifer Cobb

 February 3
Monday

1st ♈

☽ v/c 5:19 am

☽ → ♉ 10:33 pm

Color of the day: Ivory
Incense of the day: Narcissus

Note to Self

In today's fast-paced world of social media influencers, it's hard to feel like we are "enough" just being who we are. Today's spell is about reflecting on the things we enjoy about ourselves and putting them away to read at a later date. These "notes to self" can be anything—a good memory of when you were recognized for an achievement, a physical compliment, a compliment about your character, etc.—so get creative!

Set up your space. Light a candle or incense, and focus on the best qualities you have. When you feel you have written enough notes, either put them in an envelope for safekeeping to pull out when you're feeling blue, or stash them in hiding places to come upon for a little surprise. I like to put mine in random books or in my sock drawer.

Amanda Lynn

February 4
Tuesday

1st ♉

Color of the day: Scarlet
Incense of the day: Basil

Conjuring Confidence

Today is Rosa Parks Day, celebrated in honor of the acclaimed civil rights activist on her birthday. To evoke the qualities of courage, fortitude, and self-confidence exhibited by Ms. Parks, hold a hematite crystal in your dominant hand (the hand you write with) while raising your athame (ritual blade) aloft. State firmly:

I am confident! I am brave!
I have tenacity!

Add any other qualities you wish to embody. Visualize yourself surrounded by golden light. Keep the hematite stone on your person when entering situations where self-confidence is needed.

A.C. Fisher Aldag

 # February 5
Wednesday

1st ♉

2nd Quarter 3:02 am

☽ v/c 10:29 pm

Color of the day: Yellow
Incense of the day: Lilac

Make It Rain

Have fun raising energy for this easy, no ingredients money spell. All you need is your favorite song that has the word "money" in the title, a way to play it, and a place to work your magic. Make sure the words of the song fit with having money and not losing it, as we want to be sending the right message out into the universe!

Raise energy dancing to and singing your song. Give it your all and cut loose! You know what they say: dance like no one is watching. As you dance, imagine yourself already in possession of the money you seek. What do you need it for? How will you spend it? Visualize yourself doing these things while you dance and sing. When the song ends, release your built-up energy into the universe around you and trust it to bring to you the funds that you need. Give yourself time to sit down, relax, and ground afterward.

Kerri Connor

 # February 6
Thursday

2nd ♉

☽ → ♊ 1:44 am

Color of the day: White
Incense of the day: Carnation

A Potion for Good Health

This simple potion will help you guard and preserve your health during the final weeks of winter.

Squeeze the juice of half a lemon into a sturdy mug. Add a large spoonful of honey, ½ teaspoon grated fresh ginger, and a sprinkle of red pepper flakes. Fill with near-boiling water and add a cinnamon stick as a swizzle, stirring sunwise (clockwise).

Sip your tonic while it's very hot, imagining the benefits of the lemon (vitamin C), the honey (antiviral properties), the ginger (antioxidants), and the cinnamon (antiinflammatory), each of which will boost your health. Breathe the steam as you sip, and offer this charm:

This brew is cleansing me.

This brew is nurturing me.

This brew is strengthening me.

This brew is filling me with well-being.

I am magically empowered.

Susan Pesznecker

February 7
Friday

2nd ♊

Color of the day: Purple
Incense of the day: Orchid

Incense to Ease Communication

Burn this incense when you are struggling to communicate your thoughts, feelings, or ideas. This can include improving communication with a partner, child, coworker, boss, etc. You can also use this to improve communication with spirits, guides, ancestors, or deities if you can't hear/feel their messages. You will need:

- A black pen or marker
- A piece of white paper, 5 inches square
- A silver bowl or a bowl with a silver item placed inside so that it directly touches the paper (a silver ring, chain, etc.)
- 1 part dill seed, dried
- 1 part fennel seed, dried
- 1 part frankincense resin
- Mortar and pestle
- A jar or bag

Using a black pen or marker, write your full name (First, Middle, Last) on each edge of the paper square. Write your name on one edge, turn clockwise, write your name, turn

clockwise, etc. Then draw four arrows that each begin in the center of the square and go outward toward each of the four corners. Place the paper in a silver bowl or in a regular bowl with a silver item touching it. Crush and mix the three incense ingredients together (slightly—don't powder), then pour the mixture onto the square in the bowl. Say three times:

My words, the words of the sun.
My words, the words of the wind.
My words, the words of the stars.

Leave overnight, then the next day, package the incense in a jar or bag along with the paper square. When it is burning, close your eyes and visualize a warm white light radiating from your throat.

Brandon Weston

February 8
Saturday

2nd ♊

☽ v/c 2:52 am

☽ → ♋ 6:04 am

Color of the day: Blue
Incense of the day: Rue

Dream a Little Dream
Prophetic Dream Sachet

Herb-filled sachets, when tucked near your pillow as you slumber, are a wonderful way to induce sleep, encourage pleasant dreams, or release anxiety. Another way to use them in your craft is to induce prophetic dreaming.

Before you go to sleep, use a dream journal to write down questions you would like the answer to. Then tuck your herbal sachet near your pillow and see what your dreams reveal. Remember to write down your revelations as soon as you awaken so you won't forget them.

To make a prophetic dream sachet, you will need:

- A 3-to-4-inch purple organza drawstring bag
- 2 parts mugwort
- 1 part sage
- 1 part lavender
- 1 small amethyst stone

Mix the herbs together and fill the bag with them. Add the amethyst.

Charge your bag by saying something like this:

Bring me visions, second sight,

Dreams of the future on this night.

Other herbs to consider include yarrow, crocus, peppermint, bay, ginkgo, borage, thyme, and cinnamon.

Monica Crosson

NOTES:

February 9
Sunday

2nd ♋

Color of the day: Gold
Incense of the day: Eucalyptus

Skull Charm for Intelligence

If skulls are part of your fashion choices, this charm will blend flawlessly into your wardrobe. Skulls aren't necessarily a symbol of death. They can also be a symbol of intelligence, as they hold and protect our brains. This spell encourages logic, learning, intelligence, and study.

You will need a purple candle and a piece of skull jewelry or a skull trinket that is small enough to put in your pocket.

Safely light the purple candle and hold the skull near the flame, without allowing it to touch. Let the skull become just slightly warm from the light of the candle. Place the skull against your forehead and feel the charm on your skin. Imagine the heat entering your own skull and permeating your brain, lighting it up with a gentle glow. This glow is your brain awakening, opening up, and absorbing and storing new information. Extinguish the candle.

Wear or carry the skull charm in learning scenarios like school or job training. Repeat the process with the candle as needed.

Kate Freuler

February 10
Monday

2nd ♋

☽ v/c 8:49 am
☽ → ♌ 12:01 pm

Color of the day: Gray
Incense of the day: Lilac

Twilight Wish Spell

No matter what time of year it is, when you are outside in the evening there is a truly magical time that occurs between day and night. Twilight happens when the sun has set but there is still a golden glow on the horizon. In these moments when the light is close to fading, right before the night sky turns dark and the stars start to shine, there is magic in the air! This is a perfect time to make a special wish, especially if you feel stuck in the current phase of your life, hoping for a new, exciting time period to begin. It is up to you to decide when the time is right for this spell. Once you have determined what you want to wish for, and have made your words clear and concise, use these words during twilight:

In this magical moment
between day and night,

I send my wish to the universe
so it may take flight.

Sapphire Moonbeam

February 11
Tuesday

2nd ♌

Color of the day: Red
Incense of the day: Cedar

Block It with Ice Spell

At this time of year in many regions, ice is a powerful element. It can clog rivers or block harbors. This spell will help you block a bad habit with ice.

You'll need a small piece of paper, a pen, a spray bottle of water, and a small freezer bag. On the paper, write the habit you wish to block. Mist the paper with the water, then seal the paper in the freezer bag. Toss the bag in the freezer and allow the paper to freeze. When it is frozen, remove the bag from the freezer. Take the frozen paper out of the bag. Crush the paper with your hand or tear it to bits. Quickly gather the pieces of paper and return them to the freezer bag. Seal the bag again and toss the bag and the paper in the trash. Your habit will gradually fade away.

James Kambos

 # February 12
Wednesday

2nd ♌
Full Moon 8:53 am
☽ v/c 2:12 pm
☽ → ♍ 8:07 pm

Color of the day: Brown
Incense of the day: Marjoram

Night-Blooming Moon Magic

To charge your favorite perfume with the mysterious powers of the moon, after the sun has set, find a comfortable spot to meditate for five to ten minutes. Holding the bottle, close your eyes and imagine a temple dedicated to the moon, in whatever form feels most evocative. Conjure up details for all of your senses. Can you see the altar bathed in moonlight? Is that the trickling of a sacred fountain you hear? The air is fragrant—can you smell your perfume? Feel a cool breeze or the warmth of a fire on your skin? Is there something to taste, like mulled wine or fresh fruit?

With the scene vibrantly alive in your mind, visualize yourself placing the perfume on the altar, where it will absorb magical energy from this temple of the moon. Gently come out of the meditation and place the physical bottle on a windowsill where it will be bathed in moonlight while you sleep.

Melissa Tipton

February 13
Thursday

3rd ♍

Color of the day: Purple
Incense of the day: Balsam

Comfort Cooking

Every time I was ever sick as a child, my grandparents or parents would always make me soup to help me get well. With a little magical intention, you can create a potion that will work not only on the body but on the spirit as well.

As you choose your ingredients for the soup, be sure to stir clockwise to promote healing. Simple ingredients could be chicken, noodles, carrots, and broth. Stir in herbs such as rosemary, ginger, and garlic to promote protection and healing. If you are not culinary inclined, that's okay. Just grab a can of your favorite soup. Let the soup simmer on the stovetop, stirring occasionally in a clockwise direction. Let your intention for love and healing flow from you into the soup and say:

Heal the heart, warm the soul.

*Let go of all that is wrong
as you empty your bowl.*

Serve the soup to your loved one so they can begin to heal.

Charlynn Walls

February 14
Friday

3rd ♍

Color of the day: Coral
Incense of the day: Cypress

Valentine's Day

Self-Love for Valentine's Day

People tend to think of Valentine's Day as a holiday for couples, but it celebrates love in general too. That includes the love you have for yourself. Thus, it's possible to celebrate Valentine's Day even if you aren't part of a romantic relationship or can't spend the day with the person you love. Do loving things for yourself today. Read a favorite book or watch a movie about self-discovery. Buy yourself something luxurious to wear. Take yourself out to dinner. Love your body with a spa day or something else you find relaxing.

For this spell, you'll need a white vase and a purple flower, such as tulip, carnation, or pansy. Put the vase on your altar and say:

The first love is love of the self.

Add the flower and say:

*For only when you love yourself
can you love others.*

Lean forward and smell the flower. Finish with this:

I will remember to love myself, no matter who else I may also love.

Elizabeth Barrette

February 15
Saturday

 February 16
Sunday

3rd ♏

☽ v/c 3:36 am

☽ → ♎ 6:45 am

Color of the day: Indigo
Incense of the day: Magnolia

Spell to Smash Obstacles

Use this spell to help you achieve your goals and smash any obstacles that stand in your way. You'll need some ice cubes, a hammer, and goggles or safety glasses. Put on the goggles or glasses and take the ice cubes outside. Place the ice on the ground or on another hard surface that won't get damaged by the hammer. Hold your hand over the ice and think about the obstacle you need to overcome. Pick up the hammer and state:

*This ice is my obstacle, and I
smash it up completely!*

Whack the ice with the hammer to thoroughly smash it until it's no longer identifiable as ice cubes. Imagine victory as you do so. After the ice is smashed, affirm adamantly:

The path is clear! Success is mine!

Melanie Marquis

3rd ♎

Color of the day: Gold
Incense of the day: Eucalyptus

Break the Dark

By mid-February, the Northern Hemisphere has a slew of dark, cold, short days, which feel like they will never end. We get the Winter Wearies. This spell will help lift the mood and remind us that spring is coming. Gather these supplies:

- A 7-day orange jar candle
- A knife (for carving)
- Citrus essential oil (My favorite is tangerine.)
- Matches

Carve the sun into the candle. Dress the candle with citrus oil, visualizing the warmth and the light's return.

Place the candle in the room where you spend most of your awake time. Light the candle, saying:

*With this light and scent
I break the dark.*

*I welcome warmth and
my own inner spark.*

Let the candle burn while you are in the room. Extinguish it when you are not in the room. Relight the candle whenever you spend time in the room until it burns all the way down.

Cerridwen Iris Shea

February 17
Monday

3rd ♎︎

☽ v/c 6:24 pm

☽ → ♏︎ 7:19 pm

Color of the day: Silver
Incense of the day: Rosemary

Presidents' Day

Random Act of Kindness

Today is Random Acts of Kindness Day. Performing a kind action that benefits society is a powerful spell. Pick up and dispose of litter, pay for the person behind you in line, donate gently used clothing to a charity, volunteer at an animal shelter, read to children, or do any other good deed. As you perform your random act of kindness, envision a warm, benevolent pink glow of positive energy surrounding yourself and your loved ones, and kindness spreading throughout the bountiful universe.

A.C. Fisher Aldag

 ## February 18
Tuesday

3rd ♏︎

☉ → ♓︎ 5:07 am

Color of the day: Black
Incense of the day: Bayberry

**Swept Away Spell
for Self-Reflection**

As a tree connected with the goddess Brighid, birch reminds us to be courageous as new opportunities present themselves. Birch is also a tree of thresholds, and traditional birch besoms were once used to sweep away the old year. This spell is designed to guide you to sweep away old ways of thinking, fear, and negative self-reflection and to help open you up to new opportunities. You will need a charcoal tab, a heat-safe container, some ground birch bark, and a besom or broom.

On a table, light the charcoal tab in the heat-safe container and drop ground birch bark onto it to release its smoke. When ready, pick up your broom and work in a clockwise circle around the table with a sweeping motion. As you do so, say something like this:

I call upon the spirit of the birch to sweep away the old, and the power of courage to make me bold.

As I do this, new opportunities will open for me. I as will it, so mote it be.

Monica Crosson

February 19
Wednesday

3rd ♏

Color of the day: White
Incense of the day: Bay laurel

hello, Pisces Season!

Pisces season is here and it's all about getting in touch with your emotions, allowing yourself to feel deeply, tapping into your generosity and empathy, and connecting with your creativity. You don't need to have a Pisces placement to enjoy this spell. Being a water sign, I think a fun way to do this is to take a luxurious bubble bath and fill it with Pisces energy, allowing yourself to soak in all the dreamy vibes. I like to use a blend of essential oils associated with Pisces, such as sandalwood, clary sage, bergamot, orange, and jasmine.

Take your favorite oils and put a few drops of each in your bathwater. As you do this, call into the water your intentions for the season. When you are in the tub, allow the water to calm you and prepare you for the season ahead. If you don't have a bathtub, make a steamer by placing a small amount of warm water in a cup and adding the essential oils to this. Place the cup off to the side and the aroma will fill the shower.

Amanda Lynn

February 20
Thursday

3rd ♏

☽ v/c 5:06 am

☽ → ♐ 7:55 am

4th Quarter 12:33 pm

Color of the day: Green
Incense of the day: Mulberry

Calling on the Muses

The nine Muses, daughters of Zeus and Mnemosyne, are associated with inspiration, creativity, and intelligence. Do you need to be motivated in taking on a new project? Completing an existing one? Or maybe in just getting through a daily routine? Call upon the Muses.

You may do some research to find the Muse that best fits your needs or goals. Better yet? Just speak to all of them.

Select nine small white pillar candles or tealights and a mirror big enough to hold them. Set the candles in a circle on the mirror and safely light them, speaking a Muse's name as you light each one: Calliope, Clio, Erato, Euterpe, Melpomene, Polyhymnia, Terpsichore, Thalia, and Urania. Then repeat this charm:

Muses nine,

Sisters of divine creativity,

I humbly call on you, asking you to share your gifts.

May these symbolic flames
ignite my inspiration.

With gratitude and reverence
I make this request.

Extinguish the candles, giving thanks.

Susan Pesznecker

NOTES:

February 21
Friday

4th ♐

Color of the day: Pink
Incense of the day: Yarrow

Broken Candle Spell

Sometimes life can throw painful things our way, and there's no way to overcome them but to live through them. This simple spell is designed to help you move through difficult times on your journey to healing. All you need is a chime or taper candle. (Chime candles are best, as they burn much faster.)

Find a quiet moment and while holding the unlit candle, think about your current difficulty. As you do, allow yourself to feel the frustration, pain, or anger associated with it, and very gently break the candle without severing the wick. The break in the candle represents your current hardship. Place the candle in a holder and light it. Imagine yourself as the flame, burning with strength and life force. Watch how the flame easily burns past the broken part of the candle while maintaining its brightness the whole time. You are like that flame, working through the difficulties with power. Notice how after it passes the breakage, the flame is unharmed and still thriving. You will be too. Repeat as needed.

Kate Freuler

February 22
Saturday

4th ♐

☽ v/c 3:38 pm

☽ → ♑ 6:09 pm

Color of the day: Brown
Incense of the day: Ivy

Nutmeg Amulet for Success

Here is an amulet to assist you in being successful in all you do, but especially in education, legal matters, and religious or spiritual callings. Perform this ritual when the Moon is in Sagittarius—before it moves into Capricorn at 6:09 p.m. EST. Here is what you will need:

- A whole nutmeg nut
- A nail or needle for carving
- A small red cloth bag with a drawstring top, or you can use a piece of red cloth 7 inches square and some string
- Personal identifying materials: hair, fingernail or toenail clippings, spit, blood, etc.
- Sage essential oil

Hold the nut in your right hand and say:

In far lake is an island. On that island is a mountain. On that mountain is a garden. In that garden is a silver tree. On that silver tree is a golden nut. I pick that nut and put it in my pocket.

Take the nail or needle and carve your initials (First, Middle, Last) onto the nutmeg nut. Then add it to your bag or place it on the cloth. Also add your personal identifying materials. Place three drops of sage essential oil onto the nutmeg nut. Tie the bag closed with three knots to the drawstring, or wrap the materials into a bundle and tie closed with string and three knots.

Don't let anyone see your amulet. Carry it in your right pocket or in a purse or bag. Feed three drops of sage essential oil (dropped onto the outside of the bag) at every new and full moon.

Brandon Weston

NOTES:

February 23
Sunday

4th ♑

Color of the day: Yellow
Incense of the day: Almond

Awaken the Earth Spirit Spell

At this time of year, many of us are anxious for winter to end. Help end winter with this spell.

You'll need a small bare twig. Go to a place outdoors where you won't be disturbed. Pick up a small bare twig off the ground. Tap the earth with it three times. Stand as you hold the twig and say:

Earth Spirit, hear my plea.

Arise, let darkness and cold flee.

Enter every bud and blade of grass.

Let the frosts and snows pass.

Snap the twig in half and toss it aside. Walk away. The Goddess has heard you.

James Kambos

 February 24
Monday

4th ♑

☽ v/c 10:28 pm

Color of the day: White
Incense of the day: Clary sage

Healing Financial Imbalance

Financial abundance is a dance between giving and receiving, and this spell tempers the extremes of under-earning and overspending. You'll need two candles in different colors and a crystal. Quartz, pyrite, citrine, malachite, or tiger's eye are excellent options. This spell can be done on your altar or any place where you can safely burn candles.

Holding one candle, close your eyes and tap into the thoughts and feelings you associate with under-earning. Ask the candle to bring this experience into proper balance, and send the energy down your arms and into the candle. Repeat this process with the other candle, focusing on the experience of overspending.

Situate the candles two feet apart, and place the crystal in between. Intend that as you light the candles, between them is a field of interplay between earning and spending where the perfect balance for you is generated and absorbed by the crystal, which you can then carry to inspire smart financial choices. Snuff the candles out when done.

Melissa Tipton

 ## February 25
Tuesday

4th ♑

☽ → ♒ 12:40 am

Color of the day: Gray
Incense of the day: Cinnamon

National Quiet Day

Today is National Quiet Day.
Taking time to step away
from the noise and distractions of
the world is important for self-care.
When you intentionally immerse
yourself in silence and solitude, it can
help foster a sense of inner peace.
When the mind is quiet and free
from distractions, many answers
can be found in the quiet moments.
This spell is a way to help clear your
mind and become silent in order to
cultivate revelations of wisdom and
bliss. This spell can be used prior
to your meditation practice, before
you do a task that requires focus, or
even before venturing out on a nature
walk. Repeat these words to prepare
your mind for moments of solitude:

My mind is calm, my thoughts are free

*From the things that
normally consume me.*

A quiet moment is what I seek

To help my wisdom be at its peak.

Sapphire Moonbeam

 ## February 26
Wednesday

4th ♒

☽ v/c 5:04 pm

Color of the day: Topaz
Incense of the day: Lavender

Home Cleansing Spell

Use this spell to help remove
negative energies from the
home. Conjure a feeling of love in
your heart, then place your hands
over a bucket or bowl of water.
Let the feelings in your heart flow
through your hands and into the
water. Next, choose a washcloth and
place your hands on it. Repeat the
same process you did with the water,
filling the washcloth with loving energies. Then get the washcloth slightly
damp with the water, and run the
cloth all along the lengths of the base-
boards in every room of your home.
Envision the washcloth cleaning
away and absorbing any negativity.
Whenever the cloth gets visibly dirty
and after each room is cleansed, rinse
it out in the water. When you're
finished, immediately and thoroughly
wash the washcloth.

Melanie Marquis

February 27
Thursday

4th ♒

☽ → ♓ 3:46 am

New Moon 7:45 pm

Color of the day: Crimson
Incense of the day: Myrrh

Clean Sweep

The new moon is a time of endings and beginnings. This makes it a great time for cleaning. You remove the old to make room for the new, just as the moon renews itself each month. The familiar cycle of the moon helps remind you to keep up with cleaning, too.

For this spell, you will need a new broom. Preferably, choose one with natural straw and a wooden handle, although it can be any size. You also need a few drops of essential oil in any scent associated with cleansing, such as lemon, mint, or pine. Anoint the bristles with a few drops of oil and say:

New moon and new broom,

So much to see, so much to do.

Clean sweep and clean room,

Out with the old, in with the new!

Sweep your floors with the new broom. Smell the sweet scent of the cleansing oil carried by the bristles as they work. Dispose of the dirt outdoors.

Elizabeth Barrette

 February 28
Friday

1st ♓

Color of the day: Rose
Incense of the day: Violet

Ramadan begins at sundown

Fertility Charm

February is known as the month that deals with affairs of the heart, and with today being Friday, it is also a day associated with love. We can utilize these properties to produce a wearable fertility charm. This could be a charm to birth in the traditional sense or it could represent the birth of an idea. Whichever path you choose is fine, but make sure your intention is clear.

You will need some clay to shape your charm and a cord to create a bracelet or necklace to wear. The charm you mold should have a spiral on it. The center of the spiral represents that from which everything emerges. As you shape the charm, see it take root, take shape, and then emerge. Make sure the charm has a hole punched in it, then allow it to dry or bake it in the oven so it can harden. String it and wear it until the charm works.

Charlynn Walls

March

March is upon us! March is a month of unpredictable weather. Will the weather spirits decide to bring us a last hurrah of winter in the form of a blustery snowstorm or instead bring us signs of spring's beginning in the form of budding trees and perhaps rain showers sprinkled with mild, sunny days? There really is no telling! However, for those of us who follow the Wheel of the Year, the spring equinox is a time of new beginnings, regardless of the weather.

Rituals of spring and new beginnings will take place around the globe this month. Druids still gather at Stonehenge to welcome the rising sun on the morning of the equinox. March also is the time to celebrate the festival of Holi, popular in India and Nepal. People engage in paint fights, covering each other in festive splatters of vibrant color, welcoming the arrival of spring and all its vibrancy.

In March, however you choose to celebrate, work the magick of new beginnings!

Blake Octavian Blair

March 1
Saturday

1st ♓

☽ v/c 3:05 am

☽ → ♈ 4:52 am

Color of the day: Black
Incense of the day: Sandalwood

Divination for the Coming Month

The first day of any month sets a stage for fresh starts and new beginnings. You can use the Tarot to consider what March might bring.

Find a quiet place in which to work. Spread a cloth for your cards and shuffle the deck. Deal one card face up on the cloth. This card represents you and your current condition. Deal a second card face up to the left of the first card: this represents past issues that may spill into or influence the current month. Deal a third card face up to the right of the first card: this represents the coming month.

Look at the cards carefully, capturing your first impressions of meaning. Then consider the numbers, court cards, symbolism, etc. Use guidebooks for additional information.

Journal or record your reading or just leave the cards on your altar. Return throughout the month to reflect on the cards' meanings.

Susan Pesznecker

 # March 2
Sunday

1st ♈

☽ v/c 8:52 am

Color of the day: Gold
Incense of the day: Heliotrope

Wish on the Wind Spell

March arrives, and with it so do the winds of March. Long ago, magicians would release their spells and charms to the wind. To do this, you'll need a strip of fabric and a marker. Write your wish on the fabric. Go to a shrub or tree and tie the fabric/wish around a branch. As you do this, say:

> Wind, carry my wish high
> above the ground,
>
> Beyond the horizon's farthest bounds.
>
> Wind, carry my wish
> beyond where eagles fly,
>
> Beyond the clouds, beyond the sky.

Walk away and forget about your wish. When the wish manifests itself, untie the fabric/wish and discard it. The wind carried your wish to the Divine.

James Kambos

March 3
Monday

 # March 4
Tuesday

1st ♈

☽ → ♉ 5:37 am

Color of the day: Lavender
Incense of the day: Hyssop

Warming Boost

We are just over halfway through flu season—hurrah! Grab a cup of your favorite warming drink, such as tea, hot cider with a dash of cinnamon, or even a latte from your favorite local coffee shop, and find a nice comfy, quiet spot to sit for a few moments. Hold the drink in both hands. Feel the warmth in your fingertips and palms. Visualize the path this warmth will take with each sip—past your lips, down your esophagus, and into your stomach. From your stomach, see the warmth extending into the other parts of your body—down into your legs and up into your arms. Know that this warmth is healing, protecting, and keeping you and your body healthy and safe. With every drink you take, follow the pathway it takes, feeling the healing warmth radiating throughout your body. As you finish your drink, repeat these words in your mind:

Healing warmth, spread through me.

Healing warmth, protect me.

Kerri Connor

1st ♉

Color of the day: Maroon
Incense of the day: Ylang-ylang

Mardi Gras (Fat Tuesday)

Unique Name Spell

Today is Unique Names Day. It is the perfect time to find a magical name. Some practitioners prefer to keep their magical name a secret, but others decide to share it and even change it to their legal name, like I did. In order to discover your unique magical name, try this spell.

Use a pendulum, or make one with a string and a heavy object, such as a key. You can use a pendulum board that has letters, or you can write the alphabet on paper, drawing alphabet letters on the outside of a circle. Establish trust with the pendulum and practice using it by asking it to answer several yes-no questions before you begin. Begin with the pendulum in the middle of the circle and ask it to guide you to the first letter of your magical name. Once you are ready, say these words:

May my magical name be shown to me. Guide this pendulum to reveal the first letter, blessed be!

Use the pendulum to help you discover additional letters in your magical name or just for the first letter.

Sapphire Moonbeam

March 5
Wednesday

1st ♉

☽ v/c 5:53 am

☽ → ♊ 7:29 am

Color of the day: Yellow
Incense of the day: Honeysuckle

Ash Wednesday

Burying Your Troubles

This is a cleansing rite utilizing the grounding power of Taurus. You will need:

- A red pen or marker
- Paper strips, white
- A piece of white cloth, about 1 foot square (I like to use unbleached, natural cloth since this is going into the earth.)
- Frankincense and myrrh resin, equal parts
- White string
- Incense charcoal and burner
- Matches or lighter
- A shovel or spade

Using a red pen or marker, write on your paper strips all the things you'd like to release or be cleansed of. Each strip should have only one item. These might be deep issues you'd like to finally release, or current illnesses, or even influences from an enemy. Place each strip onto the middle of the white cloth. When you're finished, add a pinch of your frankincense and myrrh resin, then gather the cloth around the paper strips and tie into a bundle using the string.

Find an area outside where it's safe for you to dig a hole big enough for the bundle. Light your charcoal and add the frankincense and myrrh mixture. Dig your hole, then drop the bundle inside. Spit three times onto the bundle, then cover completely with dirt.

Brandon Weston

NOTES:

 **March 6**
Thursday

1st ♊
2nd Quarter 11:32 am

Color of the day: Turquoise
Incense of the day: Jasmine

Prompting Wealth

Today is a day of abundance. Thursdays are effective days to work toward wealth and prosperity. The day is closely aligned with the planet Jupiter. To complete this spell, you will need a piece of paper, a green pen, and a few pennies. Take a sheet of paper and draw in green ink the seventh pentacle of Jupiter. You could also print a copy of the pentacle and trace it in ink. The seal goes on one side of the paper, and on the other you write out your request.

Take the paper and place it on your altar. Then put on top of the paper a few coins and say:

Jupiter, hear my plea and help me to prosper in all my current endeavors.

Leave the seal on the altar and occasionally add a few coins, an oak leaf, or other tokens of wealth and prosperity to reinforce the spell. Make sure to do the mundane work as well to help you procure prosperity, such as applying for that promotion you want or filling out the bank paperwork to get a loan to start your own business.

Charlynn Walls

 March 7
Friday

2nd ♊
☽ v/c 9:57 am
☽ → ♋ 11:29 am

Color of the day: White
Incense of the day: Alder

The Magic of Spirit Stones

The relative permanence of stones provides a vehicle for remembering and honoring the ephemeral (think: tombstones). If you have a garden or potted plant, you can include a stone as a touchpoint for helpful spirits. This can be a simple unadorned stone, or you can use paint pens to decorate it, using waterproof sealant to protect the design.

Hold the stone in your palm, close your eyes, and feel its weight and temperature, bringing your awareness to the physicality of stone on flesh. Then shift focus to your breath, where it enters and exits your nostrils, moving your awareness from more to less solid experiences. Intend that this stone act as an intermediary between the worlds of flesh and spirit, allowing communication in accordance with the highest good, harming none.

When you see the stone in your day-to-day life, take a moment to give thanks to the spirits of the land, your ancestors, or any other beings you wish to connect with.

Melissa Tipton

 ## March 8
Saturday

2nd ♋

Color of the day: Indigo
Incense of the day: Patchouli

International Women's Day Meditation

Many times historically, women workers protested, demanding fair working conditions and equal rights. Women workers protested child labor, exploitation, and dangerous working conditions. These protests eventually led to March 8th being declared International Women's Day, which is celebrated today.

Sit quietly, with spine aligned. Close your eyes. Practice a deep, long inhalation, followed by a longer exhalation. This breath will slow the heart rate, reduce blood pressure, and promote calm within the system. Let each inhale pull strength, grounding, and energy up from the earth, through the chakras or spinal cord. With an exhale, cascade your energy around you, enveloping you. Successively expand the radius of the energetic exhale to encompass your house, neighborhood, town, state/province, and country. With a final deep inhalation, exhale and send energy to connect with women worldwide. Envision equity and safety for all women, everywhere.

Dallas Jennifer Cobb

March 9
Sunday

2nd ♋

☽ v/c 5:32 pm
☽ → ♌ 6:59 pm

Color of the day: Yellow
Incense of the day: Juniper

Daylight Saving Time begins at 2:00 a.m.

Rest and Restore Spell

Today is the start of Daylight Saving Time, which sometimes throws me off for weeks. In order to lessen the exhaustion and disorientation of "springing forward," try the following.

Upon awakening, take a few extra minutes in bed. Say:

Today I look forward to _____.

Then list all the things you look forward to in the coming day (even if one of them is "going back to bed tonight").

In the evening, before bedtime, do the legs-up-the-wall pose from yoga, where you place your legs upright against the wall, or drape your knees over a chair seat, with your back flat on the floor, for twenty minutes. In the pose, say:

Today I enjoyed _____.

Then make a list of all the good things in your day.

Do this variation on gratitude practice each morning and night for one week, starting today. Continue if you wish.

Cerridwen Iris Shea

NOTES:

March 10
Monday

2nd ♌

Color of the day: Gray
Incense of the day: Clary sage

Five Pennies Prosperity Spell

Choose a small bowl or decorative dish that appeals to you, and cover the bottom of it with a thick layer of cinnamon. Place five pennies on top of the cinnamon, then cover them with a mixture of nutmeg and ginger. Use your finger or wand to stir the pennies within the spices, making a clockwise motion. As you move the pennies, envision a flow of money coming your way. Next, place a penny at each of the four cardinal directions in your town, beginning with north, then east, then south, then west. Sprinkle some of the spice mixture on and around each penny you place, and ask the spirits of the land that dwell there to bring you the resources you seek. Return the remaining penny to your living space and place it just outside the entrance. Sprinkle any remaining spice over the threshold and around the entryway. Money will come to you.

Melanie Marquis

March 11
Tuesday

2nd ♌

☽ v/c 4:16 pm

Color of the day: White
Incense of the day: Ginger

Lucky Me Container Garden

An iconic harbinger of spring, daffodil's bright, cheery flowers can't help but make us smile. That's why they're the perfect addition to any good luck spell.

In most regions, pots of daffodils (and other flowering spring bulbs) can be found in grocery stores or garden centers at this time of year. To imbue your home with luck, happiness, and loving vibes, transplant daffodils, tulips, and hyacinths into a large container and set by your front door. Tuck in a lucky charm (a coin, wishbone, clover charm, etc.), a rose quartz, and a citrine around the base of your plants. As you do so, say something like this:

Daffodils for luck. (Place lucky charm.)

Tulips for love. (Place rose quartz.)

Hyacinths for joy. (Place citrine.)

*Bless this Witch's home
and all who enter here.*

Here are some popular bulbs and their associations:

- *Daffodil:* Love, abundance, fertility, luck

- *Tulip:* Love, renewal, protection
- *Hyacinth:* Protection, love, happiness
- *Crocus:* Psychic powers, love, strength, wisdom
- *Snowdrops:* Hope, grief, friendship
- *Fritillaria:* Love, healing, wisdom

Monica Crosson

NOTES:

March 12
Wednesday

2nd ♌

☽ → ♍ 3:56 am

Color of the day: Topaz
Incense of the day: Lilac

Incense Divination

To gain insight into a simple yes-no question, get a piece of paper, a pen, stick or cone incense in a holder, and a lighter. Draw a straight line down the center of the page. On the left, write "no," and on the right, "yes." Find a place indoors where no direct wind or draft will impact the incense smoke. Place the incense holder on the line in the center of the page. Light the incense, and as the smoke begins to billow, ask your questions out loud or in your mind. The direction that the smoke favors is your answer.

It's helpful to use a timer for this, so perhaps set it to three or five minutes or however long you can sit and look at the smoke. You will notice that the smoke leans in one direction more than the other. If the smoke is equal or flows straight up, the answer is more complicated than yes or no and needs more detailed divination such as tarot.

Kate Freuler

March 13
Thursday

2nd ♍

Color of the day: Purple
Incense of the day: Clove

Purim begins at sundown

A Spring House Cleansing

Why is it that the coming of spring awakens in us the urge to clean and freshen our life spaces? Through cleansing, we sweep away winter's detritus and open ourselves to a purified sacred space and fresh inspiration. Select a broom, a small bowl, salt, and loose lavender petals. Mix salt and water in the bowl. Move sunwise (clockwise) through your dwelling, sweeping each space with your broom and sweeping toward the main door. As you sweep, envision negativity and past misfortunes being swept out of your home. Take the bowl of salt water and again move sunwise through your home, casting salt water drops in each room and at each door, saying:

This room is clean. Let no harm enter this space. So mote it be.

Lastly, go outside and move sunwise around the boundaries of your property, sprinkling lavender blossoms and repeating:

I cleanse these bounds and set them safe. All harm will vanish with no trace.

Susan Pesznecker

March 14
Friday

2nd ♏

Full Moon 2:55 am

☽ v/c 1:47 pm

☽ → ♎ 2:59 pm

Color of the day: Pink

Incense of the day: Mint

Lunar Eclipse

Full Moon Divination Incense

This is a smoke mixture to aid with full moon divination sessions. You will need:

- 1 part juniper berries or eastern red cedar (*Juniperus virginiana*)
- ½ part lavender flowers, dried
- 1 part rosemary leaves, dried
- Optional: 1 part sweetgum resin (*Liquidambar styraciflua*, often called storax or American storax)
- Mortar and pestle
- Matches or lighter
- Incense charcoal and burner

Lightly crush all your incense ingredients together (doesn't need to be powdered) using a mortar and pestle. Before beginning your divination session (or before sleeping in the case of dreamwork), light the charcoal and add some of the incense mixture. Place your hands over your eyes and say these words:

From dark moon to light. My eyes closed are now open.

Remove your hands and divine. If you're using divinatory dreams, repeat the charm, let the incense burn briefly before extinguishing the charcoal, then go to sleep. You can store this incense mixture for future use.

Brandon Weston

NOTES:

March 15
Saturday

3rd ♎

Color of the day: Blue
Incense of the day: Sage

A Pinch of Protection

The Ides of March has a negative connotation thanks to William Shakespeare and his play *Julius Caesar*, but before that, "ides" referred to the first full moon of the month, with the Ides of March also being celebrated as the new year. That being said, Shakespeare's version does remind us that there is nothing wrong with a little added protection and a reminder to check your back every now and then.

Several culinary herbs double great as protection herbs, including sage, rosemary, bay leaves, and, of course, salt. Add a pinch of each to a small 2-inch-by-2-inch square of fabric. As you add the ingredients, say:

A pinch here, a pinch there, keep me protected everywhere.

Tie up the square and carry it with you for the day in your pocket, a bra, or somewhere else close to your body.

Kerri Connor

 March 16
Sunday

3rd ♎
☽ v/c 5:53 am

Color of the day: Amber
Incense of the day: Marigold

Herbal Shower for the Spring Equinox

The spring equinox is coming, so now is a great time to think about renewal and rebirth. Taking a hot shower with fresh springtime herbs is a fabulous way to bring in new ideas and energy. This is very simple to do.

Gather a bundle of your favorite fresh herbs, such as rosemary, lavender, peppermint, thyme, or eucalyptus. Wrap the bundle in twine and let it hang from your showerhead. Start the water and let the steam bring out the essence and scent of the herbs. Step into the shower and feel the water cleanse you. Take deep breaths, allowing the scent of the herbs to fill your lungs, bringing newness, freshness, and clarity. When you exhale, release any tension or unwanted energy you need to get rid of. Continue this until you feel calm and refreshed. Dry yourself off, and if you feel so inclined, save the herbs to dry and burn as incense at a later time.

Amanda Lynn

March 17
Monday

3rd ♎︎

☽ → ♏︎ 3:30 am

Color of the day: Ivory
Incense of the day: Narcissus

St. Patrick's Day

Good Luck Spell

Most of us could use some extra good luck. Your thoughts are powerful regarding luck. This spell will help you increase your luck with your thoughts and a good luck charm. If you don't already have a good luck charm, this is your sign to choose one. A good luck charm can be a favorite necklace/talisman, a lucky coin, or a charm from a bracelet, for instance. Once you have your good luck charm, you can add your intentions for this item to bring you extra luck:

*Grant me good luck with
these words that I speak.*

*Make good luck appear
each day of the week.*

*I believe good things will
happen wherever I go.*

*I don't just believe, this is
something I know.*

Repeat these words whenever you want to boost your good luck and to reinforce the intention that good luck and good things will happen for you.

Sapphire Moonbeam

 # March 18
Tuesday

3rd ♏︎

Color of the day: Red
Incense of the day: Geranium

Let the Water Flow Spell

As winter begins to release its icy grip, water starts to flow. Ice turns to water. Frost oozes from the earth, brooks begin to flow, and rivers run again. Water, the giver of life on this planet, flows again. Without it, everything—and I mean everything—on this Earth would perish. The seed would not sprout, and crops would wither. We spend the first half of March in Pisces, the zodiac sign ruled by watery Neptune. This is a perfect time to honor the element of water.

All you need for this ritual is your ritual cup—filled with water. Place the cup in the center of your altar. Scry into the water-filled cup. See the rivers, streams, lakes, and oceans of our abundant Earth. See them flowing and waves crashing. Then say:

I thank the water from every source

For being our Earth's life force.

End by walking outside with your cup. Gently pour the water upon the earth.

James Kambos

March 19
Wednesday

3rd ♏

☽ v/c 3:28 pm

☽ → ♐ 4:17 pm

Color of the day: Brown
Incense of the day: Bay laurel

Clear the Way

A regular practice of road-opening magic paves the way for success, both magical and "mundane." After all, no matter where you're trying to get to, the smoother the road, the faster your progress. You might use this spell daily for seven consecutive days, starting on a new moon, or at any personally meaningful interval.

Sit in meditation and release tension on your exhales, inviting peace with each inhale. Envision a brilliant star above and a star below, glowing in the core of the earth. Each star emits a column of infinite vertical light, and you are balanced between the above and the below, within this column. Envision light from your heart extending infinitely to the right and left so you are situated at the center of a cross of light. In this place of perfect balance, chant the following as many times as feels right:

The way is clear. My path is sure.

When done, release the mental imagery.

Melissa Tipton

March 20
Thursday

3rd ♐

☉ → ♈ 5:01 am

Color of the day: White
Incense of the day: Nutmeg

Spring Equinox – Ostara

Spring Equinox Altar Spell

U se this altar spell to attract good fortune throughout the spring season. Cover the altar with a green or white cloth. In the middle of the altar, place a basket. Choose some items to symbolize the blessings you hope to enjoy this spring. For example, you might choose a favorite toy or stuffed animal to represent happiness and laughter, candy to represent sweetness, colored eggs to represent fertility or new beginnings, and flowers to represent love and sexuality. Place the items in the basket. Focus on the items in the basket for a few minutes and envision having more blessings in your life this spring. Add more items to the basket as you feel called to do so, and refresh any flowers, eggs, or other perishable items as needed.

Melanie Marquis

March 21
Friday

3rd ♐

Color of the day: Coral
Incense of the day: Vanilla

World Poetry Day

Poetry comes from the spirit. It offers a way to see the world a little slant, to make sense of the mystical. It also plays a major role in magic. Most spells include elements of poetry. So do many rituals. This is because the mechanics of poetry, like rhyme and alliteration, provide more traction for moving energy, the same as they give that little "aha" in your head when you hear them.

You can celebrate World Poetry Day in a variety of ways. Read a book of poems. Look through your collection of spells and rituals for ones that feature verse. Start a songbook of shadows to gather poems, chants, and songs that you can use in creating rituals or other events. Here's an invocation to start with:

O Calliope,

Muse of Poetry,

Turn to us your face,

Lend to us your grace.

With sweet words of praise,

Blessed make our days.

Elizabeth Barrette

March 22
Saturday

3rd ♐

☽ v/c 2:53 am

☽ → ♑ 3:29 am

4th Quarter 7:29 am

Color of the day: Gray
Incense of the day: Ivy

Magical Cleanup

When we do a spell, it can leave both physical and metaphysical residue that needs to be cleaned up. Getting rid of our magical messes can sometimes be tricky. The physical remnants can usually be burnt and the ashes buried, or the remains can be thrown in the trash. Make sure to clean the physical space first before doing this spell to remove the built-up magical residue.

Since today is Saturday, it is the perfect time for banishing negative energies. Take some sweetgrass or sage incense or spray, and apply it in a widdershins (counterclockwise) movement around the workspace three times. As you do so, say:

All lingering energy or spirits,
be gone from this space.

Let only positive energy
now enter this place.

Reset all your furniture and altar items in your workspace. Then you are ready to continue working magic.

Charlynn Walls

March 23
Sunday

4th ♑

Color of the day: Orange
Incense of the day: Almond

Bright Blessings Spell

While many of us say "Blessed Be," one member of my coven always says "Bright Blessings." I love this saying, and decided to write a spell that carries the intonation and intention of the words.

Bright Blessings I call upon us all.

May you be bright and filled with might,

May the good moon inspire psychic insight,

May you be blessed and touched with grace,

May the good sun shine brightly upon your face,

May you be strong, grounded, and sturdy,

May you be firmly rooted, connected, and earthy,

May the directions inspire you to travel far,

May the elements empower you to be who you are,

May all bright blessings be bestowed upon thee,

To sustain you in wealth, health, and prosperity.

Bright Blessings I call upon us all.

Blessed Be.

Dallas Jennifer Cobb

NOTES:

ᛉarch 24
Monday

4th ♑
☽ v/c 11:01 am
☽ → ♒ 11:25 am
Color of the day: Silver
Incense of the day: Lily

Posy Potion Spell

While spring's energy pushes us forward, this Posy Potion gives us a few minutes to sit and mindfully cultivate our mental and emotional gardens. Choose a tea blend that includes either hibiscus (relaxation, love, dream magic) or jasmine (prosperity, love, dreams). Let the tea steep so you have a strong, flavorful infusion. Sit with your mug of tea in place where you won't be disturbed for twenty minutes. As you drink your tea, imagine a cottage-style garden, with a profusion of plants and flowers. In the center of each flower is an image of something you want to grow/achieve/experience in the coming cycle. The garden is growing and flowering; the energy is that of accomplishment. Fill yourself with the sensation of satisfaction, as though it's already achieved. Let it fill your senses, so you will remember it.

Finish your tea, wash out your cup, and carry the sense of fulfilment with you as you take action to grow your desires tangibly.

Cerridwen Iris Shea

 ᛉarch 25
Tuesday

4th ♒
Color of the day: Black
Incense of the day: Cinnamon

Blessing and Farewell

Moving to a new place to live can be emotional, sentimental, and bittersweet all at the same time. When you are in the midst of a transformation, consider performing this blessing and farewell spell after the last box has been removed from your home. This is a way to say goodbye and release the energy of your living space.

Stand silently in the room of your choice and reflect on the memories. Close your eyes and remember a magnificent memory in that space in the past. Think about the events that transpired in that room. Use these words to say farewell to your home's energy:

I stand and say goodbye to
this space as I prepare to move
to a brand-new place.

The memories will not be left
behind. I will carry the most
precious ones within my mind.

I release the energy as I proceed to go.

I am excited for my new
beginning, I am ready to go.

Sapphire Moonbeam

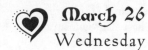

♥ March 26
Wednesday

4th ♒

☽ v/c 6:15 am

☽ → ♓ 3:31 pm

Color of the day: White
Incense of the day: Honeysuckle

Open Your Heart

It's spring and love is in the air—partly due to the increase in daylight, which slows the production of melatonin. Spring also brings with it an increase of dopamine and serotonin, the hormones of love and pleasure. Take advantage of these natural energies to open yourself to love of all kinds.

Picture your heart in your mind. Place your hand on it. Feel your heartbeat and experience the connection. Envision a pink light at the center of your heart. Allow the pink light to grow, slowly encompassing more and more of your heart. Let the light continue to grow until it emanates from all around your heart. Imagine that this light allows your heart to grow in capacity. It is more open to love, and it has more love to give. Say to yourself:

I am open to giving and receiving love.

Repeat it as many times as you like.

Kerri Connor

⬠ March 27
Thursday

4th ♓

Color of the day: Green
Incense of the day: Apricot

Loosen the Tongue Truth Spell

I am a Witch who tries to be kind, open, and honest with everyone I meet. I especially do not like it when my world is sullied by the residue of lies. To loosen tongues and get to the truth of the matter, try this spell.

You will need:

- 2 scraps of red cloth (cut to resemble a tongue)
- A needle and blue thread (truth and wisdom)
- Crumbled oak leaves (truth)
- Scissors

Loosely stitch together the scrap material, leaving one side open. Fill with oak leaves, then stitch up the opening. (If oak leaves are not available, you could use alder or violets instead.) *Optional:* Write the name of the person who is lying on your "tongue" poppet. Now use scissors to carefully cut the stitches and reveal the truth. As you do this, say:

Loosen the tongue and reveal the truth. The lies that are told are so uncouth. As I cut away each and every stitch, the truth will find this powerful Witch.

Monica Crosson

March 28
Friday

4ʂ ♓

☽ v/c 4:30 pm

☽ → ♈ 4:36 pm

Color of the day: Purple
Incense of the day: Orchid

Witches' Hair Rinse

Rosemary, a common herb, is known for making hair shiny and healthy. Make this rosemary rinse to beautify your locks while benefiting from its magical properties. Rosemary is associated with love, friendship, protection, and beauty. It's an all-purpose magical herb and very versatile, which means you can adjust its purpose to whatever your needs may be.

To make the rinse, just place three sprigs of fresh rosemary in two cups of water, bring to a boil, and then let simmer for about five minutes. Once cooled, pour the brew into a jar that has a tight-fitting lid. Add a rose quartz for beauty to the jar, and place the jar under the light of the moon for one night to charge it with lunar energy.

After washing and conditioning your hair, gently pour the infusion into your locks. Let it sit for ten minutes while visualizing your goal, then rinse. Now you have healthy hair, as well as a halo of energy aligned with your needs.

Note: You can do this spell even if you don't have hair by just pouring the brew over your head.

Kate Freuler

NOTES:

March 29
Saturday

4th ♈

New Moon 6:58 am

Color of the day: Brown
Incense of the day: Pine

Solar Eclipse

New Moon Eclipse
Cleansing Rite

The new moon represents endings and beginnings, and an eclipse of the sun is the perfect time to remove undesirable influences from your life. Prior to this astronomical event, physically clean your home. Next, open windows and doors to release unwanted energies. Smoke-cleanse your home using dry juniper boughs, sage, or hazel wands, being careful to catch any sparks or ashes in a safe, fireproof container. Walk widdershins (counterclockwise) around the space while chanting:

I remove, banish, vanquish,
and cleanse any baneful
conditions from this locale!

After smoke-clearing, walk around widdershins once again while ringing a bell, speaking the same words of power.

Finally, place iron railroad spikes or long, thick steel nails in the corners of the area, with their points facing inward toward the main part of the room. Iron is used in folk magick and Conjure traditions to ward away harmful entities. Close all the windows and doors, carefully extinguish the burning herbs in a safe container, and state:

As I will it.

If the solar eclipse is visible in your area, poke a round hole in a sheet of paper and hold it above another sheet of paper, outdoors, to capture the effect of the moon occluding the sun. Later, use that paper in written spellwork to banish any further unwanted conditions.

A.C. Fisher Aldag

NOTES:

March 30
Sunday

1st ♈

☽ v/c 5:18 am

☽ → ♉ 4:16 pm

Color of the day: Gold
Incense of the day: Marigold

Eid al-Fitr begins at sundown
(Ramadan ends)

Citrine Manifestation Charm

Citrine is a great stone to work with if you're looking for some inspiration, wisdom, creativity, and abundance. Gather the following items to create your manifestation charm:

- A small glass bottle with a cork lid, no larger than 2–3 inches in height
- Citrine chips (for manifestation)
- Coarse salt (for cleansing)
- Bay leaf (for wisdom)
- Rosemary (for focus)
- Cinnamon (for success)
- A yellow candle (for clarity and inspiration)

Combine all the small ingredients in the bottle and place the cork on top. Light the yellow candle and carefully drip the wax around the lid to seal in your intentions, then extinguish the candle. Place the bottle on your altar or any sacred area and let charge for three days.

Carry the charm with you any time you need a little pick-me-up, want to get a boost of creative energy, or need to manifest something new and exciting. Carry the charm in a small pouch to protect it from breaking.

Amanda Lynn

NOTES:

March 31
Monday

1st ♉

Color of the day: Lavender
Incense of the day: Neroli

A Shield of Allheal

Yarrow has many nicknames, including bloodwort, green arrow, sneezeweed, nosebleed, green adder's mouth, soldier's woundwort, and allheal. These indicate its rich history as a healing herb. Modern research supports its astringent, anti-septic, anti-inflammatory, vulnerary, and other qualities. It also attracts beneficial insects and has deep roots in magic. Yarrow sprouts early in spring and is easy to cultivate. The best way to enjoy its benefits is to grow your own. Plant the seeds in sun to part shade.

Yarrow is often used in spells for health. You can dry and press a spring leaf or a summer flower. If you don't have either, use a photograph. Hold the image and meditate on its healing qualities. Then say:

Sprig of allheal,

Be my shield,

Sun and shadow,

Wood and field,

By the power

That you wield.

Tuck the image into your purse or wallet to carry with you. It will help protect your health. Growing yarrow will also encourage the herb to think well of you for mutual support.

Elizabeth Barrette

NOTES:

April

This month we move from dark to light, from cold to warm, from brown to green. April is a magical month that starts with April Fools' Day and ends on the eve of May Day, begins with a joke and ends with an outdoor sleep-out. Here in Ontario, Canada, the average temperature at the beginning of April is close to freezing. It's common to have snow on the ground. Throughout April a magical transformation occurs: the temperature climbs as high as 66 degrees Fahrenheit (19 degrees Celsius) and flowers bloom.

Post-equinox, the days grow longer. Between April 1 and 30, the daylight increases from 12 hours and 46 minutes to 14 hours and 8 minutes. As the sun travels northward, it climbs in the sky. Not only do days lengthen, but shadows shorten as well. It is inviting to get outdoors. Like the plants that need sunlight to conduct photosynthesis, we humans need sunlight to help manufacture vitamin D.

This month, make time to enjoy the outdoors. Get out in the daylight, take evening walks in the twilight after dinner, contemplate your garden, and turn your face toward the sun at every chance. With winter coming to an end, now is your time to transform.

Dallas Jennifer Cobb

April 1
Tuesday

1st ♉

☽ v/c 1:43 pm

☽ → ♊ 4:26 pm

Color of the day: Scarlet
Incense of the day: Cedar

April Fools' Day – All Fools' Day

A Trickster Coloring Spell

Today is the day to honor the Trickster. One positive thing the Trickster can teach us is that we can be creative, and that we can use our creativity to turn our dreams into reality. If you wish it, create it!

For this spell you'll need a sketchbook or plain paper and artist markers/colored pencils, etc. Sit down with your art supplies. Think of what you have and what you want. Let's say you live in a small apartment but want a house. With your markers, sketch a drawing representing your apartment. Beside it or on another page/paper, sketch your dream home. Do this for anything—a new car, job, etc. As you sketch, think:

This is what I have. But this is what I will receive.

Gradually what you want will become reality. The Trickster inspires us to use our creativity to get what we want. It works well if you perform this spell in your Book of Shadows.

James Kambos

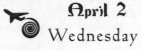 April 2
Wednesday

1st ♊

Color of the day: Topaz
Incense of the day: Lavender

National Walking Day

Walking has many advantages. It provides exercise for good health. It encourages people to slow down. It gives you an opportunity to observe the surrounding environment. It promotes connections with nature and magical energies, and it's good for you.

Today is National Walking Day this year, so take the time for a nice walk. Outdoors is ideal, but in inclement weather you could walk through a mall or other building instead. Feel your body and its connections to everything around you. Each footstep links you to the earth beneath your feet and the air that flows over your skin. Watch for a new flower or a new store. As you walk, say:

Walking feet are busy feet,
Following ancestors' beat.

Busy feet are healthy feet,
Strong and sturdy, fast and fleet.

Healthy feet are happy feet,
Facing challenges they meet.

Remember that walking connects you with all the people who have gone before and will come after.

Elizabeth Barrette

April 3
Thursday

1st ♊

☽ v/c 2:26 pm

☽ → ♋ 6:50 pm

Color of the day: Turquoise
Incense of the day: Carnation

Abundant Growth Spell

U se this spell to create a special
watering can to help your plants
grow better. First, use a permanent
marker to write the word "growth"
on the bottom, sides, and inside of
the watering can. Fill the can with
water and place three large pieces of
raw citrine inside it along with some
fresh mint. Put the can outside during the day and invite the sunlight
to enter it. Think about the sunlight
fusing into the structure of the watering can as it warms in the sun. Before
sunset, remove the citrine and place
the pieces around or near your plants.
Remove the mint and leave it outside.
Pour the water onto your houseplants
or your garden to increase growth.
The watering can will remain effective
for several months before the magick
needs to be refreshed.

Melanie Marquis

April 4
Friday

1st ♋

2nd Quarter 10:15 pm

Color of the day: Rose
Incense of the day: Thyme

hit Reset and Move On Spell for Renewal

Periwinkle (*Vinca minor*) is sometimes called the sorcerer's violet for its connection to use in both protection and love spells. It is also known as the flower of death, as the low-growing groundcover with star-like flowers can still be found growing in many a graveyard, as it is an easy alternative to grass. For these reasons, periwinkle is the perfect addition to spells for renewal.

After a hard week at work, a horrible first date, or just a bad day, brew a cup of tea, queue up some soothing music, and light your favorite calming incense. When you feel ready, surround a pink candle, inscribed with your name and anointed with a few drops of rose oil, with periwinkle blossoms and a few rose quartz crystals. Light the candle and say something like this:

Herb of renewal, reset this mess.

I'll take the good and forget the rest.

Life is funny, full of ups and downs.

Thanks for the reminder to straighten my crown.

Extinguish the candle when done.

Monica Crosson

NOTES:

April 5
Saturday

2nd ♋

☽ v/c 6:54 pm

Color of the day: Blue
Incense of the day: Patchouli

Painting Your Reflection

I love a good mirror spell. There's nothing more revealing than looking deeply at yourself in a mirror to get in touch with your inner self. Today's mirror spell is a bit different because we get to do some art by painting our reflection! This is something I like to do when I want to look deeper at my divine self and see how it reflects the way I feel that day. This spell works best with dry erase markers. Sharpies also work if that's all you have (cleanup is easy with rubbing alcohol or nail polish remover).

First, grab as many markers as you can in a variety of colors if possible. If not, just a single color will do. Next, sit at your mirror with no real intention other than to draw symbols on your reflection. Look deep into your own eyes and connect with yourself. When you feel ready, start drawing on the mirror. There are no rules to this—draw what feels right. You can outline your face, draw ancient symbols, or even draw auras. When you are done, step away from the mirror to reflect on what you have created.

Amanda Lynn

April 6
Sunday

2nd ♋

☽ → ♌ 12:34 am

Color of the day: Orange
Incense of the day: Hyacinth

Abundance with Cybele

Cybele is a Phrygian mother goddess, worshipped in ancient Greece, known as the Magna Mater ("Great Mother") during the Roman Empire. She is a matron of the harvest, whose symbols are the phiale (a dish for offerings), the cornucopia, and lions—appropriate because today the moon is in Leo! Cybele was revered during the Megalesia, the festival held in her honor from April 4–10.

Honor Cybele by making an offering of sweet fruits and bread (preferably homemade) on a platter, and pouring a libation of red wine or sparkling red grape juice onto the fertile earth. Light three red candles in safe holders at sundown, and dance wildly to the beat of a tympania (or any small hand drum), calling upon Cybele and requesting abundance. Be sure to be specific: Do you want abundance of money or food or an abundance of kittens? Thank the goddess and extinguish the candles when your rite is completed.

A.C. Fisher Aldag

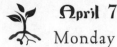

April 7
Monday

2nd ♌

Color of the day: White
Incense of the day: Rosemary

Blooming Color Magic

For this spell, you'll need a vase, water, food coloring, and cut flowers (preferably white blooms, such as roses, chrysanthemums, daisies, hydrangeas, or gardenias). You might research flower symbolism and choose one that aligns with your goal.

Fill the vase halfway with water, trim the ends of the flower stems, and choose a food coloring that matches your intention, such as blue and red (purple) for activating intuition and other third eye goals, green for the heart chakra or money spells, etc. As you add 10 to 15 drops of food coloring to the water, concentrate on the successful attainment of your goal. Stir to incorporate, continuing to focus on your spell's completion.

Place the flowers in the water, and ask the spirit of the flower to aid your magic. As the dye transforms the white blossoms, it transmutes the energy of your intention into physical reality, a living (and beautiful!) representation of your spell's successful unfolding.

Melissa Tipton

April 8
Tuesday

2nd ♌
☽ v/c 12:08 am
☽ → ♍ 9:40 am

Color of the day: Red
Incense of the day: Basil

Take Action Spell

Tuesday is ruled by Mars, the fourth planet out from the sun. Mars is known for "go out and get it" energy. Also, in Aries season, the influence of Mars is accentuated, because Mars is the ruling planet of Aries. It brings assertive energy, leadership, and courage to the day and the Aries season.

The thumb has long been associated with this energetic planet. An upright thumb symbolizes what is good and desirable. Pointed down, it represents what is not. Invoke Mars by putting both thumbs up. Intone:

With Mars in tow, I am good to go, ready to pursue my goals.

Now get to it.

Throughout the day, as needed, harness Martian energy. With thumbs up, repeat the affirmation. Each repetition connects you to the assertive Martian energy. Use it repeatedly for your own progress and gain.

Dallas Jennifer Cobb

April 9
Wednesday

2nd ♏

Color of the day: Brown
Incense of the day: Lilac

Awen Magic

When you are starting to run dry on ideas and need inspiration to strike, you can head to the Cauldron of Cerridwen. Today, Wednesday, corresponds to knowledge and inspiration and will aid in helping to draw inspiration to us. Cerridwen tended her cauldron to create a potion that would grant inspiration. We are fortunate that we can create our own.

You will need a small cauldron or mixing vessel. Into the cauldron you will put water and a stone of your choice. Blue lace agate, opal, or apatite would work well. You can also put in a pinch of basil and/or coriander to promote creativity. Once these ingredients have been added, stir them together and say:

Cerridwen, I seek the Awen.
Let the inspiration flow in.

Place the potion in a small airtight container. When you need new ideas, anoint your forehead with the mixture to open yourself up to inspiration.

Charlynn Walls

April 10
Thursday

2nd ♏

☽ v/c 3:49 pm

☽ → ♎ 9:12 pm

Color of the day: Crimson
Incense of the day: Balsam

Feel the Breeze

Take 10 to 15 minutes to stand outside with your feet planted firmly on the ground. Close your eyes and feel the air around you as it touches your body. Is it windy? A light breeze? Does the air feel totally still? Focus only on the air around you. Let any other thoughts float away. How does it feel? Cold? Warm? Wet? Dry? Simply take this moment to relax, center, and connect with the life-giving air around you. Identify and appreciate the characteristics you feel in the breeze today. Is there a message you need to hear?

Kerri Connor

April 11
Friday

2nd ♎

Color of the day: Coral
Incense of the day: Cypress

Invasive Weeds Spell

During the spring in the Northern Hemisphere, weeds start to appear in gardens. Weeds are plants that are not valued in the space where they are growing. While some weeds are actually herbs and wildflowers, others can be intrusive and invasive in a garden space.

When weeds appear that are counterproductive to what you want to flourish in the space, their removal can be used as a metaphor for getting rid of things in your life that are stifling your abundance and growth. If you want to change up the energy of your outdoor garden space and shake up the stagnant energy in your life, chant these words as you work with clippers in your garden:

As I cut these invasive weeds,

I am removing things that do not serve my needs.

I make space for the things that I want to grow.

These weeds are not welcome, they must go.

Sapphire Moonbeam

April 12
Saturday

2nd ♎

🌕 **Full Moon 8:22 pm**

Color of the day: Gray
Incense of the day: Magnolia

Passover begins at sundown

Full Moon Balance

The full moon is a tipping point between what we've brought in during the waxing moon and what we release during the waning moon.

For this spell you will need two small, shatterproof bowls and paper and pen. On one sheet of paper, make a list of what you've grown/manifested during the waxing moon. On the second sheet, make a list of what you release during the waning moon. Put one list in each bowl.

Stand balanced, feet on the ground. The left palm holds the waxing moon bowl at waist height. The right palm holds the waning moon bowl, same height. Breathe in and out three times. Slowly raise the waxing moon bowl up as you lower the waning moon bowl, as far as is comfortable without dropping the bowls. Bring your arms (still holding the bowls) back to center. Repeat two more times.

Burn both lists in a firesafe dish.

Cerridwen Iris Shea

April 13
Sunday

3rd ♎

☽ v/c 6:01 am

☽ → ♏ 9:54 am

Color of the day: Yellow
Incense of the day: Eucalyptus

Palm Sunday

Truth Seeking Spell

Amethyst is an easily obtained purple crystal associated with psychic ability and inner vision. When you find yourself in a situation where you feel information is being hidden from you, try this simple spell to reveal the truth.

Get a small amethyst crystal and place it outside in the moonlight if possible. It will absorb the illuminating moon rays, which cast light upon the darkness in the same way you will cast light upon the truth. Tape the amethyst crystal to the back of a mirror that you use regularly. When passing by the mirror once a day, spend a moment gazing into it and say:

Knowledge and wisdom before my eyes, I see the truth instead of lies.

Continue to do this until the situation is resolved.

Kate Freuler

NOTES:

April 14
Monday

3rd ♏

Color of the day: Silver
Incense of the day: Hyssop

Divination at the Crossroads

This is a rite for enhancing your divinations by using the power of the crossroads. You will need:

- 1 part dill seeds
- 1 part fennel seeds
- 1 part juniper berries or eastern red cedar (*Juniperus virginiana*)
- 1 part rosemary leaves, dried
- Mortar and pestle
- A divination tool, whichever you choose
- Incense charcoal and burner
- Matches or lighter

Prepare your incense mixture by lightly crushing the plant ingredients together in a mortar and pestle. Take this mixture, along with your divination tool and incense burner, to a four-way crossroads. Light the charcoal and add some of the incense mixture. Say these words while facing east:

I turn, I turn, I turn at the crossroads.

Turn clockwise, ending facing east again. Then say:

*At the crossroads, turn I,
turn I, turn I.*

Then turn counterclockwise, ending facing east again. Say:

May the truth be revealed. May all haters of the truth be turned away.

You may now begin your divination. Burn more of the incense throughout the session.

Brandon Weston

NOTES:

April 15
Tuesday

3rd ♏︎

☽ v/c 10:24 pm

☽ → ♐︎ 10:37 pm

Color of the day: Maroon
Incense of the day: Ginger

Witch Bottle

Witch bottles are wonderful protective charms with centuries of historical use. They're not only powerful, but also easy to make.

You'll need a small glass jar with a tight lid, some wine or mead, a black candle, matches, and several of the following items: tacks, bent pins, or small nails; pieces of obsidian; sea salt; bits of black wax; a red ribbon; very small pieces of broken glass or pottery (handle carefully!); cleaned bones from a roast chicken; bits of fur or feather; and sprigs of fresh rosemary. Each of these has protection, purification, or grounding properties.

Place your chosen items in the jar, then fill it with the wine or mead. (In centuries past, witch jars were filled with the spellcaster's urine. If you're adventurous, go for it!) Screw the lid on tight and seal with drips of black candle wax.

Traditionally witch bottles are buried on your property, ideally at the new (dark) moon. Or place them within your home for inside protection.

Susan Pesznecker

April 16
Wednesday

3rd ♐︎

Color of the day: White
Incense of the day: Bay laurel

Roasted Oranges Energizing Spell

This spell uses ingredients associated with the fire element to help relieve weariness and bring a quick boost of energy. Slice an unpeeled orange into round slices about ¼ inch thick. Heat a pan on the stovetop to medium temperature, then add the orange slices. Cover the oranges with a generous sprinkling of cinnamon and a light sprinkle of ginger and brown sugar. Think of the element of fire and invite these bright, strong energies to be present as you cast the spell. You might think of the hot sun, a raging bonfire, the warmth of your body, or the passion within you. Envision the fiery energies of the oranges and spices growing stronger as it heats. Cook the oranges on one side for about 2 minutes, then flip the slices over and add more cinnamon, ginger, and brown sugar. Cook for an additional 2 to 3 minutes as you breathe in the warm and vibrant aroma. Remove the fruit from the pan and let cool slightly. Eat for an easy pick-me-up that will have you feeling refreshed and alert.

Melanie Marquis

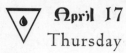

▽ April 17
Thursday

3rd ♐

Color of the day: Purple
Incense of the day: Clove

Working with the Rainy Season

April is part of the rainy season and thus a good time for water magic. Pay attention to when the rain falls, and give thanks for it. Observe where it goes, how it flows, where it pools or soaks into the ground. See how leaves and twigs follow the flowing water, how the plants soak it up.

You can celebrate rain and the element of water in many ways. Put out a birdbath to catch the rain. Plant a rain garden in a soggy part of your yard. Use rain chains to channel water rolling off a shed or other structure that doesn't have gutters. Get a rainy statue, like a frog with an umbrella, and put it outside on rainy days to charge for later use. Say over it:

Rainy day, come and stay,

Let your magic flow my way.

Water clear, water strong,

Charge this statue with your song.

At the end of the month, store the charged statue. When you need a rain spell, bring the statue out to use as a focus.

Elizabeth Barrette

April 18
Friday

3rd ♐

☽ v/c 7:38 am

☽ → ♑ 10:12 am

Color of the day: Pink
Incense of the day: Yarrow

Good Friday

Egg Coloring Divination

This fun rite is usually done around Oestara/Alban Eilir/Spring Equinox or the Christian celebration of Easter. Children can participate, too. Before boiling the eggs, bless the water by using a wand or athame dipped into the pot and saying:

All who eat thereof are hereby blessed.

Boil white eggs, then remove them from the pot. When the eggs are dry and have cooled, use a white or colorless wax crayon to inscribe sigils on each of them. These symbols can be runes, ogham letters, planetary signs, or simply small drawings of beneficial things and happy representations of good luck—a four-leaf clover, a pentagram, birds, a sun with a smiling face, hearts, cats, a triskelion, flowers, moons, and so forth.

Hide the eggs in your home or yard for participants to find. People can then color their eggs with a standard commercial kit or with natural dyes, such as onion skins for yellow, beets for pink, and grass for green. After each person has colored one or more eggs, interpret the sigils for them using correspondence books.

A.C. Fisher Aldag

NOTES:

April 19
Saturday

3rd ♑

☉ → ♉ 3:56 pm

Color of the day: Indigo
Incense of the day: Rue

An April Rain Cleaning Spell

April rains are cleansing and nurturing. This is a good time to clean your ritual tools, refresh your altar, and renew the positive energy of your ritual space. To do this, if possible place any magical tools that won't be harmed outside during a gentle April rain. Place them in a protected area. (If you can't do this, I have a suggestion for you next.) Leave your tools outside for a couple of minutes. Bring them inside and place them on a clean kitchen towel. Using a soft cotton cloth, buff them dry. Visualize any negative energy leaving your tools. Dust your altar, then place your tools back on your altar. Spritz your ritual space with any calming scent that appeals to you.

For those of you who can't place your ritual tools outside in the rain, try this. Dampen a soft cotton cloth with bottled spring water. Wipe off each tool. Visualize any dark energy leaving your tools. Follow with the remaining instructions. Now your ritual tools are as fresh as April rain!

James Kambos

April 20
Sunday

3rd ♑

☽ v/c 1:21 pm

☽ → ♒ 7:22 pm

4th Quarter 9:36 pm

Color of the day: Amber
Incense of the day: Frankincense

Easter – Passover ends

Justice for All

Easter is a time of rebirth and new beginnings. Passover is honored for overcoming adversities, recognizing justice, and appreciating freedom. April 20 (420) celebrates the cannabis plant, both its history and its effects, and renews a call for justice and freedom for the plant itself and its users. Although these three events may seem vastly different, they all have a history of persecution in common.

Choose an incense you would like to work with. If you are a cannabis user, be sure to partake while working this quick spell. Light your incense either outside or inside near an open window. Concentrate on the smoke as it swirls and then dissipates into the air. As you focus on the smoke, infuse it with your energy and words by chanting:

Justice. Freedom. Rebirth.

Imagine that justice, freedom, and rebirth are carried away on the smoke to combine with the atmosphere around you. Send these ideals out into the universe around you.

Kerri Connor

Notes:

April 21
Monday

4ħ ≈

Color of the day: Gray
Incense of the day: Neroli

Soundtrack for Success

Choose a favorite song to link to the energy of success. Pop some headphones on and either sit in meditation or go for a walk (be safe!) while you listen to the song. Conjure up the feeling of success, big and small, by recalling experiences from your recent or distant past, things like delivering a killer presentation, finding a primo parking spot, or completing a training program. Really inhabit the feeling as you visualize these successful scenarios, allowing the music to infuse and enliven your memories. State the intention "This song aligns me with the energy of success" three times, followed by "So mote it be!"

In your day-to-day life, cue up the song whenever you need a boost. Pay attention to intuitive messages and ideas inspired by the music. These are important clues leading you toward success.

Melissa Tipton

 April 22
Tuesday

4ħ ≈
) v/c 5:55 pm

Color of the day: Black
Incense of the day: Bayberry

Earth Day

Love Your Mother Earthing Spell

Depending on where you live, late April can be wintery or springlike. Regardless of the weather today, take a moment to connect to your Mother: Earth.

Attune to your internal stress level and assign it a number from zero to ten, with zero being none and ten being a lot. Now remove your shoes and socks, slippers, or boots.

Go outdoors in your bare feet. Sit with your feet on the earth, or walk slowly and mindfully for a bit.

Take several long, slow breaths. Envision the earth's energy soaking into your feet, up your legs, and flowing throughout your body.

Earthing, the practice of attuning to the vibrational energy of the earth, is known to relieve pain, improve sleep, reduce stress, encourage parasympathetic activation, improve healing, and support the natural circadian cycle.

After several breaths, reevaluate your stress level, from zero to ten, and notice if it has dropped.

Dallas Jennifer Cobb

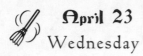

April 23
Wednesday

4th ♒

☽ → ♓ 1:07 am

Color of the day: Yellow
Incense of the day: Marjoram

herbal Cleansing Spray

Sometimes we attract funk into our energetic space, both on our bodies and in our surroundings. As magic workers, it's important to periodically cleanse our spaces. This herbal cleansing spray will do just the trick. Gather the following items:

- A 3-to-5-ounce blue or amber spray bottle
- 5 drops lemongrass essential oil
- 5 drops orange essential oil
- 5 drops lavender essential oil
- 3 drops hyssop essential oil
- 1 ounce vodka
- Purified water

Combine the ingredients in the bottle and then fill it up with purified water. Spray on yourself, on your altar, or around the room to cleanse any stale or negative energy. It can also be used to relieve brain fog and to bring happiness, mental clarity, and optimism. Shake before using and store in a cool, dry place when not in use.

Amanda Lynn

April 24
Thursday

4th ♓

☽ v/c 10:57 pm

Color of the day: Green
Incense of the day: Mulberry

A Dreaming Bath

Here is a soaking bath to aid with divinatory dreams. You will need:

- 3 cups milk (can use milk alternatives like almond or oat milk)
- 1 pearl, piece of coral, amethyst crystal, and/or sapphire (optional)
- 3 passionflowers (*Passiflora incarnata*), dried or fresh
- Purple or blue carnation flower petals from 7 blooms, dried or fresh
- A blue or purple candle, any kind, in a holder (optional)

Fill your bathtub with water to your desired temperature. Add the milk to the water. Place any of the stones you have around the rim of the tub. Add the passionflowers and carnation flower petals. Sit back and relax. I like a dark bathroom for this ritual. For me, the visions will come without even being asleep. If you don't want to soak in complete darkness, light a blue or purple candle. Soak for as long as you want, then dry off and immediately go to sleep. Be sure to extinguish the candle when done.

Brandon Weston

NOTES:

April 25
Friday

4th ♓

☽ → ♈ 3:24 am

Color of the day: White
Incense of the day: Violet

Energy Renewal Spell

Cleansing and cleaning your living space with a broom is a simple and effective way to rid yourself of lingering unwanted energies in your home. In the days of old, wise women knew it was important to use brooms to keep areas clean to prevent the members of a household from getting sick. Adding the intention to energetically cleanse your space to your spring cleaning is a great way to achieve some magical multitasking. This spell can also be used when you want to renew the energy of your space after a visitor whose energy is not compatible with your own has left.

Start in the corner of your house that is farthest from the entryway door. Use a broom to sweep your space, working your way toward the front door, and say these words aloud or to yourself:

Sweep away the negative energy, cleanse this space.

Add new magical energy in its place.

Repeat as needed.

Sapphire Moonbeam

April 26
Saturday

4th ♈

☽ v/c 12:18 pm

Color of the day: Brown
Incense of the day: Sandalwood

Cleansing Herbs

During the bubonic plague, it was believed that herbs such as juniper, lavender, and rosemary would rid the air of sickness and evil with their scent or while burning. While it's true that some herbs have antimicrobial properties, it's unclear how effective this was. However, we do know that magically speaking, these herbs can effectively rid your home of unwanted or stale energy.

After an argument, an unpleasant visitor, or just when you need to refresh your space, create a bundle of dried sprigs from each plant and tie them together with thread. Make as many as you'd like to place around your home, where they can spread their scent. Imagine that the scent is cleansing the air, neutralizing the stale energy that hangs around like fog. Replace as needed.

An alternative way to perform this cleansing is to crumble the dried herbs and burn them on a charcoal disk, going from room to room, wafting the smoke into every nook and cranny.

Kate Freuler

 April 27
Sunday

4th ♈

☽ → ♉ 3:17 am

New Moon 3:31 pm

Color of the day: Yellow
Incense of the day: Juniper

Cutting Ties

The new moon affords us the ability to start anew. In the dark of night, we can leave behind the unnecessary and come out into the light. We can let go of the things and people that hold us back from being the best version of ourselves.

For this spell you will need a length of string or thread and a pair of scissors. Before beginning, take a moment to take a deep breath and release it in order to ground yourself. List out to yourself mentally or write down what you want to cut ties with. Once you have the list, take your string in your hand and say:

*I choose to cut these ties
so that I may rise.*

Then cut a part of the thread. Repeat as many times as you have items to cut ties with. Once you have finished, take the pieces of string and throw them in the trash.

Charlynn Walls

April 28
Monday

1st ♉

Color of the day: Ivory
Incense of the day: Lily

Spring Garden Blessing

In April (in the Northern Hemisphere), we are steeped in the magick of the green as the Earth unfurls under our feet. The air is humming with the drone of bees who eagerly take nourishment from colorful blooms, and we bask under an ever-strengthening sun. Whether you have planted containers on a windowsill or a large plot of land, let's keep in mind that the Earth is truly sacred and is to be treated with honor. For it is from the Earth that all life springs.

At dawn, start in the eastern point of your garden or an eastern point in your home (or stand on your porch or balcony) and walk reverently clockwise, saying something like this:

With the universe as my guide,

*I will work with the
elements hand in hand.*

May the Goddess find favor

As I lovingly care for the land.

*By the power of the sun, of
the rain, soil, and wind,*

*Bless this garden—
let the magick begin.*

Monica Crosson

April 29
Tuesday

1st ♉

☽ v/c 1:18 am
☽ → ♊ 2:34 am

Color of the day: Red
Incense of the day: Ylang-ylang

Poem for the Self

It's both International Dance Day and Duke Ellington Day. Time for a spell to celebrate yourself!

Gather these supplies:

- Music (maybe Duke Ellington's?)

- Word magnets or a pile of cutout words from magazines or newspapers (three dozen or so). This is your "word stash."

- Blank paper or a magnetic surface

Put on your music and dance for a few minutes. Enjoy yourself! You can continue dancing as you pull words out of your word stash. Arrange them on the page or surface so the arrangement looks pleasing, without focusing on structure or content.

Read the words as they now flow, and see how they resonate, and how each word holds a meaning, memory, or possibility. Even seemingly random words will have a flow and will create something unique to you.

Photograph the poem you've created to honor yourself, print it out, and hang it where it will make you smile.

Cerridwen Iris Shea

April 30
Wednesday

1st ♊

☽ v/c 11:49 pm

Color of the day: Brown
Incense of the day: Honeysuckle

Prepare a Porta-Pagan

We magical folx often find ourselves needing to divine, cast spells, or work magic at unplanned times or when we're far away from our magical workspace. Plus, we may not feel comfortable setting up an altar or working spellcraft in public, or carrying materials with us. You can remedy some of these situations by creating a Porta-Pagan.

What's a Porta-Pagan? It's a miniature set of magical tools in a small, sturdy container. Because it's small, it can be carried in a pocket, purse, glove box, or any other easy-to-conceal space. Start your Porta-Pagan with a small metal container, like one of those hinged mint or tea containers. Fill it with small craft items like these:

- Small altar cloth
- Birthday cake or tealight candles
- Matches
- Tiny glass vials of salt, dried herbs, charged water, etc.
- Tiny mirror for scrying
- Seashells, stones, or crystals
- Miniature dice
- Miniature Tarot cards
- Small/toy athame (symbolic)

Vary the items as needed. With your Porta-Pagan, you'll be ready to work magic incongruously and on the spot.

Susan Pesznecker

NOTES:

May

Welcome to the famously merry month of May! Though it was originally named after the Greek fertility goddess Maia, the Catholic Church has since designated this month as sacred to the Virgin Mary, even referring to her as "the Queen of May" during this time. Day one of this flower-filled month is the beloved holiday of Beltane, during which the veil that usually conceals the world of the fairies fades, and our power to make contact with them reaches its yearly peak. Indeed, May's birth flower is a fairy favorite: the lily of the valley. As for our skies, this month they host the Eta Aquariids meteor shower, which reaches its peak around May 6 and is most visible before the sunrise.

May is also the month when the light half of the year begins to assert itself in earnest, and we sense the days lengthening, the sun growing warmer, and the leaves filling out the trees. This allows us to gaze bravely into our own brilliance and to courageously release anything that has been holding us back from being our most radiant, expansive, beautiful selves. Indeed, May's bright presence reminds us to claim the vital prosperity that is our birthright and our natural state.

Tess Whitehurst

May 1
Thursday

1st ♊

☽ → ♋ 3:23 am

Color of the day: Crimson
Incense of the day: Myrrh

Beltane

Beltane Garden Spell

In many places, this is the peak of spring planting season. Fall-planted flowers bloom in spring, "as early as the ground can be worked" seeds sprout, and you can start planting things that need warmer feet—especially if you pop a cover over them to trap the sun's heat and keep off late frosts. Even if you don't have room for a whole garden, you can usually manage a window box or a pot on a porch.

For this spell, you'll need one or more garden stakes, some twine or wire, garden pins, and vine seeds. They can be as small as popsicle sticks for a potted plant or as large as bean poles for a country garden. Fasten four to six pieces of line to each stake, plant the stake, and pin down the lines around it. Plant the seeds. Then say:

Maypole in disguise,

Find where power lies.

Draw it up and draw it in,

Beltane magic stir and spin.

As energy flows,

So the garden grows.

Elizabeth Barrette

NOTES:

May 2
Friday

1st ♋

Color of the day: Pink
Incense of the day: Thyme

Path to Love Spell

If you want love to follow you
everywhere you go, try rubbing
some of this pleasant-smelling oil
mix on the inside of your shoes.

Put one drop each of chamomile,
patchouli, and sandalwood essential
oils on a cotton ball, and then thoroughly wipe the inside of your shoes
with it. While you do so, visualize
a pink glow all around your shoes.
Throw the cotton ball away. Next
time you walk in your shoes, imagine
that the plant energy of the oils hidden within them makes a trail of love-
attracting footprints behind you. This
is an energetic path that will attract
the right people and circumstances
everywhere you go. Love will follow
in your footsteps and soon catch up
to you.

You can also leave a scented cotton
ball inside each shoe when you're not
wearing them, infusing them with
scent and energy for whenever you
need them.

Kate Freuler

May 3
Saturday

1st ♋

☽ v/c 4:02 am
☽ → ♌ 7:29 am

Color of the day: Black
Incense of the day: Sage

Garden Meditation

Today is National Garden
Meditation Day. It is an excellent opportunity to meditate in a
green space in nature. You may want
to meditate near your own garden or
go to a public garden. Just make sure
it is a place where you feel safe and
comfortable sitting quietly with your
eyes closed. Meditation is a way to
concentrate on the present moment
instead of being concerned about a
past event or worrying about events
that haven't happened yet. A garden
is the ideal place to immerse yourself
as you find stillness within.

Sit in a comfortable position, close
your eyes, and focus on your breath.
Take three deep cleansing breaths.
Allow any thoughts, colors, or images that you see in your inner vision
to come, observe them, and then let
them pass through your consciousness. Take all the time you need to
ground yourself and stay present in
the moment.

Sapphire Moonbeam

May 4
Sunday

1st ♌

2nd Quarter 9:52 am

Color of the day: Gold
Incense of the day: Almond

Banishing Candle

Harnessing the power of Leo and the Sun, this spell is designed to cleanse out any shadowy entities or lingering presences from your home. You will need:

- A white candle, jar-style or a votive in a holder
- 7 juniper or red cedar berries (*Juniperus virginiana*)
- Mortar and pestle
- 7 drops juniper essential oil (optional)
- Matches or lighter

Crush the 7 juniper or red cedar berries in a mortar and pestle, and sprinkle them onto the wax in your candle. You can also sprinkle 7 drops of juniper essential oil onto the wax. While facing your front door (inside), light your candle and say three times:

Light drives out all darkness.

Then make a counterclockwise circle through your entire home (the direction of removal) while holding your candle. End the circle back at your front door. Repeat for a total of three rounds, each time reciting the charm three times before you make your circle. You can then snuff out the candle or leave it lit near the front door. (Don't let it burn unattended. Snuff it out if leaving the home.) Relight the candle at your front door or on your home altar whenever your house is in need of cleansing.

Brandon Weston

NOTES:

May 5
Monday

2nd ♌

☽ v/c 9:03 am

☽ → ♍ 3:40 pm

Color of the day: Lavender
Incense of the day: Narcissus

Cinco de Mayo

A Restful Retreat

To retreat is to withdraw from the mundane while seeking quiet, rest, and rejuvenation. You can engineer your escape from daily routines and digital noise by creating a personal retreat. Plan a time and a place for it, away from home if needed. A couple of hours are good—a day is even better. Be undisturbed and leave technology off (emergency settings only). Plan what you'll do. You might read, meditate, hike, work magic, create art, or do anything that allows you to enter the liminal space of relaxation. Gather materials and a small bell, and don't forget tasty food and drink. Cleanse yourself before the retreat begins. Repeat:

To care for myself is important.
To care for myself is a blessing.
To care for myself is the best magic.

Ring the bell—and enjoy the retreat! Repeat the words and ring the bell again when you conclude. Reflect on your experience and journal about it.

Susan Pesznecker

 May 6
Tuesday

2nd ♍

Color of the day: Scarlet
Incense of the day: Cinnamon

Don't Fret the Night Away

If you've ever woken up in the middle of the night, jerking out of sleep worrying about something, you know how difficult it is to get back to sleep. Here's a spell so that you don't fret the night away.

Sit up and look around. Breathe. Cast a circle of protection around your room, imagining the room enclosed in a sphere of white light. The sphere will keep out anything negative.

Lie down again. Say to yourself:

I am here now, safe. This is my reality.

Keep repeating it until you feel calmer.

Now say:

I have these wonderful
things in my life.

Then list them. Let yourself feel calm and happy about them.
Now say:

I deserve health, happiness,
and prosperity.

Repeat this nine times. Let the protective circle melt back into the ground as you drift back to sleep.

Cerridwen Iris Shea

May 7
Wednesday

2nd ♏

Color of the day: Yellow
Incense of the day: Lilac

"Bee" Clear Tea for Clarity

Bee balm (*Monarda* spp.) is a lovely herb whose bright, earthy scent adds a touch of enchantment to any Witch's garden. It lends a citrusy flavor to recipes and is the perfect herbal ally when seeking clarity, or for working spells for success, prosperity, contentment, or peace.

Rise early and make yourself comfortable on your deck, porch, or balcony with a cup of "Bee" Clear Tea (recipe below) and take in each and every note—the sun stretching golden fingers above the eastern hills, shortening shadows, and a dew-kissed landscape. Relish in the sounds that go unnoticed— the drone of insects, the snap of a twig, or the subtle rustle of a gentle breeze. Take deep breaths and clear your mind of clutter and/or chaos and draw in the wisdom of nature.

"Bee" Clear Tea for Clarity

- 2 parts bee balm
- 1 part calendula
- ½ part yarrow

Use one teaspoon of loose tea per cup of hot water. Let steep for approximately five minutes and strain.

Monica Crosson

NOTES:

May 8
Thursday

2nd ♍

☽ v/c 12:11 am

☽ → ♎ 3:06 am

Color of the day: White
Incense of the day: Jasmine

Milk and Honey Abundance Spell

Milk and honey are two signs of abundance. Adding them to your garden encourages your plants to grow and produce abundantly.

Create a simple abundance sigil that is personal to you. What represents an abundant garden to you? If you sell your produce, perhaps a dollar sign or money bag. I use a large bowl shape and "fill" it with outlines of produce—big round tomatoes, string bean lines, and ovals of squash.

Use the milk first, slowly, and gently pour it onto the ground, drawing your sigil into the dirt at the center of your gardening area. As you work, visualize what your abundant garden will look like and say:

Bless this garden to grow and thrive.

Help my plants to stay alive.

Help them produce food for me.

Praise the Goddess and blessed be!

Repeat the process with the honey.

Kerri Connor

 May 9
Friday

2nd ♎

Color of the day: Rose
Incense of the day: Vanilla

Simple Pendulum Divination Spell

Using a pendulum for spiritual insight is an age-old form of divination. Make a simple pendulum using string tied to a ring. You can also use a necklace with a crystal pendant or sacred symbol.

Form a relationship, saying:

Pendulum, help me understand,
magnify energy through my hand.
Working with me for the good of
all, pendulum, hear my call.

Hold the string loosely in your dominant hand, allowing the ring to hang in space.

Train your pendulum by stating the obvious: "My name is _____." See how it moves. That is "yes."

Now state something untrue, such as "I'm 721 years old." See how it moves. That is "no."

Now that you know your pendulum's yes and no, use it to divine answers to spiritual questions, test food or supplement suitability, and confirm intuition.

Build your relationship through regular pendulum use and conscious engagement. More practice means the more attuned you both become.

Dallas Jennifer Cobb

May 10
Saturday

2nd ♎

☽ v/c 2:17 am

☽ → ♏ 3:58 pm

Color of the day: Blue
Incense of the day: Magnolia

World Migratory Bird Day

Birds relate to the element of air. If you like working with air, then helping birds can improve your connection with that element. Many bird species migrate twice annually. In spring they leave their winter roosts for summer nesting grounds, and in autumn they and their fledged chicks fly to warmer refuges. On these journeys, most of them rely on finding food, water, and resting spots along the way to keep them going.

Today is World Migratory Bird Day this year. You can help migrating birds by providing bird feeders with assorted food, a birdbath with water, and perches such as a trellis or garden sculpture among bird-friendly landscaping. Offer high-energy food such as sunflower seed, peanuts, peanut butter, and suet. Some birds prefer sugary foods such as nectar, jelly, or fruit. To attract their attention to your offerings, say this charm:

Birds flying high,

Drop from the sky

And stay for a spell.

Stop for a snack

On your way back,

Wherever you dwell.

           Elizabeth Barrette

NOTES:

May 11
Sunday

2nd ♏

Color of the day: Amber
Incense of the day: Hyacinth

Mother's Day

Manifesting the Mother

On this Mother's Day we can practice tarot meditation with the Empress card in order to engage with the mother energy in our lives, whether we honor a mother or give birth to an idea. Pull the Empress card from your favorite tarot deck. You will want to set this up on your altar with a journal and pen. Find a comfortable position in which to sit or lie where you can still see the imagery on the card.

Sitting or lying down starts the process of unwinding. When you are ready, take a deep breath, and as you exhale, relax the muscles in your body. Look closely at the Empress card and then close your eyes. Hold the image in your mind's eye and say:

Empress, give me insight.
Let me manifest what is right.

Focus on the imagery that is presented in your mind. When you are ready, open your eyes and write down what you envisioned. Write down how you feel you might manifest the mother energy presented to you.

Charlynn Walls

May 12
Monday

2nd ♏
Full Moon 12:56 pm

Color of the day: Gray
Incense of the day: Clary sage

Make Your Own Wand

A wand can be a powerful tool for magical work. It can focus and direct energy, amplify intention, open and close a sacred or ceremonial space, and more. Many are happy purchasing a pre-made wand, but making your own is extra special.

The classic wand is made of wood, ideally a thick "found branch" from a wooded natural space. Use the length between your elbow point and middle fingertip as a measure. Remove the bark with a pocketknife, sand the branch smooth with sand paper, and then rub with beeswax to smooth and seal.

From this point, use the wand as is or embellish it with any number of additions. Use superglue to embed a crystal in the wand tip. Wrap it with wire, perhaps strung with seed beads. Use a woodburner to inscribe symbols or words. The sky's the limit when personalizing your own wand.

Consecrate your wand by leaving it on your altar through a full lunar cycle and then blessing it with the four elements.

Susan Pesznecker

May 13
Tuesday

3rd ♏

☽ v/c 2:37 am

☽ → ♐ 4:35 am

Color of the day: Maroon
Incense of the day: Cedar

Beltane Scrub

It's still Beltane season, a time when we like to feel sexy and romantic! A great way to bring that feeling in is to create a salt or sugar scrub with some wonderful aphrodisiac essential oils. Gather the following items:

- 1 cup carrier oil (almond, apricot, jojoba, etc.)
- ½ cup sugar or salt
- A combination of your favorite sensual essential oils (or a single oil), such as jasmine, ylang-ylang, sandalwood, neroli, and rose
- A small glass bowl
- A metal spoon
- A glass jar with a lid

Gather your ingredients in the bowl and mix well with the metal spoon. Feel free to adjust the measurements so you get a texture and aroma you like. Prepare a shower, and use the scrub all over your body (minus sensitive areas). Envision your ideal intimate experience. Breathe in deeply the aroma of the scrub as you allow yourself to feel sexy and desirable. Rinse off and store the remaining scrub in the glass jar.

Amanda Lynn

NOTES:

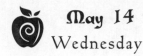

May 14
Wednesday

3rd ♐

Color of the day: Topaz
Incense of the day: Bay laurel

A Vagus (Nerve) Vacation

Lie on your back on a carpet or exercise mat, somewhere comfortable yet firm (not a couch or mattress). Bend your knees so your feet are planted on the ground, and close your eyes. Visualize a web of light surrounding and supporting you, pulsating with healing energy. As you relax, your body, mind, and spirit are able to receive more of this nourishing energy.

To facilitate this relaxation with a vagus nerve exercise, cradle the back of your head in your hands, fingers gently clasped. Without moving your head, look as far as you can to the right, maintaining this orientation until you experience a deep sigh, swallow, or yawn. Bring your gaze back to center and rest a moment, then repeat by looking as far as you can to the left. Return to center, and soak in this healing energy for as long as you wish, bringing your hands to rest on your belly.

Melissa Tipton

May 15
Thursday

3rd ♐
☽ v/c 2:29 pm
☽ → ♑ 3:58 pm

Color of the day: Green
Incense of the day: Balsam

A Pansy Love Spell

Pansies aren't just planted for their cheerful colors. They've been linked to love magic since the Victorian era. To attract romance, try this spell. You'll need a small vase of pansies (any colors you wish), a sheet of pink stationery, a pen, and a few drops of rose water. Set the vase of pansies on your altar. On the stationery, write this charm:

Pansies, draw to me a romantic spark.

Let Cupid's arrow hit the mark.

Sprinkle the stationery with a few drops of rose water. When the pansies fade in a few days, discard them. Hide the written charm and let it work. You may have a prophetic dream. When love finds you, thank the charm and discard it.

James Kambos

May 16
Friday

3rd ♑

Color of the day: Purple
Incense of the day: Rose

Mind Your Business Spell

This protection spell is intended to help turn away unwanted attention from another. There is a fine line between a friend who is interested in you to cheer on your success and one who is only there to hear the details and gossip to others about you. This spell can also be used when you sense that someone around you is envious. Place a black tourmaline stone, for protection, on a piece of paper. Around the stone, draw a circle and then add lines with arrows pointing out from the circle and away from the stone. Sit and contemplate your reason for wanting to do this protection spell. It might be best to just completely ignore the situation and not give it any energy at all. However, if you feel you need to influence the energies, safely light a black candle for protection and say these words:

Take your attention away from me,
remove your interest from what you see.

Mind your business and tend to your
own, pay attention to the "seeds"
you have watered and grown.

Extinguish the candle when done.

Sapphire Moonbeam

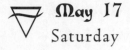 **May 17**
Saturday

3rd ♑

Color of the day: Indigo
Incense of the day: Ivy

Spell for Stability

Use this spell to help bring comfort and restore stability when needed. Find a small stick on the ground, and hold it as you reflect on the current situation that has you feeling troubled. Let your worries and other emotions flow into the stick. As you sit in contemplation, break the stick into smaller pieces. Poke each piece into the ground, making the outline of a circle with the pieces. Cover the ends of the sticks completely with a thick layer of dirt, making sure any sharp ends are buried deep. Pat the ground down firmly and envision any stress in your body flowing out through your hands and into the earth. Spend a few moments in reflection. This spell will help shift current patterns to help you feel more grounded and centered.

Melanie Marquis

May 18
Sunday

3rd ♑

☽ v/c 12:27 am

☽ → ♒ 1:29 am

Color of the day: Orange
Incense of the day: Almond

Setting Boundaries

Use this chant while you scatter salt to set a protective border around your home.

Walk the boundary outside of your home. If you live in an apartment, walk around the entire outside of your building. While walking, scatter a bit of salt on the ground and visualize your own energy mixing with the energy of the salt to form a barrier. You may visualize this barrier any way you like: as a brick wall, a bright radiant light, or whatever works best for you. Chant:

Set this barrier into place

To protect my family, home, and space.

Upon this ground my strength does pour

To protect those here for evermore.

Kerri Connor

NOTES:

May 19
Monday

3rd ♒

Color of the day: White
Incense of the day: Neroli

Victoria Day (Canada)

For Establishing Boundaries

Here is a smoke-based ritual for establishing a magical boundary around yourself. You will need:

- 1 part dogwood bark (*Cornus florida*), dried
- ½ part holly tree bark (*Ilex* spp.), dried
- 1 part mullein leaf (*Verbascum thapsus*), dried
- ½ part Solomon's seal root (*Polygonatum* spp.), dried
- 1 part sweetgum resin or bark (*Liquidambar styraciflua*, often called storax or American storax), dried
- Mortar and pestle
- Incense charcoal and burner (that can be held)
- Matches or lighter

Mix all the plant ingredients together and lightly crush in the mortar and pestle. Go outside at midnight. Light your charcoal and place it in your burner. Hold in your right hand (make sure it's a handheld burner that won't burn you). Add your incense mixture and face the east. Say:

In the east, a mountain.

Then turn clockwise to the west and say:

In the west, a mountain.

Turn clockwise to the south and say:

In the south, a mountain.

Turn clockwise to the north and say:

In the north, a mountain.

Then turn clockwise to the east and say:

A mountain on all sides. No evil can cross them. No sicknesses can cross them. (Name of enemy or target) cannot cross them, even if (he/she/they) had all the power in all the world! Stand firm, until the foundations of the earth fall away.

Let the incense burn out naturally, then return home.

Brandon Weston

May 20
Tuesday

3rd ♒

☽ v/c 7:59 am

4th Quarter 7:59 am

☽ → ♓ 8:28 am

☉ → ♊ 2:55 pm

Color of the day: Gray
Incense of the day: Basil

Nurture Nature Spell

It's May, and things are growing! This is a perfect time to do a nurture nature spell. You will need a small houseplant or a cutting from a friend or neighbor, rooted and planted in a pot. Hold the potted plant in your hands and follow your breath for a few minutes until you feel calm and aligned with the living plant in your hands. Introduce yourself, and give the plant a name. Then, calling it by name, say:

> I promise to nurture you to the best of
> my ability during this growing season.

Put the plant in a special spot where it will get the sunlight it needs. Water it regularly. Feed it. Stop and speak to it every day, and build a relationship with it. Draw it, photograph it, write about it.

As you nurture the plant, it will give you joy in return. If it's an annual or it does not survive, give thanks and compost its remains.

Cerridwen Iris Shea

May 21
Wednesday

4th ♓

Color of the day: Brown
Incense of the day: Lavender

Morning Magic Spell

We have all heard the horrors of how our brains are being rewired by constant cell phone use. Try changing your routine this morning, and instead of reaching for your cell phone and getting the cortisol hits that come from each email, or seeking the endorphin hits from likes and shares, envelop your morning in magic. Choose a quiet, self-soothing activity to begin your day, such as tea on the back deck, journal writing, or a few moments of prayer or meditation. Let your eyes seek out an object of beauty. Let your hands reach for comfort versus stimulation.

Now pause—and assess your internal state. Feeling easy, happy, and grateful? Notice feelings of calm well-being? Yay!

Consider adding Morning Magic every day. Make a choice to begin your day stress-free. Cultivate peace and set the state of your brain and nervous system. These gifts are yours to take away, into the day.

Dallas Jennifer Cobb

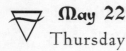

▽ May 22
Thursday

4℞ ♓

☽ v/c 12:06 pm

☽ → ♈ 12:26 pm

Color of the day: Crimson
Incense of the day: Nutmeg

Gnome Magic

Gnomes are earth elementals that can be helpful creatures, especially in the garden. They have masculine energy and can be highly protective, which aligns with the energy of Thursday. Working with gnomes means creating a space for them to occupy. A flower bed or garden area is an excellent place to invite them to stay. They enjoy the wilder parts of nature, so a spot that is shady and a tad overgrown is an excellent choice. You can put out food and drink to entice them in. You will know they have taken up residence in your garden when you start seeing your plants producing more over time. Once they are there, you can work with them to protect your property. Let them know you need their help by saying something like this:

Fierce and cunning is the gnome.
Protect and keep safe my home.

Be sure to leave offerings occasionally to show your appreciation for their help.

Charlynn Walls

① May 23
Friday

4℞ ♈

Color of the day: Coral
Incense of the day: Violet

Magical Coffee

A morning cup of coffee can be so much more than just a caffeine boost. Try giving your cup of brew a personalized magical edge based on whatever energy you need in your life that day. Just add a tiny pinch of appropriate herbs to the dry coffee grounds before starting the coffee maker while visualizing your goal. Be sure to use nontoxic herbs only, and add just a tiny bit unless you want to compromise the taste of your drink. On the other hand, some herbs and spices add a very nice flavor that you might discover you enjoy.

Here are some suggestions:

- Rosebuds, lavender, or jasmine flower for love

- Cinnamon, mint, or ginger for prosperity

- Rosemary, sage, or witch hazel for protection

- Mugwort, dandelion root, or bay for psychic ability

While you drink your coffee, sit peacefully and imagine yourself living out the goal aligned with your herb.

Kate Freuler

May 24
Saturday

4th ♈

☽ v/c 7:44 am

☽ → ♉ 1:38 pm

Color of the day: Gray
Incense of the day: Sandalwood

Protective Garden Magick

It was once said that if a person heard the bells of the foxglove ring, they were doomed to die. Of course, this is not to be taken literally, as it was folklore inspired by foxglove's (*Digitalis purpurea*) poisonous nature. But there is something that foxglove and bells have in common, and that is protective magick. Foxgloves are one of our "garden wards," and can be planted to protect your property. Bells have a long history in magick. They have been used to clear ritual space, invoke the elements, seal spellwork, send up prayers, attract positive energy, and clear away negative energy.

For easy protective magick for your home and garden, plant foxgloves in a large container and set on your porch, deck, or balcony that gets partial sun. Stick a 39-inch shepherd's hook into the container and hang a small wind chime from it. As you run your hands over the chimes, say:

I draw in positivity and banish
negative vibes. Blessed be the
Witch whose garden thrives.

Monica Crosson

 May 25
Sunday

4th ♉

Color of the day: Yellow
Incense of the day: Marigold

Fire Scrying

What's more evocative of primal magic than fire? Each time we strike a match, light a candle, or build a campfire, we're to the flame—just like moths, so the saying goes. Through this intense connection, fire also provides a powerful divinatory tool via fire scrying.

To "scry" is to open oneself to the larger world and one's place in it. Begin by kindling a fire: light a candle or, even better, kindle an indoor or outdoor hearth or campfire.

Sit before your candle or fire, dressed comfortably and prepared to sit in place for 15 to 30 minutes. As you gaze into the flame, ask whatever question is on your mind and repeat:

Flames of power, heat, and light,
Bring me guidance on this night.
May it be so.

As you scry, watch for obvious fiery symbols or manifestations. Let your mind step away from the present, too, and relax into possibility, aware of messages and intuitions that may follow. Once done, put the fire out and journal about the experience.

Susan Pesznecker

May 26
Monday

4th ♉

☽ v/c 9:52 am

☽ → ♊ 1:21 pm

New Moon 11:02 pm

Color of the day: Silver
Incense of the day: Rosemary

Memorial Day

Magical Cleaning helpers

Have you ever been envious of Snow White or Cinderella with their magical house-cleaning helpers? The rest of their situations leave much to be desired, but who wouldn't love a little magical boost when tidying up?

Set out your cleaning supplies and close your eyes, connecting to your heart space and feeling the thread that unites you to all things. Open your eyes, and circle a pointed finger around the supplies, visualizing a swirl of sparkling energy streaming from your hand like a Fairy Godmother, awakening the spirit of the supplies.

Once activated, your supplies will function on multiple levels. For instance, a vacuum can sweep up pet hair, but it can *also* collect stagnant, unwanted energy and neutralize it. As you clean, ask each tool for its help, being sure to thank it when you're done, then imagine the tool going back to sleep to enjoy a well-deserved rest.

Melissa Tipton

 May 27
Tuesday

1st ♊

Color of the day: Red
Incense of the day: Ginger

Altar Blessing

Tidy up your altar both physically and spiritually. Clean up any dust, ashes, or spills. Wash or replace your altar cloth. Dust off any statues, candleholders, or other stationary items. Replenish candles, salt, water, incense, or anything else needed. Cleanse, recharge, and/or replace any crystals or stones.

When your altar is completely clean, spritz the air above it with Florida water or another cleansing protective type of spray. Close your eyes and send energy through your power (dominant) hand, projecting it at your altar, slowly moving your hand back and forth.

Recite these words:

*Bless this altar, symbol of
my spiritual home.*

Bless this altar, window to my soul.

*Protect this altar, symbol
of my spiritual home.*

Protect this altar, window to my soul.

Kerri Connor

May 28
Wednesday

1st ♊

☽ v/c 9:01 am

☽ → ♋ 1:33 pm

Color of the day: White

Incense of the day: Honeysuckle

Spell to Attract Good Health

May 28 is the International Day of Action for Women's Health. Today's rite is intended to attract optimal health to you and your loved ones.

Use your athame (ritual blade) to cut an apple across its middle, revealing the pentagram shape at the core. Cut the apple into slices to share. Each individual takes five bites of their apple slice, thoroughly chewing and swallowing, visualizing good health while doing so. Before each bite, chant:

Earth—Health for my body.

Air—Health for my mind.

Fire—Health for my spirit.

Water—Health for my emotions.

Spirit—Health for us all.

After the rite is completed, bury the apple core near the front door of your home.

A.C. Fisher Aldag

May 29
Thursday

1st ♋

Color of the day: Green

Incense of the day: Carnation

Car Travel Sachet

When we get into our cars, we want to make sure that we get to our final destination every time. Use this simple spell to create a protection sachet to put in your car to help make sure you travel safely. You will need the following items:

- A small sachet bag (Any kind of material or fabric will do.)
- A combination of the following herbs: dried rosemary, dried mint, dried bay, cinnamon stick
- A small evil eye charm (optional)

Gather all your items inside the sachet bag and repeat the following charm. Then cleanse and charge the sachet and place anywhere you'd like inside your vehicle. Replace the herbs and repeat whenever you feel the sachet needs a boost or refresh.

As I travel in my car,

May this protect me near and far.

Keep me safe, keep me alive,

When it's time for me to drive.

Amanda Lynn

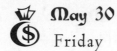

May 30
Friday

1st ♋

☽ v/c 12:50 pm

☽ → ♌ 4:17 pm

Color of the day: Rose
Incense of the day: Orchid

A Pollen Prosperity Spell

Now in the Northern Hemisphere the trees are releasing their life-giving pollen. It is the golden dust of life, covering sidewalks, porches, and windshields. Including this precious substance in a prosperity spell will draw abundance to you. You'll need a one dollar bill, a small amount of pollen, an envelope, paper, and pen. You can gather the pollen from any outdoor surface. Put the dollar and pollen in the envelope. On the paper, write this:

Precious pollen, gift of the trees,

Increase the amount of this money.

Let it multiply and come to me.

Now seal the written charm in the envelope with the pollen and money. Hide it. As money begins to come to you, sprinkle the pollen outside. Discard the charm and the envelope. Include the dollar as part of a donation to your favorite charity. May the golden dust of life bless you with abundance.

James Kambos

May 31
Saturday

1st ♌

Color of the day: Blue
Incense of the day: Patchouli

Spell for Confidence

Use this spell to boost your confidence and gain more respect. Choose a stone or a special piece of jewelry. Jade, clear quartz, tiger's-eye, silver, gold, or ruby are especially well suited, but you can choose anything that appeals to you.

Take the jewelry or stone you've chosen outside in the daytime. Hold it in your hand and envision the sun's light entering it. Picture yourself confident, a great leader who is respected and admired. Hold yourself up and stand as you would if you were absolutely bursting with confidence, shoulders back and relaxed, neck straight, and chin up. Take some full, deep breaths, expanding your chest as much as possible with each breath. Think of all your awesome qualities, and imagine your aura of awesomeness growing larger and larger, taking up a huge space around you. Put on the jewelry or slip the stone into your pocket. Wear the jewelry or carry the stone with you wherever you go, and touch it whenever you need that extra boost to remind you to stand tall and walk proud in who you are.

Melanie Marquis

June

The month of June is a time that inspires warmth, love, passion, and deep appreciation of beauty. Agricultural festivals in old Europe acknowledge and celebrate the many flowers and fruits that become abundant at this time. It is no coincidence that these plants—such as roses, raspberries, strawberries, wildflowers, and those that feature red or pink flowers or fruit—are associated with the planet Venus and the goddess Aphrodite. June is also the traditional month for weddings, and the term *honeymoon* refers to the beverage mead, made from fermented honey, that was traditionally given to the bride and groom as an aphrodisiac.

June brings the start of summer, and for thousands of years the summer solstice has been a prominent festival in many cultures. This celestial festival signifies the beginning of warm weather and abundant growth yet also reminds us of its opposite calendar festival: the winter solstice. All hail the Holly King! Spells done in June are often connected to love, romance, growth, health, and abundance.

Peg Aloi

 **June 1**
Sunday

1st ♌

☽ v/c 7:38 pm

☽ → ♍ 11:00 pm

Color of the day: Gold
Incense of the day: Frankincense

Shavuot begins at sundown

healing a Broken heart

Transmute the pain of heartbreak into the gifts of wisdom and hope, inspired by Leonard Cohen's reminder that everything is a little bit broken, but it's the cracks that let in the light. Sit comfortably and close your eyes. Focus on your breath until you feel present in your body, firmly situated in the current moment.

Place one hand over your heart and one over your belly, and attune with the rising and falling harmony of your breath accompanied by the drumbeat of your heart. Picture your heart in your mind's eye, allowing it to be just as it is, which might be a little bruised, a little cracked, a little broken right now. Visualize the energy of divine love, sparking like a seed in your heart. It glows brighter, and brighter still, until your heart is radiating with this light—light that might be more visible through the cracks of your experience. Let the imagery fade and open your eyes, knowing you are right where you're meant to be.

Melissa Tipton

June 2
Monday

1st ♍

2nd Quarter 11:41 pm

Color of the day: Ivory
Incense of the day: Narcissus

Pearl of Wisdom Spell

Pearls are associated with protection, enhancing relationships, the moon, water, harmony, divination, and manifesting abundance. For this spell, gather these supplies:

- A white or silver tealight candle in a firesafe dish
- The Moon tarot card
- Matches
- A pearl or a picture of a pearl
- Journal and pen

Sit where you won't be disturbed for twenty minutes. Place the tealight above the Moon card. Light the candle, saying:

I ask for the illumination of the pearl's wisdom.

Sit and hold the pearl (or its picture), following your breath, letting thoughts float and flow in your brain. Some will be transient monkey-mind thoughts; others will be "pearls of wisdom" on relevant situations. Absorb the knowledge. Write down what you want to remember and/or act upon.

At the end of twenty minutes, give thanks. Place your hands on the floor, grounding any excess energy. If possible, burn down the candle completely. Otherwise, burn it over the next few days. Put the Moon card back in the deck, and carry the pearl with you.

Cerridwen Iris Shea

NOTES:

 **June 3**
Tuesday

2nd ♏

Color of the day: White
Incense of the day: Bayberry

Money Bowl Spell

Attract abundance and prosperity to you with a money bowl. You will need a bowl that is pretty and uplifting to the eye, a bay leaf, a pen, and some coins or bills. Hold the bowl in both hands, saying:

Bless this vessel with wealth and wonder.

Set the bowl on your altar and say:

*May it attract abundance
and prosperity to me.*

Write a one-word wish on the bay leaf. It may be wealth, abundance, prosperity, riches, etc. Place the bay leaf in the bottom of the bowl, saying:

May bay attract what I ask.

Cover the leaf with coins or bills, saying:

*Look at all the money coming
to me. So mote it be.*

Regularly add to the bowl when you empty pockets or clean out your purse, making sure to repeat the affirmation.

Occasionally draw from the bowl as needed. Now you will always have money.

Dallas Jennifer Cobb

June 4
Wednesday

2nd ♍

☽ v/c 7:11 am

☽ → ♎ 9:38 am

Color of the day: Yellow
Incense of the day: Geranium

Communicating through Hermes

Knowing what the gods want us to do in their service can be difficult to discern. What better way to find out than to send a letter with Hermes as your emissary?

You will need a piece of paper, a pen, an herbal wash, and an envelope. The wash can be as simple as hot water poured over thyme for courage. Let the herbal wash steep for an hour and then strain. While you wait, write your letter to your patron deity or just to spirit. Ask how you can be of service and for any messages that they may have for you. Lightly cover the letter with the herbal wash. You can dab with your fingers, or use a paintbrush or a paper towel soaked with the herbal wash to lightly go over the surface. Seal the letter in an envelope and address it to the deity you wish to communicate with. Burn the letter in a heat-safe container. Take the ashes and scatter them into the wind, saying:

*Hermes, on swift feet fly. Take
my letter to those in the sky.*

Charlynn Walls

June 5
Thursday

2nd ♎

Color of the day: Purple
Incense of the day: Mulberry

Homemaking

June is a popular month for weddings because it's sacred to Juno, goddess of marriage and hearth and home. While homemaking is a crucial step in the formation of a new family, its maintenance is just as important to established families. So take some time this month to make your house a home. You can do this in many ways. Spend a day on housecleaning. Refresh your supply of towels, rugs, linens, or other homey things. Bring in vases of fresh garden flowers; this is one time to prefer cultivated over wild ones. Find a figurine of Juno—replicas of classic ones are readily available online—or a motherly figure who can stand in for her. Sprinkle the statuette with earth and ash, then say:

Juno, goddess of hearth and home,

Ruler of mirror and of comb,

*Bless this place with
your love and light*

As a refuge against the night.

Keep the figurine in your kitchen or on a mantelpiece above a fireplace.

Elizabeth Barrette

 June 6
Friday

2nd ♎

☽ v/c 9:04 pm

☽ → ♏ 10:23 pm

Color of the day: Pink
Incense of the day: Cypress

Protecting a Friend

There's nothing like a good friend, and sometimes, when we see them troubled or in a difficult situation, we want to help. You can cast a spell of protection to guide them through the tough spots.

You'll need two small pieces of obsidian, two strings (preferably black) about 12 inches long, a white pillar candle, and either a saucer or a Mason jar (preferred) to hold the candle. (For a safer candle, use a flameless battery-powered version.)

Carry out this spell with your friend. Place the stones and strings on your altar. Set the candle to one side and light it. Repeat:

Dear friend, find your way.

Be guided by this light.

Be protected from harm.

Be grounded in our friendship.

Extinguish the candle.

Give one stone to your friend and ask them to leave it in a safe place. Leave your stone on your altar. Each of you should then tie a string to each other's wrists.

Each night, light your candle and repeat the charm. Wear the strings until the concern has passed. Then you may cut each other's strings free.

Susan Pesznecker

NOTES:

 June 7
Saturday

2nd ♏

Color of the day: Black
Incense of the day: Pine

Water Spell for Good Fortune

Cast this spell for an extra boost of good luck. Choose a drinking glass that you find appealing, and fill it with fresh, cold water. Next, choose a bottle of food coloring in a color that aligns with your current goal. If it's greater prosperity, healing, increased vitality, or the aid of nature that you seek, choose green. If you're hoping for good luck in love or on an educational matter like a test, choose blue. For good fortune in gaining and arranging travel opportunities, choose yellow. For general positive energy and good luck, choose red, or a combination of red and blue to make purple.

Add just a few drops of the food coloring to the water. Swirl the glass and watch the color blend into the water as you envision yourself experiencing good fortune. Drink the water, then take an action toward one of your goals to seal the spell.

Melanie Marquis

 June 8
Sunday

2nd ♏

Color of the day: Yellow
Incense of the day: Eucalyptus

Painted heart Love Spell

For this spell, you will need a semipermanent pigment, such as henna or a nontoxic marker.

Find a quiet place and clearly imagine the kind of relationship you'd like to experience. See yourself and a partner engaging in fun activities, laughing together, or in whatever situation you desire. When you can visualize it clearly in your mind, place your hand over your heart and feel it beating. Imagine that the pulsing of your heart is sending out magnetic energy like a beacon. Draw a heart on your chest with your chosen pigment. Over the following days, the heart will fade in the shower and through wear while bringing a relationship closer. Each time you notice the heart drawn on your body, put your hand on your chest and feel your beating heart sending out the signal to attract the right person for you.

Kate Freuler

June 9
Monday

2nd ♏

☽ v/c 8:06 am

☽ → ♐ 10:56 am

Color of the day: Lavender
Incense of the day: Lily

Protection Blend for the home

Sometimes our homes can get energetically stale or we might feel like we need to power up our spiritual guard. This is when I like to call for more protection in the home. For this spell you will need:

- An assortment of the following dried or powdered herbs: bay leaf, rosemary, lavender, peppermint, cinnamon, clove, chili pepper flakes, black pepper

- A grinder (if herbs are not powdered)

- Salt

- A small to medium-size jar with a lid

If your herbs aren't powdered, you can chop them up with a spice grinder, a mortar and pestle, a rolling pin and ziplock bag, or your own preferred method. Once all the herbs are at around the same consistency, blend them with the salt and place in the jar.

Sprinkle small amounts of the mixture around your home in the corners of doorways, windows, and any area that feels mucky. Once you feel the energy is cleansed, vacuum up the herbs. Store the rest in a cool, dry place and bring out anytime you want to protect and cleanse your home.

Amanda Lynn

NOTES:

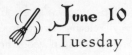

June 10
Tuesday

2nd ♐

Color of the day: Maroon
Incense of the day: Ylang-ylang

Removing Obstacles with Garlic

Use garlic's fiery nature to burn away obstacles on your path. You will need:

- A piece of white paper, 7 inches square
- A red pen or marker
- A head of garlic
- A piece of red cotton cloth, 1 foot square
- Red string, 7 feet long

Using a red pen or marker, write all the obstacles you'd like to cleanse away on the paper square. Fold the paper around the head of garlic, then place in the center of the red cloth. Spit onto the garlic and paper bundle three times. Bring the corners of the cloth up, then tie around the garlic and paper, forming a bundle. Seal with three knots in the red string. Leave about a foot of the string loose outside the knots. Tie these together to form a loop. Hang the bundle in an oak tree (or another strong, living tree) where no one will see it. As it rots away, so too will your obstacles.

Brandon Weston

June 11
Wednesday

2nd ♐

Full Moon 3:44 am

☽ v/c 3:58 pm

☽ → ♑ 9:55 pm

Color of the day: Brown
Incense of the day: Bay laurel

Full Moon Love Spell

The full moon in June is a time when love is in bloom. If you don't have a romantic partner at the moment, this spell can help attract the love that you desire. The flower of the month of June is a rose. Obtain a rose so you can use the flower petals in your spell. Red roses symbolize romance, pink roses are for adoration, an orange rose boosts enthusiasm, a purple rose has the energy of enchantment, and a yellow rose symbolizes platonic friendship. You can choose to use just one color or use all of these colors. On a piece of paper, draw a circle to represent the full moon. Place the rose petals in a circle around the moon you have drawn. Once you are clear in your intention for the love you desire, use these words to enhance the outcome:

I utilize the power of this magical full moon

So the love I desire will appear and romance will bloom.

You can dispose of the paper by safely burning it three days after the full moon. You can bury the rose petals in your garden or in the dirt of a house plant to represent planting the seeds of the love that you desire.

Sapphire Moonbeam

NOTES:

 **June 12**
Thursday

3rd ♑

Color of the day: Turquoise
Incense of the day: Apricot

Property Protection Spell

I live in a little tourist town. In the winter it is quiet and safe, and in the summer it changes. Join me in a property protection spell as the summer season approaches.

You will need about a cup of good-quality sea salt. Salt has been used for millennia to protect and bless. It has beneficial properties for healing, protection, blessing, and binding to get rid of negative energy.

Walk your property lines sprinkling salt, incanting:

Salt protects and rejects negativity.

Salt protects me and my property.

Over and over, repeat this, knowing that your action, intention, and voice vibration add to the energy you are laying down on the land. Envision the energy along the property line.

Save some salt so you can sprinkle it near each of the entrances, gates, doors, or driveways, repeating your incantation:

Salt protects and rejects negativity.

Salt protects me and my property.

Blessed be.

Dallas Jennifer Cobb

 **June 13**
Friday

3rd ♑

Color of the day: Coral
Incense of the day: Mint

Breakup Healing Spell

There are so many complicated feelings happening during a breakup. Validate those feelings and allow yourself to express the pain with this spell intended to help you sift through the raw emotions and find growth from the experience.

You will need:

- An herbal mix that includes 2 parts dried pink rose petals (self-love), 1 part lavender (peace, healing), and ½ part lemon balm (healing)

- A cup or mug

- 1 cup water

- Baking tray

- An 8 × 11 sheet of blank white paper

- A pink tealight candle

- Heatproof container

Steep your herbs in a cup of hot water for approximately five minutes. Place the sheet of paper in the baking tray, and pour the herbal water into the tray, making sure both sides of the paper are damp. Quickly remove the paper from the tray and allow it to dry overnight. Discard the herbal water.

Write yourself a letter on the paper that is now infused with healing herbs. Release painful emotions, while also reminding yourself of your strength and lessons learned. Light the tealight and use it to ignite your letter. Let it burn out in the heatproof container. As it burns, say:

Through pain I find growth.

Through growth I find healing.

Monica Crosson

NOTES:

 June 14
Saturday

3rd ℣

☽ v/c 4:52 am

☽ → ≈ 7:00 am

Color of the day: Blue
Incense of the day: Sage

Flag Day

Blood Connection Spell

Today is World Blood Donor Day. If you can donate blood, you may save a life! Whether you donate blood today or not, it's a good day to connect to your own blood and the miracle that is your body.

Lie down where you won't be disturbed for twenty minutes. Follow your breath as you inhale and exhale, relaxing. Become aware of your heartbeat. Your heart circulates your blood, which is part of your life force. Descend deeper into your own awareness. Feel how the blood flows through your veins, bringing oxygen and nutrients to your entire body. Recognize how your blood supports your body, which then gives your spirit a tangible home. Enjoy the sensation. Slowly return to your more conscious self. Say out loud:

I am a Force of Nature.

Whenever you feel anxious, repeat those words and remember the feeling of your own blood's power.

Cerridwen Iris Shea

 June 15
Sunday

3rd ≈

Color of the day: Amber
Incense of the day: Heliotrope

Father's Day

Igniting the Guidance of the Sun

This spell can be performed on a Sunday, or do an internet search for "planetary hours calculator" to find the hour of the Sun on the day of your choosing. You'll need the Sun card from any tarot deck. Sit comfortably and hold the card as you intone:

Sun of Truth,

Sun of Light,

I seek to know which path is right.

Guide and aid me, Sun!

Gaze softly at the card until the details are vivid in your mind, then close your eyes and imagine stepping into the card like a doorway, entering the Sun's realm. Feel the warm rays on your skin, infusing every cell in your body with light and igniting the wisdom of your heart, body, and soul working in perfect harmony. Ask any questions you have, and open to insights arriving as imagery, words, a felt sense, etc.

When done, thank the Sun, exit through the card, and let the imagery fade before opening your eyes.

Melissa Tipton

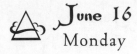 June 16
Monday

3rd ♒

☽ v/c 1:31 pm

☽ → ♓ 2:09 pm

Color of the day: Silver
Incense of the day: Hyssop

Winds of Change Spell

Cast this spell to shake up a stagnant situation and spur revolutionary changes. You'll need a short length of purple thread, about six inches long. Find a tree you like, and sit or stand beneath it with the piece of thread lying across your open palm. Think of the situation you wish to change, then add to the visualization new elements of kookiness and craziness. You might imagine squirrels leaping through the scene, a clown doing cartwheels across your mind's eye, or a dog wearing a hat playing a saxophone appearing at the forefront of your imagination. The weirder the visualization, the more effective the spell will be. State:

This situation needs to change!

Then tie the thread onto the stem of a leaf growing on the tree. Let the ends hang down to flutter in the breeze. If you don't have trees in your area, you can tie the thread to another plant. It just needs to be outside and exposed to the wind. As the air blows across the thread, the situation will transform.

Melanie Marquis

June 17
Tuesday

3rd ♓

Color of the day: Scarlet
Incense of the day: Geranium

Let the Sunshine In

The official start of summer is almost here. What better time for a quick home cleansing that will help let the sunshine in and increase positivity in your home!

In the morning, open any window coverings you have for the full day (or as long as you can if there is a safety issue). Stand in the center of each window and say:

*Let the sunshine in and bring
vibrancy and joy into my home.*

Sometime before the end of the day (as not everyone will have time in the morning), use either a vinegar and water mix or a glass cleaner to wash each window. When you do wash the windows, if it is dark out, imagine the sun shining in. Visualize the sunlight cleansing your home and leaving it brighter and cheerier than before. While cleaning the windows, say either to yourself or out loud:

*Let the light from outside
bring light to my life inside.*

Kerri Connor

 June 18
Wednesday

3rd ♓
4th Quarter 3:19 pm
☽ v/c 5:34 pm
☽ → ♈ 7:08 pm

Color of the day: Topaz
Incense of the day: Marjoram

Unlocking the Higher Self

In order to work with the divine and any guides we might encounter, we must be able to connect with our higher self. One of the ways we can connect to the higher self is through meditation. Find a comfortable place to lie down with a journal and a pen nearby.

Envision yourself walking through the woods and coming to a crossroad. Which path do you take? As you decide on the path, take note of what you see around you. Where does each path lead? To a clearing or a structure? If you see a structure, what is around it or inside it? Make this place your own. This is the interface where you can unlock your higher self.

After you have spent some time exploring, slowly start to feel yourself come back to your body as you transition out of the meditation. Write about your experience in your journal and look up anything that struck you as odd or interesting.

Charlynn Walls

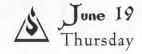 June 19
Thursday

4th ♈

Color of the day: Crimson
Incense of the day: Jasmine

Juneteenth

Summer Solstice Blessing Water

Tomorrow is the summer solstice, a time of the strengthening sun, flowers in full bloom, and the roaring heat of the season making itself known. As we prepare our rituals for Midsummer, now is the perfect time to make some Summer Solstice Blessing Water. This is a simple spell. All you need is a jar with a lid, some fresh water, and of course the sun!

Place your jar of water in a sunny spot (if possible) at noontime and let it bask in the glorious sunlight. Envision it imbued with strength, gratitude, and abundance. You can even draw a sun symbol on the jar's lid. Let the jar sit out until the sun has set and then place it on your altar. Use the water however you see fit. I like to add it to spray bottles along with a few drops of summertime essential oils (such as various citrus, lavender, tea tree, or rosemary), add it to cleansing baths, or even put a few drops in my tea. Keep the water until Winter Solstice, at which time you can dispose of it gently to the land in your area.

Amanda Lynn

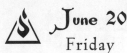 **June 20**
Friday

4th ♈

☽ v/c 9:49 pm

☽ → ♉ 9:53 pm

☉ → ♋ 10:42 pm

Color of the day: White
Incense of the day: Vanilla

Litha – Summer Solstice

A Letter to the Sun Spell

In this spell you'll write a charm asking the Sun to help bring you joy. You'll need a sheet of paper, an envelope, a pen, and a stamp. Wake up early. Facing east, feel the Sun's warmth surrounding you, even if you can't see it. On the paper, write this charm:

Glorious Sun,

Bless this spell I have begun—

Bring me joy, not hate,

And good fortune by the hand of fate.

Bring me light, not dark,

And let me know love's sweet spark.

Bring me courage, never fear,

And let me be a stranger to tears.

Bring me happiness and light.

*Glorious Sun, don't let me
fear the darkness of night.*

Fold the charm and place it in the envelope. Place the stamp on the envelope and address it to yourself. Mail it as close to noon as possible. When you receive it, open it. Read it out loud when you're alone. Hide it in a safe place, and tell no one. This is between you and the Sun. Have a blessed summer!

James Kambos

Notes:

June 21
Saturday

4th ♉

Color of the day: Indigo
Incense of the day: Magnolia

Sun Salutation

The summer solstice arrived yesterday. It's time to salute the new summer sunrise!

Check a weather app to determine the sunrise in your area. Set an outdoor altar that allows you to stand behind it, facing east. Populate the altar with solar colors and correspondences: gold or yellow cloth; pyrite, tiger-eye, carnelian, or amber; yellow candles; sunflowers; lemons; statuary; etc. You'll also need a quart jar with a lid and four tea bags of your choice. Fill the jar with water and set it and the tea bags on the altar.

Set your alarm. Yes, I know it's Saturday and you'd rather sleep in, but this will be worth it. Don yellow or gold attire if you have it. Stand behind your altar at sunrise. Facing east, raise your arms toward the sun and say:

Hail, queen of the day, bringer of light, sustainer of life. I salute you!

Add the tea bags to the jar of water and screw on the lid. Allow this to steep in the sun until noon. Chill and drink, feeling the energy of solar-brewed tea.

Susan Pesznecker

June 22
Sunday

4th ♉

☽ v/c 9:50 pm
☽ → ♊ 10:57 pm

Color of the day: Orange
Incense of the day: Juniper

Clearing Your Garden

Two days after the summer solstice, the waning moon is in Taurus, a fertile earth sign, for most of the day. The waning moon is a beneficial time to clear weeds from your garden and potted plants, and to clear unwanted conditions from your daily life. As you pull the weeds, chant:

Only that which is compatible with me remains in my garden, so mote it be.

To prevent more weeds from sprouting, place pretty stones around your garden plants—sparkly granite, smooth gray shale, faceted quartz. This helps to keep undesirable conditions from returning.

A.C. Fisher Aldag

 June 23
Monday

4th ♊

☽ v/c 4:26 am

Color of the day: Gray
Incense of the day: Neroli

Warding Against Power Outages

With summer come dry weeks punctuated by occasional thunderstorms in many parts of the US. These conditions often cause power outages. First, make sure you have a range of technology. Candles, oil lamps and fuel, matches, and other basics are essential. Camping lanterns are great. Stock food that doesn't need heat or refrigeration, like granola bars.

To ward against power outages, cast this spell. You need two pictures that will fold easily, like magazine clippings or computer printouts. One should show a sky full of lightning, and the other should show power poles with electrical lines.

First, as you fold the lightning picture away from you, say:

Lightning, stay far away.

Then, as you fold the power picture toward you, say:

Power stay on, from dawn to dawn.

Discard the lightning picture far from home, and tuck the power picture under an appliance.

Elizabeth Barrette

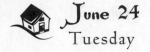 June 24
Tuesday

4th ♊

☽ → ♋ 11:44 pm

Color of the day: Black
Incense of the day: Cedar

House Spirit Blessing

Many people believe that their home has a spirit of its own. This might be an actual being or just a general feeling. You can honor your home's spirit by making a special incense dedicated to them.

If you have houseplants, trim off some of the dead bits and chop them into small pieces so you have about a tablespoon of them. Place them in a bowl. Next, find a dusty surface and run your finger along it. Add this dust to the bowl. If you have an outdoor area, take a pinch of dirt from the ground and add it. Think about adding some other things that have been sitting around your house for some time gathering energy, like an old cobweb or a bit of plaster from the walls. Things like these contain the energy of the house spirit. Mix these findings with a tablespoon of frankincense, which is often considered a sacred resin for blessing, and burn this mixture on a charcoal disk.

While the smoke billows from the charcoal, walk from room to room, using the smoke to welcome and acknowledge your house spirit.

Kate Freuler

June 25
Wednesday

4th ♋

New Moon 6:32 am

Color of the day: Brown
Incense of the day: Lavender

New Moon Cleansing Bath

In Ozark folk magic, the new moon is associated with new beginnings and cleansing. For this traditional bath you will need:

- A plastic water pitcher or small bucket
- Hot water
- A pinch of salt, any kind
- Optional herbs: hyssop, juniper, peppermint (leaves and/or berries)
- A sieve

Traditionally, this cleansing ritual is performed before sunrise. Fill your pitcher (or bucket) with hot (not boiling) water. Ozarkers will use spring water, but water from a tap is fine as well. Add your salt and optional herbs to the water and let this stand for fifteen minutes. Pour the water into a pitcher or bucket, using the sieve to strain out the herbs.

Take the pitcher to your shower or bathtub. While facing west, repeat this charm:

What is washed away
is cleansed away.

Pour some of the water over your head. Repeat the charm and water pouring a total of three times. By the end of the third pour, all the water should be gone. You can finish with a regular bath or shower. This ritual can also be performed outside.

Brandon Weston

NOTES:

June 26
Thursday

1st ♋

Color of the day: Turquoise
Incense of the day: Nutmeg

Islamic New Year begins at sundown

Summer Season Tarot Spell

Summer is here and it's a great time to allow cards from the Tarot to predict the theme of this new season. Since the moon is in the waxing crescent phase working toward becoming full, take time to look at the Tarot for the energy of the present moment, as well as a glimpse into what the future may bring. Grab your favorite deck of Tarot cards and place them on your altar or sacred space. Slowly shuffle the cards while concentrating on what you desire, and say these words:

Tarot cards, show to me the energy of how the summer will be.

I receive the messages with an open heart, reveal to me how the summer will start.

Tarot cards, show to me what the energy of the summer months will be.

Remove the sixth card from the top of the deck to represent June, the present energies. The seventh card will represent July, the eighth card will represent August, and the ninth will represent the energies of September.

Sapphire Moonbeam

 ## June 27
Friday

1st ♋

☽ v/c 1:16 am
☽ → ♌ 2:05 am

Color of the day: Rose
Incense of the day: Yarrow

Ready to Begin Again Spell

It is the day after my birthday, and there's a year until it's my birthday again. I recognize the power of cycles in my life, and celebrate consciously working with them. Not just after times of trouble, but also after great excitement and joy, I am learning how to begin again. Whether it is used with the new moon cycle, a solar return, a birthday, or even the Gregorian calendar "new year," a cyclical process of conscious renewal is powerful. On dark paper, write names of people, places, things, and practices that no longer serve you. In a firesafe dish, burn the paper, saying:

I release thee.

On light-colored paper, write things that support, inspire, and renew you, saying:

These uplift and honor me.

Place the paper someplace where you will see it regularly, so you are reminded how to resource yourself more consciously every time you choose to begin again.

Dallas Jennifer Cobb

 June 28
Saturday

1st ♌

Color of the day: Gray
Incense of the day: Rue

Spell for a harmonious home

Our world can feel chaotic at times. Struggles with work, school, and relationships may keep our emotions in flux. Though we can't escape life's difficulties, we can create sacred space for ourselves (even if it's a corner of a bedroom). Add soft light and favorite touches that give pleasure to your senses. To add a harmonious energy to your sacred space, try this spell. You will need:

- Rose and lavender essential oils

- Equal parts dried rose petals and lavender buds, mixed together

- A pretty dish

Add a few drops each of rose and lavender essential oils to the mixture of dried rose petals and lavender buds. Place your mixture in a pretty dish and set in your sacred space or anyplace where you want to add a touch of harmony to your home. When placing the dish, say something like:

I leave chaos at the door. Only peace may reside in this space.

I leave negativity at the door. Only harmony may reside in this place.

Monica Crosson

June 29
Sunday

1st ♌

☽ v/c 7:03 am
☽ → ♍ 7:44 am

Color of the day: Gold
Incense of the day: Marigold

Pack It In Protection Spell

Give your luggage some added protection from damage, theft, or loss with this quick protection spell. Create a meaningful sigil to you that represents your luggage arriving safe and sound with you at your destination/s, including back home. I use a happy stick person holding an outline of a suitcase. As you create the sigil, focus on what your trip will entail and where and how your luggage will be traveling. In your mind, lead your luggage on a quick tour of where it will go. Envision it being safe and sound and arriving intact and safe at every location it needs to. On the backside of a luggage tag, use a permanent marker to draw this protection sigil. When you are finished, say:

I place this sigil of protection to keep my belongings safe and sound.

Add the luggage tag to your already packed bag.

Kerri Connor

 June 30
Monday

1st ♏

Color of the day: Silver
Incense of the day: Rosemary

A Rain Spell

A rainy day can be depressing,
but without this vital element,
our world would be barren. Every
living thing would perish. This spell
honors rain. Perform it on a rainy
day. You'll need a small bowl or dish
and a bit of rainwater. If you're unable
to collect your own rainwater, use a
small amount of bottled spring water.
Collect some rainwater in your bowl/
dish. Place it on your altar. Stand
before the water and gaze into it.
Visualize the waters of this Earth—
oceans, rivers, lakes, ponds, even a
puddle made during a thunderstorm.
Then pause and say:

> It cleanses the land and
> sprouts the grain.
>
> It is life-giving, it is called rain.
>
> It falls, it trickles, it flows.
>
> It nourishes every animal
> and plant that grows.

End the ritual by respectfully pouring the rainwater (or bottled water)
onto the Earth.

James Kambos

July

In 46 BCE, when Julius Caesar decided to reform the Roman lunar calendar, the names of the months were numbers. He moved the first of the year back to January, and, being the egoist he was, he renamed the fifth month (the month of his birth) for himself: Iulius (Julius, today's July). He also gave it a thirty-first day. (Then he named the next month after his heir, Augustus.)

July (the month of my birth, too) is high summer. In many places, it's the hottest month of the year. It's the month in which everything blooms until the heat of the sun makes flowers—and people—wilt and nearly melt.

What do I remember from my childhood Julys? Rereading my favorite books. Dragging the big old washtub out on the side lawn, filling it with cold water, and splashing all afternoon. Helping my father tend his flowers—roses, columbines, tulips, and hydrangeas. Climbing to the very top of our neighbor's huge weeping willow tree. Chasing fireflies before bedtime and putting them in jars to glitter and wink throughout the night. Sleeping in the screened porch with all the windows open to catch every possible breeze. What are your favorite July memories?

Barbara Ardinger

 **July 1**
Tuesday

1st ♍

☽ v/c 4:47 pm

☽ → ♎ 5:16 pm

Color of the day: Maroon
Incense of the day: Ginger

Canada Day

Bead Divination

If you're a crafter, you may have a collection of multicolored seed beads (very small beads). If not, you can usually find an inexpensive bag of them at the dollar store. All you will need for this divination is the bag of beads and a tray or plate with a rim around the edge.

Reach your hand into the bag of beads while asking what theme or vibe this month will have for you. Scoop up some beads and put them on the plate or tray. Now separate them by color. Count how many beads there are of each color for some insight into what the month might bring. Many beads in one color signify a stronger influence of its corresponding energy, while very few of a color mean there is little of that influence this month.

- *Red:* Passion, courage, transformation
- *Orange:* Success, victory, goals reached
- *Yellow:* Joy, friendship, comfort
- *Green:* Growth, beginnings, new experiences
- *Blue:* Healing, peace, calmness
- *Purple:* Spirituality, magic, the unseen
- *Black:* Protection, seriousness, banishing
- *White:* Realization, manifestation, expansion
- *Brown:* Earthiness, the home, comfort

Don't forget to write down or photograph the results to revisit later in the month.

Kate Freuler

NOTES:

 ## July 2
Wednesday

1st ♎︎

☽ v/c 3:30 pm

2nd Quarter 3:30 pm

Color of the day: White
Incense of the day: Honeysuckle

Light It Up

Fire is a great tool to help us burn away the things we want to remove from our lives. Spend some time thinking about it and make a list of the things you need to rid yourself of: debt, obstacles, bad habits, etc. Be as specific as possible.

In a safe place and manner, set your list on fire. While it's burning, say:

Take these things from my life.

Up in flames I send this strife.

Allow the list to burn fully. Relight it if necessary.

Kerri Connor

July 3
Thursday

2nd ♎︎

Color of the day: Green
Incense of the day: Balsam

Wisdom of Cerridwen

This day before Independence Day in the US is also the Feast of Cerridwen in the Celtic neo-Pagan calendar. Cerridwen is the Cymri (Welsh) goddess of wisdom, sorcery, transformation, and rebirth. She possesses a sacred cauldron of *Awen*, or poetic inspiration.

Outdoors, carefully light a sparkler, which represents the flame beneath Cerridwen's magickal cauldron. Trace the burning sparkler in a triquetra shape (⟁), starting in the middle, while chanting:

Flame of Cerridwen, light my way,

Bring me knowledge every day.

Flame of Cerridwen, Awen bright,

Bring me wisdom every night.

When the spell is completed, carefully extinguish the sparkler or place it in a safe container until it has burned out.

A.C. Fisher Aldag

July 4
Friday

2nd ♎

☽ → ♏ 5:33 am

Color of the day: Coral
Incense of the day: Alder

Independence Day

Raise Your Power

In the United States, we celebrate our Independence Day with parades, fireworks, and family gatherings. Make this the day to celebrate your own independent spirit—raise your power with fire, dancing, chanting, drumming, or whatever your wild heart is drawn to do.

A simple way to raise power is by using sparklers. Whether solitary or in a group, light your sparklers and raise them high. As you do so, chant something like this:

I am one with the Air that moves me.

The Goddess/God is within me.

*I am one with the Fire that
ignites my power.*

The Goddess/God is within me.

*I am one with the Water
that flows through me.*

The Goddess/God is within me.

*I am one with the Earth
that grounds me.*

The Goddess/God is within me.

Remember, ritual doesn't have to be complicated. Be confident in your power and work your magick in a way that suits your needs, personality, and personal connection to deity.

Monica Crosson

NOTES:

 **July 5**
Saturday

2nd ♏

Color of the day: Blue
Incense of the day: Ivy

Summer Bucket List Spell

We are about halfway through the summer. If you haven't done the things you wanted to do yet this summer, it's time to start your Summer Bucket List. On paper, write down your goals for this summer. Limit your list to one to five goals. It can be anything—go to the beach, go camping, host a barbecue—but make it fun! By each item, make some notes about how you might accomplish your activities. Then say these Words of Power:

Summer is at hand, and I have a plan.

Here are the things we'll do

And the places we'll see,

Just my family and me.

Keep your list where you can see it, perhaps on your altar or on your refrigerator. As you accomplish a goal, cross it off your list. You could also do this spell with your family or friends.

James Kambos

 **July 6**
Sunday

2nd ♏

☽ v/c 6:04 pm

☽ → ♐ 6:06 pm

Color of the day: Amber
Incense of the day: Eucalyptus

The Power of Moon Dew

Early in the morning, take a clean cloth or paper towel and run it over the grass, capturing "moon dew." Use the moist cloth to rub the sides of a white or silver candle, attuning it to the moon's powers. As you do so, visualize the cloth glowing with ethereal moonlight, and the candle soaking in this energy until it's fully saturated.

The candle can be lit to tap into moon energy as needed, an energy that is well suited to divination, dreamwork, and revealing unconscious material. For instance, you might light the candle before performing a tarot reading to supercharge your intuition. Or you could spend a few minutes at your altar, gazing into the candle flame as you ask for helpful dreams that night. Make sure the candle is situated on a heatproof surface, away from anything flammable, and snuff it out when you're done.

Melissa Tipton

 **July 7**
Monday

2nd ♐

☽ v/c 5:29 pm

Color of the day: White
Incense of the day: Clary sage

Money Grow Spell

Most of us could use a little extra money. This simple spell is designed to make your money grow and multiply into more abundance.

Get a few coins and some paper money. Obtain a small houseplant that is in the early stages of growth. Choose a plant that is easy to grow so that your money will easily flow. Use a pencil and write on the paper money what you want the money for: a new car, a new house, etc. If you want money for a vacation to a far-off land, get currency from the country you want to visit for this spell. Place the coins on the outside of the plant to form a circle. The paper bill(s) can be placed underneath the plant. Once everything is in place, chant these words:

Money, money grow for me.

Multiply my abundance, appear for me!

Sapphire Moonbeam

 **July 8**
Tuesday

2nd ♐

Color of the day: Red
Incense of the day: Basil

Burning Through Obstacles to Success

Magically cleanse away obstacles on the path toward success using this fire ritual. You will need:

- A black pen or marker
- A piece of red paper, 7 inches square
- A heat-safe dish, firepit, or grill, for burning
- Lighter or matches

I recommend doing this ritual outdoors. Using a black pen or marker, write on the red paper square all of the obstacles to success in your life that you can think of. Once finished, crumple the paper into a ball. Take and rub this paper ball on your body, starting on the top of your head and ending on the soles of your feet. Do this three times. Finish by burning the paper until it's completely reduced to ash.

Brandon Weston

July 9
Wednesday

2nd ♐

☽ → ♑ 4:55 am

Color of the day: Yellow
Incense of the day: Lilac

Fighting Depression

For us to be able to work magic, we need to be in the right frame of mind. Our mental health needs to be a focus so that we can not only manage our own lives but also assist those who need us. Wednesday aligns with the element of air, which deals with issues of the mind. When we feel like we are starting to slip into depression, it can feel like we are grasping for solid ground but are left with only sand in our hands. When this starts to happen, we need to picture in our mind's eye a light at the end of the tunnel.

For this spell you will need a small white candle in a firesafe container or stand. You can anoint the candle with jasmine or eucalyptus oil to encourage an open mind. Light the candle and say:

Temporary is the dark. Illumination comes from a single spark.

Continue to burn the candle daily until you are in a better frame of mind. Let the candle burn, extinguishing it before you leave the house or go to bed. Relight until it's gone.

Charlynn Walls

July 10
Thursday

2nd ♑

☽ v/c 4:37 pm

☽ Full Moon 4:37 pm

Color of the day: Turquoise
Incense of the day: Myrrh

Full Moon Spell for Victory

Use this spell to conquer obstacles or to gain victory over competitors. You'll need a piece of paper, a pen, and a white or red candle. Write your name near the top of the paper. Place the candle in a candleholder on a fireproof surface about an inch above the top edge of the paper. Light the candle and invite the full moon's power and light to join with the flame. Envision yourself being victorious in your situation, overcoming any challenges with ease.

About 5 or 6 inches below your name, write the name of your competitor or a symbol of the obstacle you're facing. Take the candle out of the holder and drip the wax to cover this name or symbol completely, holding in mind the image of your victory as you do so. Place the candle back in the holder above your name and the top edge of the paper and state:

Victory is mine!

Snuff out the candle. Leave the paper and candle in place until the work is achieved.

Melanie Marquis

 July 11
Friday

3rd ♑

☽ → ♒ 1:21 pm

Color of the day: Purple
Incense of the day: Thyme

Journal Protection

Many of us keep handwritten journals, spellbooks, apothecaries, and grimoires. Some may prefer digital versions of these magical tomes, but there remains something special about inscribing them by hand. It's satisfying and provides a very real anchor to one's practices.

There's a drawback, though: the volumes we consider precious and want to keep secret are often appealing to others, but we don't want someone else picking up our craft journal and thumbing through it!

What to do…You might hide your journal or cast a spell of concealment. But how about a practical solution?

Locate a long cord that matches the color of your journal. Tie the cord around all sides of the journal, just as you'd tie a ribbon around a package. Fasten it snugly with one or two selected knots, for example, a square knot with a figure-eight knot on one end, saying:

Cord and knots, securely tied,

Keep this from outworlders' eyes.

Anyone picking up your journal will now have to untie the knots to get access and then retie them perfectly to cover their tracks. Problem solved!

Susan Pesznecker

Notes:

 July 12
Saturday

3rd ♒

☽ v/c 3:45 pm

Color of the day: Black
Incense of the day: Patchouli

Beat the heat Spell

It's often hot and humid in mid-July where I live. I do not do well in heat and humidity, and I do not have air conditioning. This spell helps me cope. You will need twenty minutes of undisturbed time and these supplies:

- A pitcher of cold, steeped chamomile tea
- A drinking glass
- A bowl
- A washcloth
- An amethyst

Pour yourself a glass of cold chamomile tea. Drink half of it. Pour a little of the tea into the bowl, just enough to soak the washcloth. Wring out the cloth so it's damp but not dripping. Lie down where you will be comfortable. Place the washcloth on your forehead and the amethyst on your solar plexus chakra (just above the navel). Say:

I am cool and comfortable.

Close your eyes and rest for twenty minutes. When done, drink the rest of your glass of chamomile tea.

Cerridwen Iris Shea

 July 13
Sunday

3rd ♒

☽ → ♓ 7:45 pm

Color of the day: Yellow
Incense of the day: Almond

Sigil on Your Body

I love creating sigils using the witch's sigil wheel (which you can find with a Google image search) because it's simple and very effective. Not only do I use sigils on paper for general spellwork, but they are great to put on your body as well.

For this spell, you will create a single-word sigil by using the wheel, and then take that sigil and draw it somewhere on your body. Simple sigil examples are protection, love, and clarity. I like to put them on my inner wrist, or sometimes on the sole of my foot, or over my heart. Wear the sigil for as long as you feel is necessary, redrawing it as often as you need. If you are feeling creative, you can create multiple sigils and overlap them or place individual ones on various parts of your body.

Amanda Lynn

July 14
Monday

3rd ♓

Color of the day: Ivory
Incense of the day: Lily

Money Protection Spell

Money benefits from protection. There are plenty of all-purpose protection spells or spells to ward off financial ruin. But what about ways to protect money that you carry, or at least symbols of said money, such as credit or debit cards? For this you need to get a little more creative.

The best approach is to anchor the spell to something for carrying money. You could put a protection symbol on a purse, a wallet, or a plastic sleeve holding a card. For visible marks, consider using a metallic paint pen or permanent marker. For invisible marks, salt and water work well on anything waterproof (like plastic), but for leather, use leather conditioner. It just needs to be something you can draw or write with.

Good symbols of protection include the Algiz rune (ᛉ), the pentacle (five-pointed star in a circle), Thor's hammer (a T-shape), or the udjat (Eye of Horus). Then say:

> By power divine, this money stays mine,
>
> Until comes the day I give it away.

Elizabeth Barrette

July 15
Tuesday

3rd ♓

☽ v/c 1:10 pm

Color of the day: Gray
Incense of the day: Cinnamon

Soak It Up

Pick a goal you have been working toward but haven't achieved the results you desire. Perhaps you have encountered unforeseen obstacles or other setbacks that have prevented you from being where you want to be along your goal's path. Whatever reason your success has been shortcoming, this spell is designed to give you a magical boost to move your progress along. Sit in a comfortable position, preferably outside on the ground. Draw up energy from the ground below you. Feel this energy as it moves throughout your body. Saturate your body with this energy and hold it there. While holding on to this energy, infuse it with positive thoughts of you achieving your goal. What will it look like? What will it feel like? See yourself overcoming whatever stands in your way of success.

When you are ready and feel the energy is fully infused, tilt your head back and release the energy with a deep exhalation through your mouth. Feel the whoosh of energy as it passes from you out into the universe to help deliver success to you.

Kerri Connor

July 16
Wednesday

3rd ♓

☽ → ♈ 12:32 am

Color of the day: Brown
Incense of the day: Lavender

Banishing Thorns

When you find yourself having to deal with a difficult person and cannot make peace with them in a mundane, communicative way, it's time for magic. This spell is to remove a person's prickly or upsetting attitude. Gather these materials:

- A plant or stick with thorns, such as a rose, a cactus, or a stem from a blackberry bush

- Scissors or wire cutters, depending on the size of the thorns

- Gardening gloves if needed

Hold the plant material in your hand carefully and visualize the behavior of the person who is causing problems. Allow yourself to feel annoyed, and picture that feeling going down your arm, through your hand, and into the plant. Now the plant or stem holds the unpleasant energy of the situation within it. Using the scissors, methodically cut every single thorn from the plant and gather them together. Bury the thorns in the ground if possible or throw them away. Keep the stem in a place where you can see it each day. Every time you look at it, note how its defenses are removed, leaving it smooth and harmless. The problematic person should be on better behavior soon.

Kate Freuler

NOTES:

July 17
Thursday

3rd ♈

☽ v/c 8:38 pm

4th Quarter 8:38 pm

Color of the day: White
Incense of the day: Clove

Water Blessing Chant

I live on the shore of Lake Ontario, the fifth largest Great Lake and the seventeenth largest lake in the world. As the biggest spiritual influence over my life, water is central to my magical practice.

I attend water-keeper ceremonies aimed at raising awareness and encouraging action to protect drinking water sources. I know the value of this sacred lake. Today I will teach you a chant based on a well-known goddess chant in honor of the Great Mother. I have co-opted it to honor the water:

Water, water, water, water,
Great Mother of us all.

Water, water, water, water,
Great Mother of us all.

Bless you, bless me, bless you, bless me,
bless you, bless me, bless you, bless me.

Water, water, water, water,
Great Mother of us all.

Let the sound of your voice infinitely bless the water.

Dallas Jennifer Cobb

July 18
Friday

4th ♈

☽ → ♉ 3:59 am

Color of the day: Pink
Incense of the day: Violet

Incense Meditation

Is there something in your life that you wish to change, yet you cannot figure out how to do so? This meditation can help. Find a time and place where you can sit uninterrupted for twenty minutes. Create a sacred space, such as by casting a circle. Use an incense stick or cone—frankincense, lavender, rosemary, or a commercial blend designed for contemplation. Light your incense in a safe container on a flat surface.

Sit comfortably and concentrate on the burning incense, and use your intuition to "see" images in the smoke. Incense fumes that hover low mean a condition that is "stuck" or fixed in one place; a continuous circle indicates a situation that is constantly returning to the same spot; wavering smoke can mean indecision; smoke spiraling upward designates slow, steady progress; while a rising line can indicate the situation is moving forward and upward. Jot down some of the images that you envision: faces, material objects, animals, written letters, or sigils.

A.C. Fisher Aldag

July 19
Saturday

4th ♉

Color of the day: Blue
Incense of the day: Sage

Banishing Salt

Set up protective barriers with a banishing salt made with alder charcoal and blackthorn. With its sharp thorns, blackthorn is a hedge-row tree that not many are brave enough to cross. Alder is found growing along watery borders, and when cut, its light wood turns a reddish orange. This gives the impression that the tree bleeds, linking it to war and the supernatural.

With the addition of protective bay and star anise seed, this salt is perfect to sprinkle around doorways or property boundaries and to use in banishing rituals.

You will need:

- Mortar and pestle
- 1 teaspoon alder charcoal, crushed (available online)
- ½ cup sea salt
- 1 bay leaf
- 1 star anise pod
- 3 blackthorn thorns (available online)

Using a mortar and pestle, crush the alder charcoal to make 1 teaspoon of powder, and mix with the salt. Crush the bay leaf and remove the seeds from the points of the star anise pod. Add both the crushed bay and the anise seeds to your salt mixture. Add the three blackthorn thorns and store the salt mixture in a glass jar.

Monica Crosson

NOTES:

 July 20
Sunday

4th ♉
☽ v/c 2:43 am
☽ → ♊ 6:22 am

Color of the day: Gold
Incense of the day: Juniper

Protect Your Creative Energy

Your creative energy requires differing levels of protection as you progress through a project. When the initial idea sparks, perhaps you remain more open as you take in a range of possibilities, but then you might shut out the peanut gallery so you're not distracted by everyone else's opinions of what you "should" do.

Select a container with a lid, such as a cauldron, jar, or box. Name your project on a piece of paper and place it inside. Imagine the container glowing with divine light, dissolving anything that does not serve. This light forms a filter that protects your project at all times, *and* you can adjust how much energy is allowed in or out with the lid. For instance, if you're feeling overwhelmed by the number of tasks remaining, close the lid a bit (or all the way) so you can focus on what's in front of you. Or if motivation is flagging, open the jar to reconnect with how this project will live in the world, powering you to the finish line.

Melissa Tipton

July 21
Monday

4th ♊
☽ v/c 3:52 pm

Color of the day: Lavender
Incense of the day: Hyssop

Summer's Song Meditation

It's July, the high note of the year. Now, summer's song is being sung. It's a song you can hear, see, and sense. You can hear it in the rumble of a thunderstorm and in the cricket's drowsy trill in the warm late afternoons. You can see it in a meadow frosted white with daisies and splashed with the gold of black-eyed Susans. And you can sense it in the evening breeze, which carries the breath of August. Capture the essence of the season with this meditation.

Sit outside and get comfortable. Be aware of the sounds, sights, and sensations surrounding you. Close your eyes and ground and center. Think of something that gives you joy—career, family, home, etc. When ready, return to a daily state of mind. Open your eyes and look around you at July's bounty. Think of your meditation and record your thoughts about it in a journal or Book of Shadows. Refer to your thoughts about this meditation often when your spirits need a lift. Our memories, just like summer's song, tend to fade far too quickly.

James Kambos

July 22
Tuesday

4th ♊

☽ → ♋ 8:26 am
☉ → ♌ 9:29 am

Color of the day: Scarlet
Incense of the day: Geranium

Perspective Spell

Today is both National Hammock Day and Summer Leisure Day. Taking the time to rest and relax is important. Allowing your body to slow down is part of self-care. Lying in a hammock outside is a great way to slow down and observe the beauty of nature while putting your feet up. Lying horizontal with the ground can help you see things from a new point of view. You can look up and watch the leaves toss and turn in the air as they are blown by the breeze. When you take time to rest, it can help you solve problems or issues that you might be facing. Close your eyes and listen to the sounds of the wind, the birds, and nature. Then say these words:

*As I lie in this hammock to rest
and renew, help me see the issue
from a new point of view.*

Relax leisurely and remember that things usually have a way of working out.

Sapphire Moonbeam

July 23
Wednesday

4th ♋

☽ v/c 8:42 pm

Color of the day: Green
Incense of the day: Carnation

Connecting with Spirit Guides

As practitioners of the old ways, we are fortunate to be able to connect and communicate with our guides in this lifetime. In order to receive their messages, we need to be open to them. One place where we can be receptive is in a dream state.

By practicing lucid dreaming, we can open ourselves up and interact with our guides. One way to start out is by thinking about a dream state that you want to happen. You could imagine a scenario where you are chatting with a guide in a cafe, and include one odd detail as a cue so you know it is a dream. For example, maybe there is a blue rose on the table. Before falling asleep, say what you want to dream about and that you want to remember it. Think about this several times before falling asleep. Say:

*What I see is what I dream.
What I dream is what I see.*

If you see the cue, you know you are dreaming and then can control the interaction. Upon waking, write down what you remember and learn from your guides.

Charlynn Walls

 **July 24**
Thursday

4th ♋

☽ → ♌ 11:28 am

New Moon 3:11 pm

Color of the day: Green
Incense of the day: Carnation

The Joyful Fool Spell

Today is a new moon, which is a great time for new beginnings and the Fool tarot card.

If you have more than one tarot deck, choose the Fool card who looks the most celebratory. Sit where you won't be disturbed for about twenty minutes.

Stare at the Fool card with soft focus, and follow your breath until you feel relaxed. Let your mind and imagination wander around the card. What do you want to start on this new moon? How will you embody a joyful Fool who trusts the universe to try something new? Let yourself consider possibilities.

At the end of twenty minutes, place your hands on the floor and ground any excess energy back into the earth.

Put the Fool card where you can see it every day during the waxing moon. Be alert for new opportunities. When the right one appears, jump!

Cerridwen Iris Shea

 **July 25**
Friday

1st ♌

Color of the day: Rose
Incense of the day: Vanilla

Get in Touch Spell

Cast this charm when you need to get in touch with someone but they're not responding as quickly as you'd like to calls or messages. Find a leaf, and on one side of it write the person's name you are trying to reach. Write your own name on the other side of the leaf. Think about the person and their energy as you hold the leaf. Visualize having with this person the conversation you desire, be it by phone, message, mail, or an in-person meeting. Imagine the details of the exchange you wish to have. You might visualize seeing the email or receiving a message notification, or imagine hearing your phone ring or opening your mailbox to find the letter you've been awaiting. Then hold the leaf toward the sky and say:

Winds, hear me! Have (state person's name) contact me!

Throw the leaf straight up over your head as you walk forward beneath it.

Melanie Marquis

 July 26
Saturday

1st ♌

☽ v/c 7:02 am

☽ → ♍ 4:55 pm

Color of the day: Indigo
Incense of the day: Sandalwood

Bowl of Felicity

The word *felicity* means happiness, joy, and delight. We all can use some encouragement at times, and this bowl will do the trick.

Select a small bowl of your choice—no bigger than a cereal bowl, and smaller if possible. Over time, add items that please you: ceramic figures, crystals, natural items (acorns, seeds, etc.), pins, beads, marbles, or anything. The only criterion is that each makes you happy.

Each time you add an item, say:

> *Precious bowl of felicity,*
>
> *Treasured items are given thee.*

Purify the bowl with your choice of salt, smoke, or dried herbs and keep the bowl on your desk or altar. When you need inspiration, select an item, hold it in your hand, and say:

> *Precious bowl of felicity,*
>
> *May this treasure inspire me.*

Care for the bowl, and it will continue to bring delight.

Susan Pesznecker

 July 27
Sunday

1st ♍

Color of the day: Amber
Incense of the day: Frankincense

Sleep Circle

This protective spell is especially helpful for parents with small children who may have trouble falling asleep at night. Envision a bright, sparkling silver sphere of glowing protective energy around, above, and below the bed, as your child is snuggled beneath comfy blankets. Point toward the east, and draw a circle around the bed. Then make a circle from ceiling to floor. A flashlight beam can also be used to point and draw the circles. Chant:

> *Circle, circle, 'round my bed,*
>
> *Where I rest my weary head.*
>
> *In its glowing silvery light,*
>
> *I will spend a restful night.*

For children who fear the dark or monsters under the bed or in the closet, use water infused with lavender, rose petals, and /or mint. Strain the herbs out and pour the water into a spray bottle. Draw a colorful label that says "Monster Repellent." Use it to squirt around and under the bed. Children can join caregivers in chanting:

> *All harmful forces, go away!*
> *Only blessings will remain!*

A.C. Fisher Aldag

 **July 28**
Monday

1st ♍

☽ v/c 8:57 pm

Color of the day: Silver
Incense of the day: Rosemary

Cleansing home Incense

Juniper has long been used in the Ozark Mountains for smoke cleansing, especially in the home. We use our native red cedar, which actually isn't a cedar, but a juniper, *Juniperus virginiana*. Common juniper works just as well. You will need:

- 1 part juniper berries or red cedar berries, crushed
- 1 part frankincense resin, crushed
- Mortar and pestle
- Incense charcoal and holder
- Lighter or matches

Crush the berries and resin together in a mortar and pestle. Light your incense charcoal the add a pinch of the incense mixture. Beginning at the front door of your home (inside), move through the entire home in a counterclockwise direction (the direction of removal). End at the front door. Step out the door with the incense burner. Let this burn out completely. Throw any cooled ash into a moving body of water.

Brandon Weston

 **July 29**
Tuesday

1st ♍

☽ → ♎ 1:43 am

☽ v/c 11:59 pm

Color of the day: White
Incense of the day: Ylang-ylang

Pick a Page

Witches are always looking for fun new ways to do divination. Tarot cards and reading tea leaves are great tried-and-true traditions, but I think it's fun to try something unconventional to see what we can ascertain from it.

Pull out a random book from your collection and flip to a random page to get your message. This works best with novels or poetry books, but try it with whatever you have lying around. You can pick a book at random for something more exciting, or if you have a novel where you know the theme, go ahead and go with that.

Start by asking yourself a question, or if you want to keep it interesting, just flip to any page! Start at the first paragraph on the page and read until you feel you have enough information. Take some time to see how the question and the message connect. Keep an open mind and get as creative as you'd like with the interpretation. The point is to have fun!

Amanda Lynn

July 30
Wednesday

1st ♎

Color of the day: Yellow
Incense of the day: Lilac

International Friendship Day

It takes approximately 40 to 60 hours of togetherness to go from acquaintance to casual friendship, 80 to 100 hours to establish a regular friendship, and over 200 hours for a close friendship. In a world where people have little time for themselves, that's hard. The result is widespread loneliness, which undermines health and happiness.

Today is International Friendship Day, a time to celebrate friendship as a way to inspire peace efforts and build bridges between communities. Devote some time to nurturing the friendships you already have—go out for lunch, walk in the park, have a game night, whatever. You could also cast a spell to attract new friends. Make three braids of pink yarn, then braid those together. Say:

By the might of three times three,
gather in new friends for me.

Wear the braid as a bracelet or carry it in your pocket. Then go places where you could meet potential friends, like a bookstore, hobby class, or club meeting. Choose at least one person to talk with.

Elizabeth Barrette

July 31
Thursday

1st ♎

☽ → ♏ 1:25 pm

Color of the day: Purple
Incense of the day: Apricot

Beautiful Inside and Out Spell

I spent years feeling ugly. It's taken focus to reduce the hypnotizing effect of early, negative messages. Midsummer is a great time to cast a beauty spell under the brilliant sun, in summer's warmth and the happy vibes of Leo. This isn't about artificial, surface-level beauty, but rather deep-inside self-worth beauty.

You'll need good-quality oil to anoint yourself with. Begin with your feet, gently rubbing them with oil, luxuriously, saying:

Someone's been deceiving me.
Told me I am ugly. But look, look,
look and see, I see only beauty.

Anoint your legs, knees, and thighs, repeating your incantation. If you have privacy, anoint your bum, belly, and breasts. Anoint down your arms to your hands. Finally, with your warm, slightly oily hands, gently anoint your face, saying:

Someone's been deceiving me. Told me
I am ugly. But look, look, look and
see, I see only beauty. Blessed be.

Dallas Jennifer Cobb

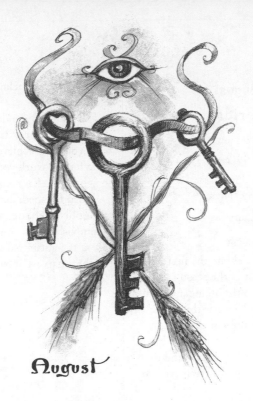

August

Summer is at its height of power when August rolls in, bringing with it the first of the harvest festivals, Lughnasadh (or Lammas), on the first of the month. Lughnasadh is a festival of strength and abundance, a reflection of August itself. Lugh and the Corn God are highly celebrated during this month and are particularly good to work with in spells or rituals for abundance, prosperity, agriculture, marriage, or strength. The Earth Mother in her many forms is ripening and overflowing with abundance. While we often see the first harvest as being associated with corn, there is much more that has been harvested by this point. We must remember not to overlook anything or take anything for granted in our lives, and the harvest is an excellent reminder of that. It is a time to begin focusing on expressing appreciation and giving thanks for all that we have.

The full moon this month is most often called the Corn Moon, but also goes by the Wyrt Moon, Barley Moon, or Harvest Moon. The stones carnelian, fire agate, cat's eye, and jasper will add extra power to your spells and rituals at this time. Use the herbs chamomile, St. John's wort, bay, angelica, fennel, rue, barley, wheat, marigold, or sunflowers in your spells. The colors for August are yellow, gold, and the rich green of the grass and leaves.

Kerri Connor

August 1
Friday

1st ♏︎
2nd Quarter 8:41 am

Color of the day: Pink
Incense of the day: Thyme

Lammas

The First Harvest

Today we celebrate the first official harvest of the season. It is a time to celebrate the abundance you have gathered. Whether this is the fruits of your garden or the fruits of a harvest in other areas of your life, now is the time to celebrate and be thankful for all you have achieved so far this year.

Create a small collage with pictures, words, statements, sigils, stickers, or anything that represents your achievements for the year. This will need to be placed on your altar or in another prominent location in your home where you will see it daily when it is done. Take this into consideration when choosing the size and background of your creation.

Fill your collage with images of what you are proud of achieving. These are things you worked for, and recognition is deserved. We often forget to recognize our own achievements or congratulate ourselves. Instead, we are brainwashed into completing a task and efficiently moving on to the next, with little to no self-praise or self-acknowledgment of a job well done.

Tell yourself you deserved these successes. Congratulate yourself on what you have achieved. Feel appreciation for the work you performed and the goals you have accomplished.

When finished, display your collage until Yule. You may add any new accomplishments on the second harvest at the autumnal equinox or on the third harvest at Samhain.

Kerri Connor

NOTES:

August 2
Saturday

2nd ♏

☽ v/c 9:07 pm

Color of the day: Gray
Incense of the day: Rue

harvest Prosperity Rite

The Irish harvest holiday of Lughnasadh, and the Christianized celebration of Lammas in Britain, is a joyful time of gratitude for bounty.

For this rite, first verbally thank deities, ancestors, spiritual beings, or the universe itself for all the blessings you've enjoyed this year. Next, anoint a green candle with lavender and rose oil, and light it in a safe holder. Slather thick slices of bread (preferably homemade) with butter, honey, and/or jam, and prepare a platter with seasonal fruits, veggies, and nuts. Drink buttermilk or herbal tea infused with honey and lemon. Chant:

*Enough and plenty, come
to me, O come to me.*

*Blessings now, and bounty,
come to me, O come to me.*

*Wealth and prosperity,
come to me, O come!*

Dance clockwise around your candle or stand in place to play a percussion instrument while chanting. Eat some of the bread and produce, and drink the beverage. Share your harvest with loved ones. Carefully extinguish the candle or allow it to burn out safely. Finally, take some of the food outdoors to offer to spiritual beings, using biodegradable containers. Thank them once again for hearing your request.

A.C. Fisher Aldag

NOTES:

August 3
Sunday

2nd ♏

☽ → ♐ 2:00 am

Color of the day: Yellow
Incense of the day: Marigold

Nature Blessing

We all live on this Earth, and there is no Planet B. We rely on nature for the air we breathe, the water we drink, the food we eat, and everything else we need. It is important that we take care of nature so it can continue taking care of us. For this blessing, you need symbols of nature. Take a walk around your yard or neighborhood and collect small things to represent the world around you. This might be a leaf, a flower, a pebble, a small jar of rainwater, or other things depending on your locale and the season. If you can't get outside, use pictures instead. Gather your nature symbols in a basket and say:

> Blessed be the Earth,
> Planet of our birth.
>
> Blessed be the air,
> In which we all fare.
>
> Blessed be the land,
> On which we all stand.
>
> Blessed be the sea,
> And blessed be me.

Then return the symbols to nature.

Elizabeth Barrette

August 4
Monday

2nd ♐

Color of the day: Gray
Incense of the day: Neroli

Find Your People Spell

The August long weekend (the first Monday of the month) is called Civic Holiday here in Canada. It's when the annual Kaleidoscope Gathering takes place. In a huge forested campground by a river, hundreds of pagans come together to share learning and tools, perform rituals and trials, and celebrate and feast.

Coinciding loosely with Lammas/ Lughnasadh, the traditional first harvest celebrations included feasting, competitions, and games, plus stories and song around a bonfire.

Have you been struggling to find community? Let the power of Lugh/ Lammas help you. State:

> I am magnetized magically.
> I draw my people to me.

Can you gather with other witches today in festivity? Search online for pagan festivals near you. Plan to attend. List magical people and events in your community. Reach out. Add events to your calendar. Call people. Invite community together to share rituals, ceremonies, and sabbats.

> My community begins with me.

Dallas Jennifer Cobb

August 5
Tuesday

2nd ♐

☽ v/c 11:29 am

☽ → ♑ 1:04 pm

Color of the day: Red
Incense of the day: Basil

Ritual Bath for Empowerment

Awaken the senses with this fabulous herbal bath to help you recenter and find your inner joy, confidence, and self-empowerment. This bath salts recipe is perfect to use during a waxing moon phase, when our energy is focused on drawing in—attracting and increasing.

Set the mood with candles, a bright citrusy incense, and your favorite music. Add one cup of the herbal bath salts to your bath (recipe below). As you do so, say something like this:

Herbs of mirth, confidence, and strength,

Enable me with clarity, empowerment, and grace.

By the power of root, stem, and bud divine,

May your magick wash over me and allow my light to shine.

Empowerment Bath Salts

- 3 cups Epsom salts
- ½ cup baking soda
- 1 ½ cups pink Himalayan salt
- 25 drops lemon balm essential oil
- 10 drops calendula essential oil
- 1 tablespoon dried chamomile
- 1 tablespoon dried rose petals
- A large glass bowl
- A spoon
- Glass containers

Mix the ingredients in the bowl, and store the salts in glass containers in a cool, dark place. Makes 5 cups.

Monica Crosson

NOTES:

August 6
Wednesday

2nd ♑

☽ v/c 1:40 pm

Color of the day: Brown
Incense of the day: Marjoram

Divining Answers

When we need answers to our burning questions, we may not always know where to turn to get them. One quick way is to divine the answer. But this is not done with a tarot or oracle deck. All you need is a pack of playing cards. Pull out the aces, lining them up in a row on the table in front of you, as if you were playing solitaire. Here are the meanings of the aces:

Ace of Hearts = "yes"

Ace of Spades = "no"

Ace of Diamonds = "maybe"

Ace of Clubs = "so"

Shuffle your deck of playing cards, and as you do so, ask aloud the question to which you need an answer and state:

As I will the answers,
so shall they be known.

Start turning over the cards and placing them one at a time on the aces you set out. Continue flipping cards over until one matches the suit of an ace. If you end up with "so," then you need to clarify your question and try

again. Ask as many questions as you like, reshuffling as necessary.

Charlynn Walls

NOTES:

August 7
Thursday

2nd ♑

☽ → ♒ 9:18 pm

Color of the day: Turquoise
Incense of the day: Jasmine

Mirror Spell for Abundance

Use a red lipstick or gold eyeliner to draw a ring of dollar signs or other money symbols on your mirror so that the reflection of your face is framed by the symbols. See yourself putting cash in your pockets. Visualize your purse or wallet stuffed with money. Envision making a large deposit in your bank account, seeing in your mind's eye a deposit slip or receipt showing a huge balance. Imagine yourself free of financial concerns and how you will feel when you are more prosperous. Say to your reflection:

I am rich! I live a life of abundance!

Give your reflection a kiss. Notice throughout your day the abundance and riches you already have, however humble they might be. Leave the symbols on the mirror as long as you like, but when you do clean it off, do so only during a full or waxing moon. Wipe off the symbols with a small piece of tissue and burn the paper safely in a fireproof dish, expressing thanks as you do so. You will soon see your wealth and abundance increasing.

Melanie Marquis

 ## August 8
Friday

2nd ♒

Color of the day: Coral
Incense of the day: Rose

Praise the Goddess Ritual

Now we begin to experience the power and the glory of the harvest season. It's the power of a lush, bountiful Earth about to bring forth its abundance. And it's the Goddess—the Great Mother—who provides this abundance for us.

For this ritual, drape your altar in green fabric. Decorate it with symbols of the season. This could be a vase of seasonal flowers or bowls of fresh fruits or vegetables. On your altar, have one glass of red wine or grape juice. Stand before your altar and meditate on the Goddess for a moment. Think about the many civilizations that have worshipped her by many names through the ages. In a gesture of praise, raise your glass and say:

Bringer of the rain,

Mother of the grain,

Mother of every bud, flower, and seed,

Giver of all that we need,

To you I raise a toast with my hand.

Thank you, Great Mother, for the bounty of the land.

End the ritual by drinking your wine/juice.

James Kambos

August 9
Saturday

2nd ♒

☽ v/c 3:55 am

☽ Full Moon 3:55 am

Color of the day: Blue
Incense of the day: Magnolia

Full Moon Embodiment Spell

I love full moons so much, as they are a symbol of big energy, completion of cycles, and general fulfillment. I love taking the richness and boldness of the moon into my being and giving thanks for all things related to full moon energy. Embodying full moon energy is great for when we want to keep that vibe going for a few more days, or also to simply thank the moon for its divine support on our magical journey.

For this spell, you will sit somewhere comfortable inside or outside, and if possible, directly under the moon. If that is not an option, don't fret! The energy of the full moon is still with you. When you have created your sacred space, repeat the following chant until you feel you have successfully brought full moon energy into you, then give one last thanks and go about the rest of your night feeling that lovely lunar glow!

Orb of night, shining bright,

Bathe me in your silvery light.

Infuse me with your luscious glow.

I give you thanks this sacred night!
                                    Amanda Lynn

NOTES:

August 10
Sunday

3rd ≈≈

☽ → ♓ 2:50 am

Color of the day: Orange
Incense of the day: Frankincense

Inner Strength Spell

Today is World Lion Day. The lion symbolizes powerful courage and strength. If you need extra help with your inner strength, this spell will assist you. Your words and thoughts are powerful. What you tell yourself is very important. Sometimes we need to do extra work on our inner dialogue to convince ourselves that we can handle challenging life situations with strength.

Stand or sit in a comfortable position. Grab your favorite stone or crystal and place it in your dominant hand. Close both hands into fists, with your fingers curled together tightly. Then say these words internally or aloud:

I am strong, I am strong, I can make it through this day. I can handle any challenge that life throws my way.

Let this affirmation help you, and use it on any day when you feel like you need to remind yourself of your courage and strength.

Sapphire Moonbeam

 August 11
Monday

3rd ♓

☽ v/c 2:55 am

Color of the day: Ivory
Incense of the day: Clary sage

Gratitude-Tinted Glasses

Sometimes it's easy to get a little fixated on someone's flaws—especially if you live with them! This spell helps you refocus on what's working well in a relationship, so you can expand on that energy. It's not intended to be a magical spackle over issues that need attention; think of it as a tool for connecting to clear-eyed gratitude and, if needed, a positive, problem-solving attitude.

Sit comfortably and close your eyes. Place your hand over your heart, connecting to your heartbeat. Draw energy up from the earth and down from the sky to stream into your heart. Visualize the energy as a soft pink glow as you repeat three times:

I wish I may, I wish I might,

See what's working with loving sight.

Bring the relationship to mind and allow any insights to arise. If, say, you're reminded of how this person texts you "good luck" before big meetings, tell them how much you appreciate this to magnify positive energy.

Melissa Tipton

August 12
Tuesday

3rd ♓︎

☽ → ♈︎ 6:33 am

Color of the day: Scarlet
Incense of the day: Cedar

Charging the Waters

Good spellwork often uses specially charged waters. Charged waters may be naturally occurring, as when one collects rainwater, or created intentionally, as when one leaves water out under the full moon to gather the moon's energies.

It's easy to begin a collection of your own charged waters. Start with an assortment of tight-lidded jars and spring water, purchased or obtained locally from the wild.

- *Sun-charged water:* Leave a jar of spring water under the full sun, from sunrise to sunset.

- *Moon-charged water:* Same process, but leave from moonrise to moonset.

- *Other types of celestial-charged waters:* Leave water out under eclipses, comets, meteor showers, or conjunctions.

- *Other options:* You may also charge waters with correspondences by adding crystals, herbs, waterproof objects, and/or objects of certain colors and leaving the jar in a window. Consider the impact of the celestial event's compass direction—north, south, east, or west—to power up your correspondences.

Label your waters and enjoy using them in your magical practices.

Susan Pesznecker

NOTES:

August 13
Wednesday

3rd ♈

☽ v/c 6:54 pm

Color of the day: White
Incense of the day: Lavender

Hecate's Divination Ritual

Hecate (or Hekate) is a triform goddess worshipped in ancient Greece, although her origins may be much older. In modern neo-Pagan traditions, tonight is dedicated to Hecate, who rules over the realms of mystery, sorcery, and augury. A simple divination rite can be performed in her name using three silver or copper coins that are stamped with heads and tails.

At sundown, light a red candle and some incense of black storax, patchouli, or myrrh (or commercially made "Hecate incense") in safe containers. Drop your three coins onto a black cloth while asking your question.

Meanings:

• *Three heads:* Yes

• *Three tails:* No

• *Two heads, one tail:* Likely

• *Two tails, one head:* Unlikely

• *One tail in the middle of two heads:* A problem may be encountered halfway through the endeavor, with an eventual positive outcome.

• *Tail, head, tail:* Wait until later.

Carefully extinguish the candle and incense or allow them to burn out. Thank Hecate, and make an offering to her of dark bread and red wine or pomegranate juice.

A.C. Fisher Aldag

NOTES:

August 14
Thursday

3rd ♈

☽ → ♉ 9:22 am

Color of the day: Crimson
Incense of the day: Clove

Crystal Clear-Out

Have you ever wondered what to do with crystals you've accumulated but aren't using? It's difficult to part with pretty things, but sometimes it's very satisfying to clear out your magical space. If you have a few crystals you don't need, consider giving them a new life by leaving them in a place where a random person will find them. Imagine sitting down on a park bench and discovering a rose quartz next to you or noticing an amethyst in the cracks of the sidewalk. How would you feel? Would you take it home? Would you feel it had special meaning? Perhaps it would simply bring a sense of delight.

When you imagine all the different ways that finding a crystal might impact a person, the possibilities are fun to think about. Consider leaving one on the outside windowsill of a business, or "forgetting" one in your favorite coffee shop, or placing one under a tree at a park. Whoever finds it will surely feel something positive and maybe give it a new home. It's a good way to spread a bit of magic.

Kate Freuler

August 15
Friday

3rd ♉

Color of the day: Rose
Incense of the day: Mint

Burying Illnesses in Apples

Apples are a traditional Ozark container for magically removing all different kinds of illnesses and hexes. These would have been readily available in most hillfolk cabins alongside another favored container, the potato. You will need:

- An apple, any variety
- A shovel or spade

This ritual begins with an apple. It can be any variety, but it needs to be whole. Rub the apple over your entire body, starting at the top of your head and ending on the soles of your feet. You need only touch the areas you can actually reach. While rubbing the apple over your body, repeat over and over for the entire ritual:

Into apple, into ground.

Repeat the rubbing from head to foot three times in total. When finished, bury the apple in the dirt outside. (The illnesses and curses that were removed might kill your plants, so bury it anyplace where there's dirt and not plants you want to save.) Burying the apple in a graveyard is also traditional.

Brandon Weston

August 16
Saturday

3rd ♉

☽ v/c 1:12 am

4th Quarter 1:12 am

☽ → ♊ 12:01 pm

Color of the day: Brown
Incense of the day: Ivy

Anger as a Positive Catalyst Spell

Instead of being afraid of our anger, we can use it as a positive catalyst.

Today the sun is in Leo, the lion. The word *catalyst* begins with *cat*. For this spell, you will need twenty minutes of undisturbed time and the following supplies:

- A stuffed lion or a picture of a lion
- The Strength tarot card with a lion on it
- A pillow
- Pen and paper

Place the lion and the Strength card where you can see and reach them. The pillow is beside you. The pen and paper are within reach.

Concentrate on something that makes you angry. Feel yourself burn with intensity. As the anger builds, consider ways to resolve the situation without causing more harm (power of the Strength tarot card).

Feed the anger into the lion. Punch the pillow if you need to release extra anger/energy to ground. Make a list of the positive steps you can take to resolve the situation, and take the first step.

Leave the lion where you can see it every day until the situation is resolved, then feed positive, healing energy through the lion to cleanse it.

Cerridwen Iris Shea

NOTES:

August 17
Sunday

4th ♊

Color of the day: Gold
Incense of the day: Hyacinth

Clarity Bath Meditation

When you need to see a situation with the utmost clarity, turn to a water bath meditation.

Set your scene with minimal lighting. If you use candles, ensure they are in a firesafe container with nothing nearby to light. For background sound, try an internet search for "clarity binaural beats." (While binaural beats are best used through headphones, you want them only as background, so skip the earbuds.)

Fill your bath with warm water and sprinkle in a handful of sea salt. To maintain the clarity of the water, do not add any other herbs or oil.

When you are ready, undress and climb into the tub. Close your eyes. Think about the situation you are seeking clarity on while using a finger from your dominant hand to slightly stir the water next to you gently and as quietly as possible.

Do not focus on your finger stirring, but on the silence you can achieve while doing so. Every now and then, gently lift your hand from the water. Listen for the drops of water sliding down your fingers to splash back into the water. When you feel relaxed and ready, drain the tub.

You may find, while you are quiet and listening or soon after, that new clarity will come to you.

Kerri Connor

NOTES:

August 18
Monday

4th ♊

☽ v/c 7:53 am

☽ → ♋ 3:05 pm

Color of the day: White
Incense of the day: Hyssop

honoring the Journey

For many of us, August is the beginning of the harvest season. The raucous growth of midsummer has mellowed as we settle into the golden light of late summer. If we're paying attention, we'll find that the signs of autumn are emerging.

As the moon wanes, this is a good time to look back with gratitude and honor the fruits of our past efforts and embrace the changes that mark our journey ahead. For this spell, you will need three tealight candles.

Light the first candle and say:

*I look back upon my journey
with gratitude and honor
for my past endeavors.*

*I thank the Goddess/God
for my many blessings.*

Light the second candle and say:

*I honor my current path as I continue
to grow in strength and power.*

*I thank the Goddess/God for the light
that leads me through darkness.*

Light the third candle and say:

*I honor the threshold of
new possibilities.*

*I thank the Goddess/God for
guidance as I release those things
that no longer serve me.*

Extinguish the candles when done.

Monica Crosson

NOTES:

August 19
Tuesday

4th ♋

Color of the day: Black
Incense of the day: Geranium

heart of the Matter

Everyone has a heart—not just a body part, but something at the core of their identity that gives their life meaning. It may be a career, religion, home, virtue, code of honor, another person, or any other key feature. People who haven't found theirs may feel empty, unfulfilled, adrift. So it's important to know and nurture your heart.

For this spell, you need a heart-shaped bead, a way to write on it, and a ribbon that will fit through it. Look for a big pendant-type bead of glass, metal, wood, or stone. First, string a loop of ribbon through the bead and knot it. Write your heart on the back. You can write more than one thing, but choose wisely because you don't have a lot of space. Take some time to meditate on what you treasure the most. Then say:

Heart of mine, always known,

Safely kept as my own.

Hang the pendant where you'll see it, and remember to pay attention to your heart.

Elizabeth Barrette

 August 20
Wednesday

4th ♋

☽ v/c 8:27 am

☽ → ♌ 7:17 pm

Color of the day: Yellow
Incense of the day: Honeysuckle

Back to School Spell

If you have back-to-school jitters, try this spell. Start this spell about one week before school begins. Each morning, stand and face east. Raise your power (dominant) hand out. As you turn clockwise, visualize a protective stream of blue light streaming from your hand, surrounding you with a shield of protective energy. Stop turning when you are facing east again. Now, still facing east, say with a smile:

I'm free to be me,

And you're free to be you,

And I'm as confident as I can be!

Go back to school with your head up. Remember the protective shield of energy that's surrounding you, and wear that smile!

James Kambos

August 21
Thursday

4th ♌

☽ v/c 2:13 pm

Color of the day: Green
Incense of the day: Myrrh

Saying Goodbye to Leo Season

Leo season is full of boldness, creativity, and daring to express yourself—a month of fabulosity indeed! With only one more day left, you may find the urge to scramble and fill it up with as much Leo energy as possible. Let's do that in a fun way.

Today is a fantastic day to embrace your inner Leo energy. This can be done by dressing up as boldly and fiercely as possible. Or maybe it's not about clothing, but about how you take on the day. Feel the pride and confidence of the lion when you walk down the street. It may even be fun to give yourself a little "rawr" anytime you see your reflection just to remind yourself how extraordinary you really are! However you choose to show off your lion self, the point is to be the main character of your day today.

Amanda Lynn

 August 22
Friday

4th ♌

☉ → ♍ 4:34 pm

Color of the day: Purple
Incense of the day: Cypress

Trouble Be Gone Spell

Use this spell to gain protection against a specific enemy. You'll need a wooden match. Light the match and hold it as you think of your adversary. Think of their essence and their misdeeds as you are holding the match, and imagine it is this enemy you are holding in your hand. Firmly say, "Be gone!" and blow out the match. Once it has cooled, dispose of the match in the trash or compost.

Melanie Marquis

 August 23
Saturday

4th ♌
☽ → ♍ 1:24 am
New Moon 2:07 am
Color of the day: Indigo
Incense of the day: Pine

The Power of Freewriting

Did you know that a certain kind of writing can access the creative parts of your brain as well as forgotten or hidden memories? Welcome to freewriting! Use this when wrestling with a problem or before divination or magical practices.

You'll need paper, a pen or pencil, and mint tea or candy. Before beginning, focus on your problem, issue, or desire and condense it into one or two words: this is your "prompt."

Sip the tea or chew the candy to heighten your senses. Begin writing in response to your prompt. Don't worry about writing perfectly, and don't stop to correct or edit. Just write whatever comes to mind, even single words. Keep the pencil moving, even if you hit a temporary block. Doodle, draw squiggly lines, or do whatever keeps the pencil moving on the paper—this is important. Continue freewriting until you feel done, then stop and read what you wrote. Consider how the words respond to your prompt: you may be surprised.

Susan Pesznecker

 August 24
Sunday

1st ♍
Color of the day: Yellow
Incense of the day: Heliotrope

Sunday Miracles

The Oxford Dictionary of Phrase and Fable defines a miracle as "a surprising and welcome event that is not explicable by natural or scientific laws and is therefore considered to be the work of a divine agency." I believe miracles occur every day.

They say that what we focus on grows. Start the day with a moment of quiet focus to invoke the miraculous. Vow to pay attention to the "surprising and welcome events that are not explicable" today. Find treasures as you walk. See miraculous flowers blooming. Delight in butterflies and hummingbirds visiting the zinnias and sunflowers. Celebrate the vibrant dance of nature in its late summer beauty. Can you find a wild raspberry or pluck a calendula flower to tuck behind your ear? Hunt for a fossil in a pile of stones, and look through your eyelids at the sun. Miracles surround us. Today, attune to the miraculous, and see it.

Dallas Jennifer Cobb

① August 25
Monday

1st ♍

☽ v/c 9:53 am

☽ → ♎ 10:08 am

Color of the day: Silver
Incense of the day: Narcissus

Mining the Energy of habits

Write down your goal as concisely as possible, such as "perfect new job." Be sure to focus on what you *do* want, not what you don't (for example, "short work commute" rather than "no more long work commute").

Next, choose an easy habit, like drinking coffee or brushing your teeth, and focus on your written-down goal while doing this activity. For example, you might tape the goal to your bathroom mirror, gazing at it while brushing your teeth, visualizing the energy of brushing empowering your goal (imagine the words expanding into the cosmos with each swipe of your toothbrush).

Once the goal and the habit are linked, each time you carry out this activity, give thanks for *already* having achieved your goal—for instance, saying to yourself, "I love my perfect new job. Thank you!" Picture enjoying the new job, making regular deposits to this energy each day.

When/if you want to unlink the goal and habit, simply tear up and dispose of the written-down goal, intending that the two are now disconnected.

Melissa Tipton

NOTES:

August 26
Tuesday

1st ♎︎

☽ v/c 10:06 pm

Color of the day: Maroon
Incense of the day: Ginger

Make Your Own Luck

Today is Make Your Own Luck Day. One of the best ways to make your own luck is to remain optimistic. Sure, you can carry a lucky penny or place a horseshoe above your door, but you already have everything you need for good luck. The most potent and magical ingredient or element of any spell is always you. Lucky people have an inherent belief that they are, in fact, lucky. This spell will help you increase your optimistic attitude.

Get a lodestone or a small magnet. Place it on your altar or other sacred space to attract good luck energy. Safely light a small white tealight candle and then chant these words to reinforce your belief in your own luck:

The luck I attract begins with me.

I believe good luck and opportunities will be attracted to me.

Extinguish the candle. Remember that you have the internal power that fuels all of your personal luck and magick.

Sapphire Moonbeam

 August 27
Wednesday

1st ♎︎

☽ → ♏︎ 9:27 pm

Color of the day: Brown
Incense of the day: Lilac

Boosting Mobile Communication

In the modern era, we find ourselves surrounded by information. We are constantly bombarded with emails, texts, snaps, tweets, and more. Responding to them can sometimes seem like a daunting task, especially when you feel like what you are trying to communicate could be misinterpreted. Wednesday is a good day to foster better communication between individuals. Here is a quick spell to help the intent of your words to get through.

Read the message carefully. See what the sender is saying and what they need from you in response. Thoughtfully compose your response, and read it through twice. Doing your due diligence beforehand will help your spell be more successful. Before hitting the send button, say:

Let my intent ring true, so my words do not go askew.

Send your message with confidence.

Charlynn Walls

August 28
Thursday

1st ♏

Color of the day: Turquoise
Incense of the day: Mulberry

Animal Companion Blessing

Our pets give us so much affection and joy. Today is Rainbow Bridge Remembrance Day, a time to honor beloved animal companions who have crossed over and to do a spell of protection for our living pets. Gently stroke your animal friend from the top of their head to right before their tail in a soothing manner. When your pet is relaxed, raise your dominant hand (the one you write with) to the sky to receive energy. Place your receptive hand on your pet. Channel the energy into your friend and chant:

My Dear One, I love you so,

You'll be safe where'er you go.

I bless you as you sit with me,

As my will, so it must be.

For additional safety, whisper this spell into an amulet of protection to be worn on your buddy's collar. The amulet can be a charm, the pet's name tag, a pentagram, a Mjölnir (Thor's hammer) or other symbol of faith, or even your animal companion's license tag.

A.C. Fisher Aldag

August 29
Friday

1st ♏

☽ v/c 8:47 pm

Color of the day: Coral
Incense of the day: Yarrow

Connecting to the Spirit of Place

The "spirit of place" refers to the energy within the area where you reside. This can include the earth, trees, weather, animals, and even the people. Understanding the spirit of place takes work, meditation, and time. This simple spell is designed to aid in making that connection.

Get a brown candle and place it somewhere in nature where you will be able to retrieve it. You can find a spot on the ground where few people go, hide it in a tree, or conceal it under a rock. Leave it there overnight to absorb the various energies present. The next day, retrieve the candle, along with a small bit of dirt or plant material from the area. Be sure not to disturb any wildlife. Place the candle in a holder and surround its base with the earthy bits you collected. Every time you light the candle, you are drawing the spirit of place to the flame by honoring and acknowledging it. Light it for a few minutes per day until it is gone.

Kate Freuler

August 30
Saturday

1st ♏

☽ → ♐ 10:04 am

Color of the day: Blue
Incense of the day: Rue

A Spell for the Disappeared

August 30 is International Day of the Victims of Enforced Disappearances, including those imprisoned in inhumane conditions, those who have been murdered for their beliefs, and/or victims of trafficking. For this spell, gather these supplies:

- Black, red, and green candles in safe holders
- A representation of Medusa
- A firesafe dish
- 3 small strips of paper
- Matches

Place the candles behind Medusa, with the dish and the strips of paper in front. Light the candles, saying:

Black for banishment, red for blood, green for justice.

Meditate on victims of enforced disappearances, the loss of those lives, and the loss to family, friends, and the community.

Light the first strip of paper in the black candle, saying:

May the abusers be banished.

Drop it in the dish.
Light the second strip in the red candle, saying:

May the blood shed by the disappeared ignite the fires of action in the world toward justice.

Drop it in the dish.
Light the third strip in the green candle, saying:

May Medusa's ferocity bring healing.

Drop it in the dish.
Let the candles burn down safely.

Cerridwen Iris Shea

NOTES:

August 31
Sunday

1st ♐

2nd Quarter 2:25 am

Color of the day: Orange
Incense of the day: Juniper

Divining Your Calling

This form of scrying uses a candle flame and a mirror. It's a great divination for finding your calling—perhaps for life or perhaps just for the present. You will need:

- A chair to sit in

- A table

- A white taper candle, any size, in a holder

- A mirror, big enough to see your head and upper body

- Matches or lighter

Position the chair at the table. Place the candle near the center of the tabletop. Place the mirror on the other side of the candle so you can see your reflection. If you're using a wall-mounted mirror, place the table and chair near enough to the mirror so you can clearly see your head and upper body.

Light the candle. All other lights in the room should be out. Look through the candlelight at your reflection in the mirror for a few seconds. While doing this, say:

Light, illuminate my true path.
Darkness, let me see.

Then blow out the candle. It's believed that when you are suddenly plunged into darkness, you will see yourself wearing the clothes of your true calling or holding items related to this path.

Brandon Weston

NOTES:

September

The equinox happens toward the end of this month, heralding the beginning of autumn in the Northern Hemisphere and the start of spring in the Southern Hemisphere. An equinox happens when the sun crosses the celestial equator, an imaginary line in the sky not unlike our Earth's own equator. It's on the equinox that the sun rises due east and sets due west. This is why people often go to famous landmarks to watch the rising or setting of the sun on the equinoxes and solstices. In our ever-changing world, it's nice to know there are at least some constants!

Astrologically, the autumnal equinox is when the sun sign of Libra begins. It's fitting, as this is the time when day and night are of equal length, and Libra is the sign of the scales. The full moon that corresponds with this event is called the Harvest Moon or the Corn Moon. The few days around the equinox and the full moon bring a period in which everything is ripening and full of energy. It all seems to be coming into fullness, preparing either for the coming of winter or the start of the growing season.

Charlie Rainbow Wolf

September 1
Monday

2nd ♐

☽ v/c 9:39 pm

☽ → ♑ 9:45 pm

Color of the day: Ivory
Incense of the day: Rosemary

**Labor Day (US) –
Labour Day (Canada)**

All Is Well Spell

I love long weekends. An extra day off—with pay! Need I say more?

Cast an "All is well" spell. Taking stock and harvesting energetic awareness can help you see the bigger picture. Instead of practicing manifestation, which begins with a sense of lack and a desire for more, begin with the awareness of how rich you are. State what you have, see, enjoy, use, and own. Specifically name what uplifts you. Acknowledge the abundance present in your life, saying "All is well." Stretch it out into a secure future, adding "and all will be well." Intone:

*Yay, an extra day off, with pay!
All is well, and all will be well.*

*I have a home and feel safe here.
All is well, and all will be well.*

*I'm supported by family,
friends, and neighbors. All is
well, and all will be well.*

I'm blessed. So be it.

Dallas Jennifer Cobb

September 2
Tuesday

2nd ♑

Color of the day: Red
Incense of the day: Cinnamon

Chill Out

Have you ever received a frustrating text or email, and you *know* you should chill out before replying, but it's so darn tricky to keep your fingers from typing? This spell is for you! First, fill a cup with cool water to dip your fingers in, or put your hands under running water for a few seconds. Feel the urgency begin to dissipate with this change in sensation. I like to imagine my fingers with beet-red, furious faces that melt into blissed-out smiles under the water.

Second, take a minute to move around—go for a walk around the block or stretch in your chair. Changing your physical position helps alter your state of mind. Visualize the text or email surrounded by a soap bubble, floating off on the breeze. It will return if and when needed, but for now, it's not your concern. Repeat the mantra:

All in good time.

Give yourself some serious appreciation for taking the time to connect with and nourish yourself before choosing your course of action!

Melissa Tipton

September 3
Wednesday

2nd ♑

Color of the day: Topaz
Incense of the day: Bay laurel

Safe Travel Talisman

Almost everyone travels, whether for work or for pleasure. When we do take off by plane, train, or automobile, we want to do so in a manner that is as safe as possible. One way we can attempt to keep ourselves or our loved ones safe is to create a safe travel talisman.

You will need a moonstone, a quartz crystal, or another stone that is protective in nature. You can also take some air-dry modeling clay to put a protective rune around the stone. The Algiz rune (ᛉ) would be ideal, as it is thought to wrap the wearer in a protective shield. (The stone can be embedded in the clay, with the rune drawn on the border.) When working with the clay and the stone, say:

> As this clay wraps around
> this stone, let the protective
> energy envelop the bearer.

Once the clay has hardened, the talisman can be placed in the individual's bag or pocket, ready to protect them as they head out of town.

Charlynn Walls

September 4
Thursday

2nd ♑

☽ v/c 6:08 am

☽ → ♒ 6:32 am

Color of the day: Green
Incense of the day: Carnation

Divination Tea

Mugwort is great to work with for divination. It helps you slip into a relaxed dreamlike trance state, opening yourself to receive and interpret messages more easily. Lavender, sacred lotus, and rose petals make ideal accompaniments to add to the tea, in both flavor and power.

Mix these ingredients together, adjusting quantities according to your own personal taste and what you have available. Sacred lotus may be a bit expensive and can be a little difficult to find. Mugwort tea can be bought already bagged, or you can use any other food-grade quality mugwort along with the other dried flowers.

When you are ready to use the tea, let it steep in hot water for 3 to 5 minutes. While it is steeping, carefully hold the cup in your hands, or hold your power (dominant) hand over the cup, and say:

Help me to divine the truth.
Help me to see the unknown.

This blend not only works as a tea, but also can be smoked on its own or combined with cannabis for even more potent effects.

Kerri Connor

NOTES:

 # September 5
Friday

2nd ♒

☽ v/c 4:51 pm

Color of the day: Rose
Incense of the day: Thyme

A Charm for Quick Wit

We all have those moments of wishing that we felt confident with an answer or could retrieve a bit of information on the spot. Luckily for us, we can create a portable charm to give us a boost in those moments.

You'll need a 5-inch circle of cloth, a 12-inch length of string or yarn, a pinch of ground coffee, and a half-teaspoon of at least five of these: allspice, cinnamon, ginger, matcha, mint, rosemary, sage, and thyme (each ground or powdered).

Place the coffee and herbs/spices on the cloth. Gather the edges and tie the bundle closed with the string. Repeat:

When ideas or words elude me,

May this charm bring clarity.

Sniff the aroma of the bundle as you incant. Keep it with you and breathe deeply of it as needed.

Susan Pesznecker

September 6
Saturday

2nd ♒

☽ → ♓ 11:54 am

Color of the day: Gray
Incense of the day: Sage

Soothing Rose Oil

The scent of roses is commonly associated with romance and seduction. But did you know that in aromatherapy, it can also represent peace and calming energy as well as happiness and joy? Because of its versatility, I love to use rose essential oil for so many things, especially to help me unwind. For this spell we will be making a soothing rose oil. You will need the following:

- ½ cup of your preferred carrier oil (I like almond or jojoba.)
- A small Mason jar with a lid
- 10–15 drops of rose essential oil
- 5–7 drops of an accompanying oil, such as lavender for calm, orange for uplifting, or even sandalwood for grounding

Pour the carrier oil into the jar and then add your essential oils. Feel free to adjust the amount of each to your liking. Let sit overnight, then store in a cool, dry place. Apply to pulse points on your wrists and temples anytime you need to de-stress.

Amanda Lynn

☽ **September 7**

Sunday

2nd ♓

☉ **Full Moon 2:09 pm**

Color of the day: Gold
Incense of the day: Almond

Lunar Eclipse

Full Moon/Lunar Eclipse Release Spell

When we have a full moon with a lunar eclipse, that's always a good time to clear, banish, or release anything we no longer need. That may include a habit, a relationship, or a fear. For this spell you will go to an apple orchard and select a windfall apple to aid you in the spell. If that's not possible, you may use a small rock instead. Think of what it is you wish to release from your life and follow the instructions in this verse:

Go to an orchard where forgotten
apples may be found,

Brown and soft and scattered
upon the ground.

Select one to help you with this deed.

It will help you release what
you no longer need.

Whisper to it what it is
you must release,

Then throw it far away—
now you'll find peace.

Walk away and don't look back. Your problem has been harmlessly released.

James Kambos

Notes:

September 8
Monday

3rd ♓

☽ v/c 1:44 pm

☽ → ♈ 2:37 pm

Color of the day: Lavender
Incense of the day: Lily

Thorny Protection Bag

Here is a protection amulet that harnesses the fiery protection of Mars. Create your amulet after the Moon moves into Aries at 2:37 p.m. EDT. You will need:

- A red taper candle in a holder
- Matches or lighter
- 3 thorns: honey locust thorns (*Gleditsia triacanthos*) or thorns from roses, pear trees, cacti, hawthorn, or any others you might have available
- Wax paper
- A small cloth bag with a drawstring top, red or blue
- Cinnamon essential oil

Light your candle. Gather your three thorns together on a piece of wax paper, with the points facing the same direction. Carefully drip wax from the candle onto the thorns until they are completely covered. While dripping, repeat:

Little spears. Little swords.
Little arrows. Protect.

Let the wax dry, then peel the waxed thorns from the paper. Place them in the cloth bag. Drip three drops of cinnamon essential oil onto the thorns. Pull the bag closed, then tie the strings into three knots. Carry in your pocket, purse, bag, etc. for daily protection. Feed with three drops of cinnamon essential oil dropped onto the cloth of the bag at every full and new moon.

Brandon Weston

NOTES:

September 9
Tuesday

3rd ♈

Color of the day: Scarlet
Incense of the day: Basil

Wonderful Weirdos

Today is National Wonderful Weirdos Day. Who knew?! This day is a great time to celebrate what makes you unique, interesting and, yeah, kind of weird. The concept of normal is outdated and lacks originality. There is no need to completely conform and present yourself to be like everyone else. Our differences and weirdness are truly what makes life intriguing. Be proud of what makes you weird and different from others. Honor the fact that you don't necessarily fit in, and celebrate it! This chant will help boost your confidence and help you be proud of who you are:

> *I proudly present myself to the world,*
>
> *With my weirdo flag
> completely unfurled.*
>
> *I will not be pressured to be
> like the accepted norm.*
>
> *I will continue to be me
> and not conform.*

Be true to you, you wonderful weirdos!

Sapphire Moonbeam

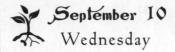

September 10
Wednesday

3rd ♈

☽ v/c 2:54 am

☽ → ♉ 4:03 pm

Color of the day: Brown
Incense of the day: Lavender

Crisp Wishes Spell

Autumn is a time when the air gets cooler and our focus sharper. For this spell you will need:

- 3 autumn leaves (or small papers cut into leaf shapes)
- A Sharpie marker
- An apple
- A knife
- A small pot of earth
- An acorn
- A little water
- A glass of apple cider

Write three wishes, one on each leaf, in marker.

Cut the apple horizontally, to reveal the pentagram in the center. Dig out the seeds and put them aside. Eat the apple as you visualize the wishes achieved.

Tear up the leaves into tiny pieces. Work them into the earth with the apple seeds and the acorn with your fingers. Make sure the seeds and the acorn are covered. Pour a little water over them.

Then pour a little cider over them, saying:

> My wishes sleep under the soil
> until they are ready to grow.

Drink the rest of the cider. Tend the pot, replanting as necessary.

Cerridwen Iris Shea

NOTES:

September 11
Thursday

3rd ♉

Color of the day: Crimson
Incense of the day: Jasmine

A Prosperous Harvest

Food is the oldest form of wealth. Storing it for winter offers survival through a bleak season. The gold of grain came long before the gold of coins. Also, grain's ability to sprout when planted echoes gold's ability to grow through investment. So the oldest prosperity spells are also spells for a bountiful harvest.

For this spell, you need a square of green cloth, a handful of golden grain (such as corn or wheat), a gold-colored coin, and a foot or so of green yarn. First, place the handful of golden grain on the green cloth and say:

> May the harvest prosper.

Next, place the gold-colored coin on top of the golden grain and say:

> May prosperity be harvested.

Gather up the points of the green cloth and twist them together. Tie the green yarn around the twisted points to secure everything. Store the bundle on your altar or another sacred space. The spell lasts for one year, harvest to harvest.

Elizabeth Barrette

September 12
Friday

3rd ♉

☽ v/c 4:14 pm

☽ → ♊ 5:38 pm

Color of the day: White

Incense of the day: Mint

Cleansing Stick

Settle into an autumn state of mind with this wonderfully scented herbal stick used to cleanse and calm the energy after a long and active summer. You will need:

- 4 to 10 fresh sprigs of herbs, 6 to 8 inches long, including wood betony, rosemary, and lavender

- Natural twine

Lay out your sprigs with the stems together. Wrap twine several times around the stems and tie off. Working at an angle, wind the twine upward around your bundle. Wrap around the top of the bundle and continue wrapping back down the stems. Wrap around the bottom twice and tie off. Hang to dry in a dark place or in a paper bag for at least two weeks before use.

Thoroughly clean your home. Then light the stick and cleanse every nook and cranny, starting at your front door and working in a sunwise (clockwise) direction. As you do so, say something like this:

Summer wanes and I prepare my nest

To settle into autumn's rest.

Blessed be the weakening light

As I settle into the season's lengthening night.

Monica Crosson

NOTES:

September 13
Saturday

3rd ♊

Color of the day: Indigo
Incense of the day: Sandalwood

Unwinding Spell

Use this spell to reduce anxiety and usher in relaxation and joy. Hold the string of a yo-yo toy and let the yo-yo drop all the way down. Then slowly wind the string around the yo-yo as you think of all the stress and anxiety you're feeling. Wind the string around the yo-yo tightly and notice how your body feels physically when anxiety is at the forefront of your thoughts.

Once the yo-yo is wound, hold it against your palm and take some deep breaths. Create in your mind's eye an image of yourself feeling carefree, relaxed, and happy. Observe this image in detail and notice how you feel physically when envisioning this less stressed version of yourself. Now loop the yo-yo string around your finger and let it unwind as you hold this image in your mind.

Enjoy some time playing with the toy. If you don't know how to operate a yo-yo, that's okay. Just rewind the string and give it a few tries. Transmuting your stress through play will kick-start a transformation and make it easier to cope with anxiety.

Melanie Marquis

September 14
Sunday

3rd ♊
4th Quarter 6:33 am
☽ v/c 6:46 pm
☽ → ♋ 8:30 pm

Color of the day: Amber
Incense of the day: Eucalyptus

Friendship Rite for Pagan Pride Day

September is the month for Pagan Pride Day (PPD) events, a chance to meet new Witch and Pagan friends. This lighthearted ritual is perfect for your local PPD. Play lawn games, toss a frisbee, create a handcraft together, or share a picnic. Gather in a circle, passing along a squeeze from hand to hand clockwise. Chant:

Friendships are true,
friendships are pure.

Love and acceptance,
friendships endure.

Pass around small disposable cups filled with water or juice, and drink together. Give each participant a small token, such as a tiny crystal, an acorn, or a little charm to remember the day.

A.C. Fisher Aldag

September 15
Monday

4th ♋

Color of the day: Silver
Incense of the day: Neroli

Wishing Star Smash

Star anise is an affordable and common herb that smells like black licorice. The whole seedpods, which can be bought at many grocery stores, are shaped like stars, and within each point of the star is a seed. For this spell, think of these seeds as representing potential, hope, and growth.

Select a pod that is symmetrical and has its seeds intact. Get a hammer and find a hard surface such as a concrete floor.

Think of a wish that you can put into one bold, simple sentence.

Place the star on the hard surface and imagine that it is glowing with the power of your wish just as the stars glow in the sky. Say or think your wish, and smash the star with the hammer, releasing all its power and potential with a bang. The seedpod will burst, releasing your wish into the universe.

If possible, sprinkle the remains outdoors beneath the starry night sky, and think about how the scattered seeds mirror the scattering of stars above.

Kate Freuler

① September 16
Tuesday

4th ♋

☽ v/c 11:14 pm

Color of the day: Gray
Incense of the day: Ylang-ylang

The Smell of Success

Make an enchanted air freshener for your home or car with a piece of felt, string, essential oils of your choice, and a hole punch or scissors. Cut a shape from the felt, aligning the shape and color with your spell's intention for an added boost (for example, a pink heart for love, a gold coin for money, etc.). Create a hole in the top of the felt to loop the string through using a hole punch, or simply make a small snip with your scissors.

Set the felt shape and your essential oils before you and hover your hands above them. Feel energy streaming from your palms into the felt and "waking up" the essential oils as you state your spell intention three times. Add 10 to 12 drops of oil to the felt, then hang wherever you like, refreshing the oil as needed. When you catch a whiff, be mindful of any intuitive nudges or ideas that come to you. Take action on these messages to enhance the success of your spell.

Melissa Tipton

September 17
Wednesday

4th ♋

☽ → ♌ 1:20 am

Color of the day: White
Incense of the day: Honeysuckle

Balancing Act

With the fall equinox close at hand, the theme of balance is in the universe. Light and dark are moving toward equality. The next several days are the perfect time to evaluate the balance in your own life.

Open yourself to the balance theme with this quick meditative working in tree pose. If you are unfamiliar, a quick "tree pose" internet search will bring up images for this yoga pose, which is all about a strong base, stability, and balance.

The leg that remains on the ground is your base. Feel the strength in your base as you shift your weight to bear down solely on it. Tell yourself:

This is my base. Firm, strong, stable.

When you feel that your base is strong and steady, slowly lift your other leg and place your foot into a comfortable position against your base leg. Take your time and keep your movements completely under control. Go slow enough that you do not tip or shake, but instead feel the strength in your base leg grow as it accepts the changes and compensates for the movements in your other leg.

Continue to tell yourself:

My base is strong and stable.

Feel as you align into balance and hold your pose. How does this feel to you? How can you apply a strong, steady base to your life?

Kerri Connor

NOTES:

September 18
Thursday

4th ♌

Color of the day: Purple
Incense of the day: Clove

Prepare Your Own Herbal Infusions

An herbal infusion is a liquid in which herbs have steeped for a period of time. Infusions have many uses in the magical sanctum: they can be part of spellcasting, used to clean or consecrate items, or even consumed as a tea, whether to affect one's frame of mind or just to taste good. It's easy to make your own infusions, and by doing so, you'll always know they're fresh, safe, and ready to use.

For a simple herbal infusion, you'll need a cup of uncontaminated/filtered water, two clean lidded pint jars, a small strainer, and 1 tablespoon crushed dried herbs or 2 tablespoons chopped fresh herbs.

Add the herbs to the jar, followed by a cup of boiling water. Immediately screw on the lid, then let the herbs infuse for 4 to 8 hours. Strain into a second clean jar, add the lid, and label with date and herb. Discard the used herbs. Store in the fridge and use within 2 to 5 days.

Susan Pesznecker

September 19
Friday

4th ♌

☽ v/c 8:21 am
☽ → ♏ 8:23 am

Color of the day: Pink
Incense of the day: Orchid

Balance through Water

Daily life can be stressful, and there often needs to be a reset period where we are able to come back to a point of balance. Water can be a viable medium to facilitate bringing our emotions and bodies into harmony. Fridays align with Venus and the element of water, so this is the perfect opportunity to work on balance. Draw yourself a ritual bath. (This spell can also be done in the shower with a shower melt instead of a bath bomb.) Get the temperature of the water to where you can fully submerge yourself. Add your favorite bath bomb or oil to the water. Float in the water and allow all the stress you are under to melt away. Find a rhythm with your breathing and just be. Feel your emotions even out as the breath in your body does the same. Say aloud:

Venus, allow me release.
Please help me find peace.

Remain in the water until you feel more balanced and at peace. Then drain the tub, removing the turbulence from your system.

Charlynn Walls

NOTES:

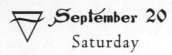 **September 20**
Saturday

4th ♏

Color of the day: Black
Incense of the day: Ivy

Sacred Transitions Spell

A few days remain in Virgo season. The added Saturnian energy of Saturday makes today a great day for to plan for sacred transition. Virgo is known for organized, detail-oriented hard work. Saturn is renowned for providing structure, clear timelines, discipline, and patience. What loose ends need to be tied up before the season changes? What vestiges of summer need to be cleaned and put away? What preparation is needed for the coming autumn?

Wash your hands with soap and water, then dry them. Intone:

*I'm ready to begin, bringing
sacred transition.*

Make a list of several small tasks you need to complete. Start with the smallest. When it is done, make a checkmark next to it, feeling a sense of accomplishment. Then move on to the next task. When you are done working for the day, wash your hands again. Intone:

I'm finished.

Relatively quickly, you have transitioned your house and property from summer to autumn.

Dallas Jennifer Cobb

☽* **September 21**
Sunday

4th ♏

☽ v/c 3:54 pm

New Moon 3:54 pm

☽ → ♎ 5:41 pm

Color of the day: Yellow
Incense of the day: Juniper

UN International Day of Peace –
Solar Eclipse

International Peace Day

Today is the International Day of Peace, established by the United Nations in 1981. It is also a new moon/solar eclipse. This is a transformational time for a new beginning. It is a day to promote peace throughout the world, but more importantly a time to consciously cultivate peace within yourself. The new moon is like a doorway, a chance to begin again and walk into the new energy with fresh ideas about how to achieve peace. Obtain a small candle, white if possible, but any color that you have on hand will work. Place the candle in a holder where it can safely burn until it goes out on its own. Say this blessing as you light the candle to send out a wish for inner peace as well as wishes for a more peaceful world:

As I light this candle flame,
I wish for peace within and I
wish for the world the same.

Sapphire Moonbeam

September 22
Monday

1st ♎

☉ → ♎ 2:19 pm

Color of the day: White
Incense of the day: Clary sage

Mabon – Fall Equinox –
Rosh hashanah begins at sundown

Balancing Mabon

Today is Mabon, a time of balance. The light and the dark stand equal, with the dark increasing. Everything is in flux, balanced on the point of a pin. It is this balance that gives power and mobility. So too must your life be balanced so that you can respond as needed.

For this spell, you will need a pocket compass, the kind with a metal pointer balanced on a post. Sunset is the best time for casting, though any time during the day will work. Cup the compass in your hands and pay attention to how the pointer wobbles and turns but always finds its way. Think about the different parts of your life and how you balance them. Then say:

As without, so within,
Turn on the point of a pin.

As within, so without,
Find balance without a doubt.

Keep the compass on your altar, and turn to it when you need more balance.

Elizabeth Barrette

September 23
Tuesday

1st ♎

☽ v/c 12:02 pm

Color of the day: Maroon
Incense of the day: Bayberry

Incense for Regaining Balance

This incense utilizes the power of the moon in Libra to aid in rebalancing the body and mind. You will need:

- 1 part violet flowers, dried
- 1 part white rose petals, dried
- 1 part yarrow flowers, dried
- Mortar and pestle
- A bowl
- Incense charcoal and burner
- Matches or lighter
- An airtight container

Crush and mix together your three flowers in a mortar and pestle, then place in a bowl. You can prepare this incense mixture during the daytime for use at night when the moon is visible. While outside under the moon (or inside looking at the moon), hold your bowl containing the incense mixture up toward the moon and say:

Balance that was lost now be regained. Let the scales be even. From head to toe. From inside to outside. Let what has been lost be regained.

You can now light your charcoal and add some of the incense mixture. Waft the smoke over your body from your head to your feet three times. This incense mixture can be stored in an airtight container and used whenever you've fallen out of equilibrium.

Brandon Weston

NOTES:

September 24
Wednesday

1st ♎

☽ → ♏ 5:00 am

Color of the day: Brown
Incense of the day: Marjoram

An Autumn Planting Ritual

It may be fall, but now is the time to plant spring-blooming bulbs. For this ritual you'll need some spring bulbs of your choice, such as tulips, daffodils, or crocus. Prepare a place for them in your yard if you need to. Remove them from their package. Look at them carefully. They're truly amazing. They may look dry and life-less, but each contains the seed of life, ready to produce a beautiful flower next spring. Mindfully begin to plant them as you say:

> Autumn leaves turn from green to gold.
>
> Soon frost will kiss the
> Earth and take hold.
>
> Now these bulbs will rest
> in Mother Earth,
>
> But they'll return as a flower
> during the season of rebirth.

When done, take a moment to realize you've taken part in the sacred cycle of life—birth, death, and rebirth. And remember that when you plant, you're affirming your belief that there will be a tomorrow.

James Kambos

September 25
Thursday

1st ♏

Color of the day: Turquoise
Incense of the day: Nutmeg

The Individual in Partnership

Today is World Maritime Day. Instead of honoring the shipping industry, honor the goddess who is the ocean herself. Amphitrite was a pre-Hellenic triple goddess honored as the sea. In Greek myth, she was demoted to nereid and married Poseidon. She kept her independence and has caves under the sea filled with jewels, tends sea mammals, creates sea monsters, and calms the winds.

You will need a stone associated with the ocean and/or Amphitrite, such as larimar, coral, cuprite, or aquamarine. If possible, go to an ocean beach. Let the waves race over your feet. When you feel ready, say:

> Thank you, Amphitrite, for showing
> me the power of adaptation,
> and the power of keeping my
> individuality in partnership.

Fling the crystal as far out into the water as possible, making a promise to remain your unique self. Walk away without looking back. Or you can take a shower, visualizing the power of the ocean. Speak the words, and throw the crystal into the next moving body of water you encounter.

Cerridwen Iris Shea

September 26
Friday

1st ♏

☽ v/c 1:44 pm

☽ → ♐ 5:37 pm

Color of the day: Rose
Incense of the day: Rose

Oh, Sugar, Sugar Sweetening Spell

A sugar sweetening spell is perfect for adding a bit of pleasantness to a souring situation, whether it's off-vibes within the home or office or a relationship that has gone stale. Sugar spells are quick and easy, so give it a try. You will need:

- 1 cup granulated sugar
- 1 teaspoon dried rose petals
- 1 teaspoon dried lavender buds
- ½ teaspoon rose quartz chips
- A bowl
- A glass pint jar with a lid
- A scrap piece of paper
- A pen or pencil
- Rose essential oil
- A pink tealight candle

Mix the sugar and the dried herbs and rose quartz chips together in a bowl. Transfer to a glass pint jar. On the scrap of paper, write who, where, or what situation needs sweetening. Anoint the paper with a little rose oil and place in your sugar jar. Fasten the lid. Light the candle and set it on the lid, allowing it to safely burn down. The wax that drips over will seal your spell.

Monica Crosson

NOTES:

September 27
Saturday

1st ♐

Color of the day: Blue
Incense of the day: Magnolia

School Success Spell

In late September, many students anticipate their first school exams and project deadlines. A spell bag can help scholars succeed. Herbs that enhance focus and concentration include ginseng, sage, rosemary, ginkgo biloba, and turmeric. Blue stones, including lapis lazuli, turquoise, sodalite, kyanite, and labradorite, can assist with mental prowess.

Create a small bag of yellow fabric to represent sunshine and air, and place several of the abovementioned herbs and crystals within. Since the moon is in the zodiac sign of Sagittarius today, call upon the power of this energy to bring about educational success. In ancient Greece, Sagittarius was associated with the centaur Chiron, a physician and instructor to Achilles, Jason, and even the god Dionysus. Using blue permanent marker, sketch an image of a centaur on the spell beg, or use the planetary symbol for Sagittarius (♐). Hold the spell bag aloft and fan it with the element of air while requesting knowledge, focus, memory, concentration, and success.

A.C. Fisher Aldag

 September 28
Sunday

1st ♐

Color of the day: Gold
Incense of the day: Frankincense

Bell Spell for Success

Cast this spell for success in reaching a particular goal. You'll need a hand bell, or you can create your own by punching a hole in the bottom of an empty food can and adding a length of string with a shiny coin tied and taped to the end of the string. Use a permanent marker to write words or draw symbols on the inside of the bell to express your goal. Go outside and look to the moon as you ring the bell at least three times. With every ring, say:

Success is mine!

You can keep the bell indefinitely or give it away after your goal is achieved. If you want to give away the bell, you can paint over the added symbols or words using blue or red paint.

Melanie Marquis

September 29
Monday

1st ♐

☽ v/c 1:44 am

☽ → ♑ 5:55 am

2nd Quarter 7:54 pm

Color of the day: Gray
Incense of the day: Hyssop

Leaves of Gratitude

Autumn is often a time when we're inspired to reflect on what we have gained and experienced throughout the year. Set aside some time to take a walk on a day when the leaves are falling. As you wander, pick up five or so dried leaves and take them home. Get a jar with a lid, a marker, and a quiet place to think. As you hold a leaf in your hand, remember an instance during the past year when you felt joy. It can be a funny scenario that made you laugh, an achievement, or a person you met. As you hold the leaf, allow yourself to feel the happiness of the memory, and then write a word associated with it on the leaf. Crumple the leaf in your hands or grind with a mortar and pestle. Put the remains in the jar. Repeat this with the remaining leaves, assigning a good memory to each one.

When you are finished, you'll have a jar of crumbled leaves infused with positive feelings. You can add this positive energy mix to incense, include it in spells for peace, or rub some between your fingers when you're feeling down to give yourself a boost.

Kate Freuler

NOTES:

September 30
Tuesday

2nd ♑

Color of the day: Red
Incense of the day: Basil

So Long, September

For many of us, fall unofficially
starts in August and makes
itself officially known in September.
In several parts of the Northern
Hemisphere, we are delighted to see
hues of amber, red, and orange as
the scenery changes around us and
the air starts to get just a bit crisper.
September is such a wonderful month
to relish in the delights of fall. It's
when school starts again and we
have the fall equinox, and it's a gentle
reminder that we have one more
month left of "Spooky Season." So
today, let's celebrate and honor the
joys of September while we still can.

All you need is your favorite fall
beverage. Apple cider and hot chocolate are just a couple of examples.
Sit in a quiet place (outside if you
can) and take a deep breath and a
nice sip of your beverage. Close your
eyes and reel in the last moments
of the month. Sit with gratitude for
September as you make way for the
rest of the coming months.

Amanda Lynn

October

D ays that turn on a breath into rapidly waning light. Wispy, high
dark clouds in an orange and turquoise sky. Bright orange pumpkins
carved into beautiful art and lit from inside. The eerie music of screeching
cats. These fond images of October burn at a Witch's heart, calling to her
even across the seasons where she's busy setting up her tent for festival.
By the time October finally arrives, Witches and other magic users have
already had discussions about costumes and parties, rituals and celebrations,
and we look forward with happiness to the whole month of both poignantly
somber and brightly playful activities.

In Celtic Europe, our ancestors acknowledged October as the last month
of the summer season, with winter officially beginning on Samhain. They
carved slits in squashes to keep light in the fields so they could finish their
day's work, and when the custom came to America, it eventually evolved
into the tradition of carving jack-o'-lanterns. American Witches often use
magical symbols to carve their pumpkins, creating beacons for their Beloved
Dead. In the spirit of the turn of energies at this time, we give candy to
children to ensure that they, our future, will remember the sweetness inside
and be good leaders when their turn comes. May we all be so blessed.

Thuri Calafia

October 1
Wednesday

2nd ♑

☽ v/c 11:33 am

☽ → ♒ 3:52 pm

Color of the day: Yellow
Incense of the day: Bay laurel

Yom Kippur begins at sundown

Balance Meditation

Yom Kippur, the most sacred holy day in the Jewish calendar, is a time for fasting, reflection, and atonement. Here is a meditation to do today, even if you are not Jewish.

If possible, abstain from food until sundown. Avoid wearing leather, jewelry, or fancy clothing. Sit on a chair with your back straight, and focus on your breathing. Inhale through your nose, and exhale through your mouth. Consciously allow toxic beliefs and harmful thoughts to dissipate with your exhalations while breathing in blessings and holiness during your inhalations.

A.C. Fisher Aldag

 ## October 2
Thursday

2nd ♒

Color of the day: White
Incense of the day: Jasmine

Pyromancy

What revelations can be found dancing in the flames or within the tendrils of smoke of your ritual fire? What secrets can be revealed in the dying embers? Pyromancy is a method of scrying using fire. There are several ways of practicing this form of divination, including the following:

- *Observing flames:* Toss herbs, bark, leaves (laurel is traditional), twigs, or nuts into your ritual fire, and ask your question. Interpret answers through the shapes formed in the flames or by the color of the fire.

- *Symbols in smoke:* The rising or settling of the smoke may be revealing. Smoke rising straight up is positive, and low-hanging smoke indicates a negative response.

- *Interpreting coals:* Throw salt into a dying fire and watch for the shapes formed in the embers.

Before practicing pyromancy, say something like this:

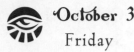

Within the heart of the dancing flame
Lies secret knowledge to be gained.
Reveal your mysteries meant for me
By spark, ember, and
flame—so mote it be.

      Monica Crosson

NOTES:

October 3
Friday

2nd ≈

☽ v/c 2:15 pm

☽ → ♓ 10:07 pm

Color of the day: Coral
Incense of the day: Yarrow

A Dreaming Tea

This traditional tea mixture uses several Ozark medicinal plants to help aid with producing divinatory dreams. You will need:

- 1 part passionflower leaves, dried (can also add the flowers)
- 1 part peppermint leaves, dried
- ½ part yarrow flowers, dried
- Mortar and pestle
- An airtight container

Crush your plant ingredients together in a mortar and pestle, then store in an airtight container. To use the tea, let 1 tablespoon of this mixture steep in 2 cups of boiling water for 5 to 7 minutes. Strain into a coffee cup or mug. If the tea is too strong, you can add sugar or honey. You can also dilute it with water. Drink the tea 15 to 30 minutes before going to sleep. As you lie in bed, repeat this charm:

Flowers of the field, let good visions
like little blossoms bloom in my
dreams. Let the true be revealed.

      Brandon Weston

October 4
Saturday

2nd ♓

Color of the day: Brown
Incense of the day: Pine

Pet Blessing

October 4th is officially recognized as the day when the Catholic Feast of St. Francis of Assisi is celebrated. During the celebration, people will often have their pets blessed, as Assisi was said to have loved animals. We can also take a moment to provide a blessing for our pets to ensure they are protected. With today being a Saturday, there is a lot of associated energy that goes into protection.

We can call upon Artemis, as she is a goddess and protector of animals and nature. All you will need for this blessing is some salt water. As you initiate the blessing, dip your finger or thumb into the salt water and then draw a pentacle or crescent moon on the forehead of your pet. As you do this, say:

Artemis, I lift my pet up to you.
Please bless and protect them.

Finish up the spell by brushing, petting, or spending additional time with your pet.

Charlynn Walls

October 5
Sunday

2nd ♓

☽ v/c 8:30 pm

Color of the day: Orange
Incense of the day: Heliotrope

Sunday Between the Worlds

I love Sundays. It often feels like a day spent between the worlds. And we all know that what happens between the worlds magically affects all worlds.

On Sundays I like to sleep in, move slowly, linger over coffee and morning pages, take long walks with my dog, and escape the constraints of my usual routines in favor of solitude, quietude, and adventure.

Even if for only an hour, can you take yourself between the worlds today? Do you know what activities and spaces provide you with a greater sense of in-the-moment well-being?

Take a walk in nature, spend time meditating, laugh with friends, practice yoga nidra, or take a delicious afternoon nap. Sit in the sun with your cat in your lap, or walk your dog.

Choose an activity that feels luxurious and releases you from the constraints of time and space, rules and roles, even for a few minutes.

Dallas Jennifer Cobb

October 6
Monday

2nd ♓

☽ → ♈ 12:48 am

Full Moon 11:48 pm

Color of the day: White
Incense of the day: Narcissus

Sukkot begins at sundown

Full Moon Clarity Spell

Sometimes we're faced with hard choices and don't know where to turn because there are so many layers to the situation. If you find yourself facing a moral dilemma but are flip-flopping in confusion and conflicting feelings, use this spell to examine the issue piece by piece.

If possible, go outdoors. Cut an onion in half from top to bottom and then repeat, creating four quarters. Pull the layers of the onion apart and arrange them in a single layer on the ground or on a flat surface. As you dismantle the onion, revealing all its many facets, ask the moon to illuminate the important details of the issue, allowing you to make a clear choice. Leave the onion overnight and then dispose of it. You will soon make your own choice in good conscience as clear facts are presented to you bit by bit. This spell may make your nose and eyes run, but no one said moral dilemmas were easy!

Kate Freuler

October 7
Tuesday

3rd ♈

☽ v/c 2:24 pm

Color of the day: Black
Incense of the day: Geranium

Nine of Cups Happiness Spell

For this spell, I like to use the Nine of Cups card in Deborah Blake's *Everyday Witch Tarot*. Elisabeth Alba's painting features a woman reading in a comfortable chair under a tree abundant with apples and pentacles, wine, and nibbles on a table beside her, happy and fulfilled in herself. To perform this spell, block off several hours for yourself, and nest in your favorite chair, a sofa, or your bed. Have a book, a beverage, a snack, a pet, and your journal handy.

Take the card and soak in the beauty of the figure, enjoying her bountiful, beautiful life. Imagine yourself as the figure in the card. Ponder the wonderful things in your life and give thanks for them.

Spend some time enjoying yourself, reading and writing in your journal about what you love about your life. Rest and do whatever you want to honor yourself and your good fortune. Keep the Nine of Cups card where you will see it every day for nine days. Each time you see the card, it will revive the sense of wellbeing.

Cerridwen Iris Shea

October 8
Wednesday

3rd ♈

☽ → ♉ 1:12 am

Color of the day: Topaz
Incense of the day: Lilac

Pentacle Spell for Clearing Energies in the Home

Use this spell to clear away stale energies in the home and welcome new blessings. Choose a favorite incense stick and light the tip as you stand inside your home facing the front door. Envision any stale and unwanted energies leaving the space as you blow out the flame. Holding the incense stick vertically, move it around in the shape of a pentacle, first making a clockwise circle in front of your face, then going up and back down, back up, straight across, and back down again to make the star shape. Now turn your body to each of the other three directions and do the same, making the pentacle shape as you turn your body to face each way. Finish with another pentacle as you face your front door.

This spell will help clear out and freshen the energies lingering in your home. Extinguish the incense when done.

Melanie Marquis

October 9
Thursday

3rd ♉

☽ v/c 8:31 pm

Color of the day: Green
Incense of the day: Balsam

Power of Prayer

Yes, of course Pagans, Wiccans, Druids, and other magical folk pray. Prayer is simply a means of having a discussion between oneself and something beyond, whether for thanks, honoring, or beseechment.

Compose your prayer by hand, using pencil and paper. First, consider who will receive the prayer: a deity, an ancestor, the universe, etc. Second, consider the purpose of your prayer. A gifting or sacrifice may be appropriate, depending on your benefactor. Third, consider how you will express gratitude. Keep your ideas brief and clear.

Rough-write each component, then read them aloud. Edit and smooth the words until they feel right.

Before delivering your prayer, compose yourself by cleansing (at least wash your hands and face, and perhaps don fresh clothing). Spend a few silent moments in a quiet, appropriate space before offering your prayer. Enter the prayer in your magic journal and describe the experience (and perhaps, in time, the results).

Susan Pesznecker

October 10
Friday

3rd ♉

☽ → ♊ 1:12 am

Color of the day: Purple
Incense of the day: Thyme

Kitchen Witch Earthy Granola

Make a batch of this granola for a quick grounding snack. As you combine the ingredients, focus on the calming, nurturing, stable correspondences associated with the element of earth. Infuse these thoughts into your working now for extra support when you eat it later. You will need:

- 3 cups of raw nuts to your liking
- ½ cup raw pepitas
- 1 cup hemp hearts
- ¼ cup chia seeds
- 1 cup finely shredded coconut
- 1 cup dried cranberries
- ¼ cup coconut oil
- ¼ cup maple syrup
- 1 teaspoon cinnamon

Place the nuts and raw pepitas in a food processor and pulse together briefly, leaving the mixture chunky. Pour into a bowl and add the hemp hearts, chia seeds, shredded coconut, and dried cranberries. Blend together.

Warm the coconut oil with the maple syrup in a microwave or on your stove. Stir in the cinnamon. Pour over the dry ingredients and blend thoroughly.

Spread a thin layer on a cookie sheet and Bake at 325 degrees F. for an hour. Allow to cool and store in an airtight container.

Kerri Connor

NOTES:

 October 11
Saturday

3rd ♊

☽ v/c 10:56 pm

Color of the day: Indigo
Incense of the day: Patchouli

Cemetery Magic

I frequent cemeteries as much as possible. I love connecting with and honoring those who have come before us. In fact, I picnic in cemeteries all the time. This was actually a common occurrence in the Victorian era before the advent of state parks.

Today I invite you to go to your local historical cemetery (a modern one is also acceptable) and have a picnic with the dead. Use your intuition to find a grave that you feel connected to, or find a grave that looks lonely or unkempt. Set up your picnic and spend some time at the grave. You can also see if you are able to find any information on who the person was. When you are finished, leave a token such as a stone at the grave to thank them for allowing you to spend time with them. If you are able, clean up the area around the grave or water any flowers that might need it.

Amanda Lynn

October 12
Sunday

3rd ♊

☽ → ♋ 2:37 am

Color of the day: Yellow
Incense of the day: Marigold

Magical Boost Simmer Pot Spell

Scent connects us to the element of air and contains magical elements. Smells interact with the memory centers in our brains. Using the same incense before you practice your craft, for instance, reinforces and reminds you to be in a state of mind that will assist your magical work. Cinnamon is a great scent to utilize in the autumn, and it carries the energies of good fortune.

Get a pan or simmer pot and fill it with water, two-thirds full. Add fresh fruit, such as slices of apple, orange sections, and cranberries. Add cinnamon sticks to the pot and heat until the water boils. Reduce the heat and allow the scent and steam to fill your kitchen with the mixture of fruit and cinnamon. This magical brew will help you get into a magical mindset and enhance your magical practice. Repeat as needed when you need a boost to get into a magical mood.

Sapphire Moonbeam

October 13
Monday

3rd ♋

4th Quarter 2:13 pm

Color of the day: Silver
Incense of the day: Rosemary

Sukkot ends – Indigenous Peoples'
Day – Thanksgiving Day (Canada)

Consecrating the Altar

I enjoy having a dedicated workspace for my rites and spells.
Spaces gain power when they are
used consistently. However, there
are times when it is necessary to
change a current altar's location due
to a move, or to reconfigure personal
space due to the season/sabbat.
When I have done this in the past,
I have always consecrated my altar
prior to using it again.

When I consecrate my altar, I
ensure that I have all the elements
represented within the space. I make
sure I have incense for air, salt/soil for
earth, candles for fire, a dish of water
for water, and a representation of the
God/Goddess for spirit. Then I stand
over my workspace and say three
times:

*I devote this space to the work
of the old ways. Let me show my
dedication throughout my days.*

After completing this, I light the candle and incense and sprinkle a little
salt into the water, then sprinkle the
salt water lightly around the altar.

Charlynn Walls

NOTES:

October 14
Tuesday

4th ♋

☽ v/c 1:05 am

☽ → ♌ 6:47 am

Color of the day: Red
Incense of the day: Cinnamon

Remove a Curse Spell

If you feel you're the subject of a curse, this spell may help. You'll need a beverage glass, one teaspoon of salt, about one cup of water, a plain white sheet of paper, and a blue ink pen. First, mix the salt and the water in the glass. Stir until the salt dissolves. Set aside. On the paper, write why you believe you're cursed—a string of bad luck, etc. If you think you know who cursed you, write their name. You are not going to curse them! This is not a revenge spell. However, you may request protection from this person. Don't worry, karma will take care of them.

When done writing, fold the paper into a small size. Now soak the paper in the salt water. When the paper is completely wet and the water turns blue, in a firm voice say:

Water salty as the sea,

Wash this curse away from me!

Spirits red and spirits white,

Spirits blacker than the night,

You have no power over me.

Dark spirits scatter, dark spirits flee.

And so it must be!

End by tossing the paper in the trash. Pour the water down the drain. Wash the glass in warm soapy water. Don't drink from it again, but you may use it for clearing or banishment magic.

James Kambos

NOTES:

October 15
Wednesday

4th ♌

Color of the day: Brown
Incense of the day: Lavender

Radish Wards

Use this time during the waning moon to embrace the restorative power of nature. Take long walks under autumn's golden sun (and don't forget to stop and play in the leaves). Gather magickal treasures, such as hazelnuts, stones, and twigs, to add to your seasonal altar. Pick up some radishes at your local farmers' market for roasting with garlic and herbs, and don't forget to save a few of the larger ones to carve. Yes, those tiny root crop favorites are a perfect protection ward to use in October as the veil thins.

So get comfy and light a candle and your favorite incense. Open a window and let the cool autumn breeze enchant your senses. When you're ready, use a paring knife to carefully carve frightening faces or protection symbols of your choice (such as a hamsa, hexagram, or pentagram) into your radishes. Invoke their protective powers by gently blowing on them. Place them on windowsills or tuck them near doors to keep negative energy at bay. Extinguish the candle when done.

Monica Crosson

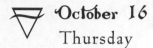 **October 16**
Thursday

4th ♌

☽ v/c 1:06 am
☽ → ♏ 2:06 pm

Color of the day: Turquoise
Incense of the day: Apricot

From Thought to Reality

To create something, we must translate the energy of thought into external reality, and we can prime ourselves for this transmutation by connecting with the body. Find a comfortable place to sit and close your eyes, focusing on your breath until you feel centered. Pay attention to where your body meets the chair or the ground, anchored in physical reality. Bring to mind your idea, and imagine it floating right above your head. The idea acts as a magnet, attracting the energies you need for its fulfillment. Sense these energies streaming into your crown, passing down through your body where they are transmuted into the desired outcome. Visualize this outcome taking shape around you, perhaps imagining yourself in a specific place or engaged in a particular activity.

Thank your body and mind for their creative partnership, and in the coming days and weeks, remain open to intuitive guidance that will help you take action on your creative idea.

Melissa Tipton

·October 17
Friday

4th ♏

Color of the day: Rose
Incense of the day: Violet

Autumn Meditation

With autumn comes the harvest. Farmers gather the last fruits, vegetables, and grains. Food is canned, frozen, and otherwise preserved for winter use. Craft materials are gathered to provide activities in inclement weather. This is a season for the final flurry of work, and then rest to take stock of accomplishments.

For this meditation, choose any fall item to use as a focus, such as a bundle of multicolored corn, some decorative gourds, or a sprig of vividly colored leaves. Sit in a comfortable spot and look at your focus. Say:

> I honor the season of harvest
> and its hard work.

Think about projects you worked on during recent months and all that you put into them. Then say:

> I honor the fruits of the
> harvest and their bounty.

Meditate on your accomplishments and the rewards that they bring you. Finally say:

> I honor the end of the harvest
> and the time of rest.

Mentally set aside the busyness of the recent months and think about something you will do to rest and recover.

Elizabeth Barrette

NOTES:

October 18
Saturday

4th ♏

☽ v/c 5:10 pm

Color of the day: Blue
Incense of the day: Sage

Petitioning the Crossroads for Open Doors

This crossroads ritual is aimed at opening doors when it seems like there are no options or discernible paths to be seen. You will need:

- ¼ part whole barley, dried
- ½ part fennel seeds, dried
- ½ part juniper berries, dried
- 1 part rosemary leaves, dried
- Mortar and pestle
- Incense charcoal and burner
- Matches or lighter

Crush and mix together the incense ingredients in a mortar and pestle.

Perform this ritual at night at a four-way crossroads. Light your charcoal and add some of the incense mixture. Face the easternmost road. Waft some of the smoke in that direction. Say:

In the east! A good door opens for me.

Continue clockwise for the three other roads, repeating the phrase but replacing "east" with the direction you're facing. Clockwise directions will be east, south, west, north.

When you're back at east, let the incense burn out completely. Leave behind the cool ashes at the center of the crossroads.

Brandon Weston

NOTES:

 October 19
Sunday

4th ♏

☽ → ♎ 12:01 am

Color of the day: Amber
Incense of the day: Eucalyptus

Stability Spell

It's difficult to watch someone you care about go through difficulty, especially when their mindset is out of control. When someone you know needs some stability but can't seem to manage it, try this simple spell to help them find balance.

Find a stick on the ground that is at least half an inch wide and less than a foot long. Paint or carve the name of the person in question into the wood while visualizing them feeling calm, collected, and rational. Imagine them making good decisions and facing their issues in healthy ways. Take the stick to an isolated outdoor area with soft earth, and push it vertically into the earth as far as you can, anchoring it in the ground. The earth enfolds their name, and stable energy enfolds their life. If you can't find earth soft enough, burying the stick is also fine. Cover it completely with dirt and pack it down.

This spell can be done with your own name if you're the one who is seeking balance.

Kate Freuler

 October 20
Monday

4th ♎

Color of the day: Lavender
Incense of the day: Lily

Protection Under Duress

There are times when we may find ourselves caught off guard, especially when we feel upset or threatened. For those times when we find ourselves under extreme stress or under duress, we can create a bubble shield for protection. The bubble shield can be used to protect from either physical or mental harm.

See either yourself or what you are trying to protect within the center of a bubble. If you need to expand the bubble to contain everything, see yourself pushing it up and out until everything is contained. Once you see that everything within your mind's eye is surrounded completely by the bubble, say:

As protected within,
so protected without.

The flexible membrane surrounds the person or item. It deflects negativity and can also prevent severe injury. You may end up having scrapes and bruises, but no major harm comes to what is within the confines of the bubble.

Charlynn Walls

October 21
Tuesday

4th ♎

☽ v/c 8:25 am

New Moon 8:25 am

☽ → ♏ 11:42 am

Color of the day: Scarlet
Incense of the day: Ylang-ylang

New Moon Spell
for Psychic Power

Use this spell to increase your receptivity and improve your psychic abilities. You'll need thirteen small pieces of raw amethyst and a small black or purple candle. Take the candle outside after dark and place it in a candleholder or on a firesafe dish. Surround the candle with the amethyst pieces, arranging the crystals in a circle.

Light the candle. Gaze at the flame and focus on your desire for your psychic abilities to grow. Think of why you want these skills to improve and how you will utilize your increasing talents. Place your fingertips to gently rest on a few of the amethyst pieces and state:

> Dark Moon, Mother of the Night,
> let me peer into the shadows!
> Lend to me your sight!

Let the candle burn down as you sit quietly in meditation, noting any visions or impressions that come to you. When the candle goes out, pick up the amethyst crystals and place them on your altar or wrap them in purple fabric to keep with you to give your psychic power a boost.

Melanie Marquis

NOTES:

October 22
Wednesday

1st ♏

☉ → ♏ 11:51 pm

Color of the day: White
Incense of the day: Marjoram

Ancestor Alignment Spell

Aligning with our ancestors can give us incredible power in our daily lives. For this spell, you will need a list of as many of your known ancestors as possible. They do not have to be those of blood; they can be ancestors of spirit or inspiration.

Yellow is often used for ancestor work, but for this spell, I prefer to use purple. Carve your name into a purple candle and dress it with frankincense oil. Put it in a firesafe holder and light it. Take a few deep breaths and say:

I am _____ (state your name).

Then say:

I honor _____ (read your list).

At the end, remember which name resonated strongest and say:

I align with _____ (name).

Watch the candle and breathe, feeling yourself coming into alignment with that ancestor. Let the candle burn down, or put it out and burn it down over 2–3 days, feeling the alignment. This is the ancestor with whom you will work in the coming cycle.

Gerridwen Iris Shea

October 23
Thursday

1st ♏

Color of the day: Crimson
Incense of the day: Myrrh

Pumpkin Burial Spell

Samhain is coming, and in modern times, we recognize this as the season of death. As we make our way through this season, we often think about what no longer serves us and how we can move on from those things. One way to do so is to hold a funeral for those items. In this case, we are not discussing physical items, but rather concepts, patterns, thought processes, etc. that we are getting rid of. For this spell you will need:

- A miniature pumpkin and carving tools
- Strips of paper and a pen/pencil
- A shovel
- Access to a secluded area of public land

Carve out the insides of the pumpkin and dispose of them. Next, write down all the things you want to bury on the paper and then place the strips inside the pumpkin. When you have filled up the pumpkin, put the top back on and take your pumpkin and shovel to an area of land where you can hold a little funeral and bury the pumpkin safely.

Amanda Lynn

October 24
Friday

1st ♏

☽ v/c 12:14 am

☽ → ♐ 12:19 am

Color of the day: Pink
Incense of the day: Alder

A Charm of Protection

There are many times in our lives when we feel the need for protection, and for a multitude of reasons. At such times, a protection charm kept close may provide emotional support as well as psychic safekeeping.

Into a small drawstring bag, place the following: ¼ teaspoon each of rosemary and clove, a paper clip, a short piece of black cord, and several of these stones or crystals: amethyst, basalt, fluorite, hematite, quartz, obsidian, or tiger's-eye. Then add small personal items that speak to you of protection: tiny toys or figures, a coin, a small key, etc.

Place the filled bag on your altar space. Sprinkle it with water and a pinch of soil from your yard or the grounds around your home. Light a candle and safely pass it above the bag from east to west and north to south, repeating:

Elementals, bless this charm.

Keep me safe from daily harm.

Extinguish the candle. Keep the charm near you at all times, envisioning each item ensnaring or warding off harm.

Susan Pesznecker

NOTES:

October 25
Saturday

1st ♐

Color of the day: Indigo
Incense of the day: Ivy

Fall Simmer Pot

The veil is at its thinnest at this time of year, so it's the perfect time to clear negative energy from your home. This simmer pot will chase away the gloomies while ushering in coziness and warmth.

Begin in the morning with a large soup pot filled ¾ of the way with water. Turn an apple sideways on a cutting board and slice it into 9 pieces so the pentagram made through the core and seeds may be seen. Place these in the pot.

Next add 1 tablespoon cinnamon, 1 tablespoon ginger, and 9 whole cloves. Stir the pot 9 times clockwise and say:

Clear my house of what should not be.
Fill it instead with comfort for me.

Set the flame to low and allow to simmer for 9 hours, adding more water throughout the day if necessary.

Kerri Connor

 October 26
Sunday

1st ♐

☽ v/c 12:42 pm
☽ → ♑ 12:53 pm

Color of the day: Orange
Incense of the day: Hyacinth

Kissing Potion

Your magick charm is worn on the lips with this kissing potion lip balm with sweet ingredients to promote love and attraction. With notes of warming nutmeg, known for its aphrodisiac properties, it is perfectly paired with vanilla, whose sweet scent and sensual flavor set the mood for love.

You will need:

- 6 tablespoons carrier oil (such as grapeseed or olive oil)
- 2 tablespoons beeswax (or candelilla wax)
- 2 tablespoons solid cocoa butter or shea butter
- 10 drops vanilla essential oil
- 5 drops nutmeg essential oil

In a double boiler, add the oil, beeswax, and butter, and heat over a low setting until melted. Add the essential oils, stirring clockwise, and say something like this:

Love on my mind and on my lips,

I draw in love with a kiss.

Carefully pour into half-ounce refillable tins. Allow to set up, and store out of direct sunlight. Will keep for up to two years. Makes 8 to 10 cups.

Monica Crosson

NOTES:

October 27
Monday

1st ♑

Color of the day: Ivory
Incense of the day: Clary sage

Magical Redecorating Spell

If you are renovating or redecorating your living space, you can add intentional magical energy to your project. Before you begin to paint the walls in a room, use a pencil to write positive affirmations on the walls. Add words that describe the energy you want to bring to the space: love, dreams, success, joy, laughter, harmony, peace, etc. You can also draw symbols for protection, such as a pentacle (a five-pointed star inside of a circle). The point of each star on the pentacle represents one of the elements: earth, fire, water, air, and spirit. Once you have your writing in place, light some sage or incense. While you allow the smoke to swirl in the space, say:

As this transformational smoke cleanses my space, bring the energy of love, laughter, and peace to this place.

Use whatever words you have added on your walls in this chant to suit your own needs.

Sapphire Moonbeam

October 28
Tuesday

1st ♑

☽ v/c 11:38 pm

☽ → ♒ 11:55 pm

Color of the day: White
Incense of the day: Ginger

To Summon a Spirit Spell

To communicate with a friendly spirit, begin by draping your altar in black. You'll also need a black candle in a holder, a pinch of culinary sage, and a dark magic mirror. If you don't have a magic mirror, try this. Place a black sheet of construction paper behind the blank glass of a picture frame. Darken the room. Sit before the mirror. Safely light the candle and sprinkle the sage around the candleholder. Call to the spirit:

> To the spirit, (say the spirit's name), I must speak.
>
> It is you that I seek
>
> As you were with blood and bone
>
> When the Earth was your home!
>
> Come in peace to me.
>
> Come now, come gently.
>
> So it must be.

The mirror/glass will mist over, then the image may appear. The spirit may look younger and healthier than you remember. Ask one question. They may answer with a gesture or a thought. Keep the session to no more than ten minutes. Thank the spirit and end the session. If the spirit doesn't appear, try again in a week. Safely snuff out the candle and let cool. Put away your supplies and discard the sage.

James Kambos

NOTES:

October 29
Wednesday

1st ♒

2nd Quarter 12:21 pm

Color of the day: Brown
Incense of the day: Honeysuckle

Communication Clarity

Wednesday is named for the Anglo-Saxon deity Wodan, who is conflated with the Norse god Oðin, the ancient Greek entity Hermes, and the Roman god Mercury. Tonight is also when Mercury reaches its greatest eastern elongation, when the planet will be visible in a clear sky in the evening.

Mercury is the god of translators, interpreters, and commerce, while Hermes is the herald of Olympus, representing communication, information, and reasoning. To help foster optimal understanding between yourself, loved ones, coworkers, and/or authority figures, call upon Mercury on this night.

Using green ink, write three key points that you wish to communicate on paper, and memorize them. Next, wrap the paper around three caraway seeds, parsley, bergamot herb (available in teas), and a star anise seed, along with a green stone, such as emerald, peridot, or jade. Carry this charm with you when you must impart crucial information.

A.C. Fisher Aldag

 ## October 30
Thursday

2nd ♒

Color of the day: Purple
Incense of the day: Mulberry

Protective Pumpkin

The end of this month and the beginning of the next feature a cluster of holidays about spooks, spirits, and tricksters. People get excited and may try shenanigans that they would otherwise know better than to attempt. That can make for some risky adventures. So this is a good time to work protection spells for safekeeping.

For this spell, you need a whole pumpkin. Medium size is ideal so you have plenty of room to work, but pie size or miniature will work if that's all you can find at this late date. Paint your pumpkin with protection symbols, such as the Triple Goddess (full moon between two crescents), Horned God (circle with a crescent above), hamsa (hand with an eye in the palm), ankh (cross with a loop for the top), or evil eye amulet (a blue eye). Place it at the entrance to your home and say:

Pumpkin strong and pumpkin sound,
Stand your guard and ward this door
From all spirits going 'round
Behind, beside, or before.

Elizabeth Barrette

October 31
Friday

2nd ≈

☽ v/c 2:15 am

☽ → ♓ 7:46 am

Color of the day: Rose
Incense of the day: Violet

Samhain – halloween

Piercing the Veil of Illusion

Samhain, when the veil between worlds grows thin, is an ideal time to see through illusory thoughts and stories that are no longer serving you. You'll need a tarot or oracle deck and incense. Light the incense and shuffle your deck, then draw a card and hold it above the incense, allowing the smoke to waft around the card, partially obscuring your view. Allow your intuition to awaken, the drifting of the smoke gently altering your state of consciousness.

State this intention:

I pierce the veil of illusion, the truth laid bare in accordance with the highest good.

Then pull the card out of the smoke. Gaze at the image, allowing your intuition to draw your attention to relevant features. What beliefs about yourself, your situation, or others need to be questioned and revised? Open to receive the messages that are correct and good for you.

Melissa Tipton

November

The sounds of nature begin to quiet down in November, but this month is far from silent. Yes, the cheery morning birdsong of spring is gone, and crickets are no longer fiddling on warm summer afternoons, but November has its own "voices." On a frosty November morning, you'll hear a faint, faraway gabble. Raise your eyes toward the sky, and coming over the horizon, in a V formation heading south, is a flock of wild geese. The sound makes you pause and wonder: how do they know it's time to migrate? As you rake leaves, the late autumn breeze stirs them, and they softly rustle as they click and swirl up the street. Few sounds say November like the wind. It may be as gentle as a baby's breath or it may roar, carrying the weight of the coming winter as it howls in the night. During the night you can also hear November's most haunting voice: the lone hooting of an owl. Yes, this month has many voices, but every evening I hear the most comforting voice of all. That voice belongs to the crackling of burning logs as my hearth fire wards off the chill of a dark November night.

During this mysterious month, let the voices of November speak to you, igniting your imagination and your magic.

James Kambos

November 1
Saturday

2nd ♓

Color of the day: Black
Incense of the day: Rue

All Saints' Day

Dreaming Bath

This traditional herbal bath aids with divinatory dreams, especially contact with guiding spirits. You will need:

- 1 part chamomile flowers, dried
- 1 part fennel seeds, dried
- ½ part lavender flowers, dried
- ½ part passionflower leaves and/or flowers, dried
- Mortar and pestle
- A mesh bag or large tea strainer (for the herbs)

Mix your ingredients together and bruise lightly with a mortar and pestle. Add the mixture to a mesh bag or large tea strainer, then add to a bath of hot water. Leave your herbs in the water while you bathe, which can be for as long as you like. (To adapt this spell to a shower, you could let the herbs steep in hot water in a plastic pitcher or large bowl and then pour it over your head.) I recommend doing this right before going to sleep. After drying off and before going to bed, recite this charm:

As I sleep, surround my bed.
Let no nightmares fill my head.
As for tomorrow, let me rise
With truthful visions in my eyes.

It's said that the dreams you have after this bath will be messages from your guardian angel, guiding spirits, and blessed ancestors.

Brandon Weston

NOTES:

November 2
Sunday

2nd ♓

☽ v/c 10:15 am

☽ → ♈ 10:39 am

Color of the day: Yellow
Incense of the day: Frankincense

Daylight Saving Time
ends at 2:00 a.m.

Conversation with Death

We are just past Samhain and the Day of the Dead celebration. Now is a good time to confront our own feelings about mortality and have a conversation with Death.

Sit where you will be undisturbed for about twenty minutes and where there is an empty chair facing you. Imagine a figure representing the personification of Death seated in the other chair. This figure is not a threat to you and has not come to claim you at this moment. Death is here for conversation. Talk about your fears surrounding this large transition, whether it's losing a loved one, leaving loved ones, not knowing what comes next, or anything else. Verbalize what frightens or saddens you. Let your intuition provide the other side of the conversation. It may be difficult, but it will bring a sense of comfort.

At the end, thank Death for their time, and let any fear or tension drain down into the ground.

Cerridwen Iris Shea

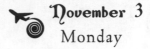 **November 3**
Monday

2nd ♈

Color of the day: Silver
Incense of the day: Neroli

Safe Journeys

This spell can be done every time you travel by automobile. Starting at the hood of your vehicle, walk clockwise around it three times. Call upon deities, ancestors, spirit beings, or the bountiful universe. Chant:

May this vehicle be protected from all of humankind, all of nature, and all of their creation. Keep this vehicle running well, functioning correctly, and safe. Guard and protect this vehicle. As my will, so it must be.

You may wish to request special protection against specific hazards, such as inclement weather.

An additional way to protect a car or truck is to use essential oils such as frankincense or patchouli to inscribe sigils on the hubcaps and bumpers. When dried, the symbol will be invisible. A rune for safe travels is Ehwaz (M), which represents transportation, motion, and a journey. Keep an amulet of protection, such as an Eye of Horus or a pentagram, on your key chain. A bay leaf in your console or glove box brings about a blessed journey.

A.C. Fisher Aldag

November 4
Tuesday

2nd ♈

☽ v/c 6:21 am

☽ → ♉ 11:16 am

Color of the day: Maroon
Incense of the day: Cedar

Election Day

A Warming Cordial

This concoction warms, heals, celebrates, and looks gorgeous as well. Start this now and it'll be ready for winter celebrations and rituals. You'll need:

- 12 ounces fresh whole cranberries (rich in vitamins and antioxidants)
- 2 one-quart canning jars with tight lids
- 1 cup white sugar
- A bottle of good vodka
- A table knife

Rinse and dry the cranberries, then chop finely—a food processor works well for this. Spoon into a canning jar, and top with the white sugar. Slowly fill the jar with vodka, removing bubbles and gaps with the knife. You'll need to keep adding more as the sugar dissolves and the mixture settles. Once the jar is filled, screw on the lid. Keep the jar on the kitchen countertop out of direct light. Shake daily.

After six weeks, strain into a fresh jar. Store in the fridge. Warm up by sipping small amounts of the brilliant red liquid, use as a celebratory cocktail mixer, or use in ritual, with the red color symbolizing blood and health.

Susan Pesznecker

NOTES:

November 5
Wednesday

2nd ♉

☽ Full Moon 8:19 am

Color of the day: Topaz
Incense of the day: Lilac

Manifestation Pomanders

Use the full supermoon's powerful energy to help you manifest your dreams for the upcoming year with these Manifestation Pomanders. Bright citrusy oranges studded with protective clove and cinnamon are the perfect vehicle for magickal intentions. Add a gold ribbon for hanging over the Yuletide season, or place them in a bowl as a reminder that magick happens for those who believe.

You will need:

- A paring knife
- Whole oranges
- Small scraps of paper
- A toothpick
- Whole cloves
- Ground cinnamon
- Gold ribbon (optional)

Under the light of the moon, use a paring knife to create a slice at the top of an orange deep enough to tuck in a small piece of scrap paper. Write your intention on a piece of scrap paper and push it into the slit. Use a toothpick to pierce holes in a pattern of your choosing around the orange.

(Spirals and star patterns work great for this kind of project.) Place whole cloves into the piercings, and dust the orange with cinnamon. Wrap gold ribbon around the orange and hang if you choose.

The pomanders will dry over several weeks. Save them until Imbolc to burn and release your intentions.

Monica Crosson

Notes:

November 6
Thursday

3rd ♉

☽ v/c 9:51 am

☽ → ♊ 10:20 am

Color of the day: Turquoise
Incense of the day: Jasmine

Successful holidays

With the holiday season comes a rush of activities and obligations. People dash here and there, trying to get everything done. One little snag can unravel a whole day's worth of plans. So it pays to plan ahead and do a little spellwork for success.

For this spell, you need a small portable holiday decoration from any event in the season. This could be a turkey for Thanksgiving or a reindeer for Yule, or more generally a leaf for autumn or a snowflake for winter. Hold it in your hands and visualize completing your holiday activities successfully. Then say:

Festive spirits of the fall
And the winter, heed my call!

Banish glitch, delay, and mess;
May my efforts meet success.

Hang the ornament where you do most of your holiday tasks. That may be your kitchen, your home office, or even your car. Whenever you need a little boost, just touch it and recite the incantation again.

Elizabeth Barrette

November 7
Friday

3rd ♊

Color of the day: Coral
Incense of the day: Mint

Bay Leaf Incense

Burning bay leaves is a common incense for many things. Today we are creating bay leaf incense for prosperity. Gather some dried bay leaves and use a Sharpie to draw your favorite symbols for prosperity on them, such as a symbol for currency, a rune prosperity symbol, or even a sigil, just to name a few examples. Either burn the leaves whole or turn them into powder using your favorite method and then burn them. Envision prosperity for yourself and all those around you while it burns. Once all of your incense has burned, take the ashes and rub them on paper currency and say the following chant:

Ash of fortune and luxury,

I send you out to spread prosperity.

By the power of 3 times 3,

Bring some wealth back home to me.

While doing this, imbue the magic of prosperity into the currency as it spreads to all who use it. In return, the magic of prosperity will come back to you!

Amanda Lynn

November 8
Saturday

3rd ♊

☽ v/c 9:32 am

☽ → ♋ 10:06 am

Color of the day: Blue
Incense of the day: Pine

Lucky Charms

Our beliefs around money, tied as they are to a sense of safety and security, can become entrenched and resistant to necessary updates. These beliefs typically appear as rules that seem synonymous with "common sense"—why would we do things any other way? To root out beliefs that are hindering your financial prosperity, take three coins (the dingier the better!) and place them in a glass bowl. Holding the bowl, close your eyes and beseech the spirit of money:

> *Money, I ask for your guidance and aid. Please show me the path to financial prosperity, clear and true. Thank you!*

Add a pinch of salt to the bowl and pour in enough white vinegar to cover the coins. Let them sit for thirty minutes or overnight, then drain the vinegar and buff the coins with a clean cloth. Carry the cleansed coins as charms, and remain open to the intuitive messages they bring, aiding you with your financial goals.

Melissa Tipton

November 9
Sunday

3rd ♋

Color of the day: Gold
Incense of the day: Almond

Stress Sack

This time of the year can be difficult when dealing with complicated family dynamics. Strained relationships are easily exacerbated with the stress of holidays. If you know you will be encountering uncomfortable situations, plan to have some backup at hand.

Gather together a small piece of amethyst, a small piece of quartz, 2 tablespoons dried lavender buds, 1 tablespoon dried jasmine buds, 1 tablespoon dried rose petals, and 4 drops of vanilla extract.

You can use a small drawstring cloth bag to hold the ingredients, or you can sew the ingredients into a small pouch or pillow. Begin by adding the stones and then the herbs. Top off with the drops of vanilla so it can soak in a little. Close and tie off the drawstring bag or sew your pillow pack shut.

Keep your stress sack with you when you know you will be in an environment where you may need it. When you feel stressed, squeeze your sack, sniff it, and squish it between your fingers. Take some deep breaths and relax.

Kerri Connor

November 10
Monday

3rd ♋

☽ v/c 12:23 pm

☽ → ♌ 12:34 pm

Color of the day: Orange
Incense of the day: Eucalyptus

Promoting Prophetic Dreams

Mondays are the day of the week to tap into the potential of the moon. The moon holds dominion over the human subconscious and our dreams. Through our dreaming state, we can access the capability of our mind to filter the will of God/Goddess. We can receive images of the past and the future as well as direct messages from deity.

To aid your prophetic dreaming, fill a small spritz bottle with water and add to it a few drops of violet and rosemary essential oils. Shake to combine and spray on your pillows shortly before bed, saying:

Let me see in the dreaming,
into the past or far beyond,
what I need to be gleaning.

Go to bed, breathing slowly and deeply. Clear your mind and let sleep take you. Upon waking, take a few minutes to write down any dreams you had in order to keep track of those that accurately predict an aspect of the future or have a message from deity.

Charlynn Walls

 November 11
Tuesday

3rd ♌

Color of the day: Black
Incense of the day: Cinnamon

Veterans Day –
Remembrance Day (Canada)

Water Emotion Spell

Water is the magical elixir of life. Not only does water from rain clouds nourish the earth, but it is also the element that is connected to our emotions. This spell will help you deal with heavy emotions. Gather up some rain water or snow (and let it melt) and place it in a bowl. Safely light a small white candle next to the bowl for the intention of purity and cleansing. The flame of the candle will add energy for transformation. Sit with your feelings, feel the feelings, and allow yourself to cry if necessary. Place your nondominant hand in the bowl, stir the water, and say:

May the light of this candle be a start

To release the heavy emotions
from my heart.

May the water cleanse and help free me.

May the flame of the candle
transform me.

Repeat this as needed. Upon completion, safely extinguish the candle and pour the water outside onto the earth.

Sapphire Moonbeam

November 12
Wednesday

3rd ♌
4th Quarter 12:28 am
☽ v/c 6:29 pm
☽ → ♍ 6:52 pm

Color of the day: Yellow
Incense of the day: Marjoram

Dice Divination

Numerology is an ancient, complex science, but you can make use of it in this simple divination spell using two dice like you'd find in a board game. Hold the dice in your cupped hands up to your mouth, and whisper your question. Shake, and then drop the dice on a hard surface. Let the number give some insight into your situation:

1: Birth, beginnings, hope

2: Partnership, balance, cooperation

3: Joy, communication, uniqueness

4: Practicality, logic, reason

5: Change, adventure, freedom

6: Love, romance, emotion

7: Spirituality, mysticism, introspection

8: Success, determination, accomplishment

9: Humanitarianism, empathy, compassion

10: Independence, self-actualization, self-sufficiency

11: Psychism, higher power, fate

12: Creativity, completion, harmony

For example, if your question is "What will my new job be like?" and you roll a 5, you can expect it to be exciting and to bring new experiences. If you ask the question "How will my current relationship play out?" and roll a 10, perhaps the partnership will highlight your strengths.

Kate Freuler

NOTES:

November 13
Thursday

4th ♍

Color of the day: Crimson
Incense of the day: Apricot

Pepper Protection Spell

Use this spell for protection. Write down on a small scrap of paper the name of the person or a description of the circumstance that is threatening to breach your defenses. Fold the paper or crumple it up tightly as you envision the threat imploding, the negative energy folding in on itself. Choose a small jar or envelope. Fill the jar or envelope with black pepper, then insert the scrap of paper, covering it completely with the pepper. Pound your fist nine times on top of the jar or envelope, stating:

> No! No! No!

Toss the jar or envelope in the trash or keep it packed away and concealed. Rub your hands with salt and wash them thoroughly immediately after casting this spell.

Melanie Marquis

November 14
Friday

4th ♍

Color of the day: Purple
Incense of the day: Vanilla

Meditation to Combat Loneliness

Every one of us will face times when we feel like we are all alone. When this is the case, I like to do a simple meditation to ground and connect me to all those I love and want to feel reconnected to. Sometimes I do this when I want to connect to ancestors or just feel the connection to other witches.

For this spell, all you need is a quiet space, a heatproof container, a lighter or matches, and a bay leaf with the following written on it:

> I am connected to all my kin, no matter who or where they are.

Get yourself in a comfortable position, and carefully light the bay leaf and recite the phrase if you choose to. Focus on feeling that connected energy to those you are sending it out to. Inhale the scent of the earthy bay leaf, and let that remind you that you are also connected to source energy. Meditate for as long as you need until you feel revitalized and united with those you love.

Amanda Lynn

November 15
Saturday

4th ♏

☽ v/c 4:08 am

☽ → ♎ 4:44 am

Color of the day: Gray
Incense of the day: Sandalwood

Cast a Wish into the Fire Spell

Fire can release a spell, charm, or wish into the cosmos, where it'll begin to work. For this spell you'll need to build a small safe fire. You may use a fireplace, cauldron, or other heatproof container. All you'll need are a few twigs. Once the fire is burning, don't leave it unattended. Before you build your fire, write your charm on a piece of paper.

When the fire is burning, speak these words into it:

*Fire, for centuries we've
tended your flame,*

And our partner in magic you remain.

I now have a wish, a request.

I ask that my need be blessed.

Upon this paper I've written a charm.

May it come to me without harm.

Into your sacred flame this charm I cast,

Send me my wish, let it come to pass.

As the charm burns, don't look away. Watch as the smoke carries your wish to the Divine. Watch the fire as it burns out. When the ashes are completely cool, discard them in the trash or compost.

James Kambos

NOTES:

November 16
Sunday

4th ♎

Color of the day: Orange
Incense of the day: Eucalyptus

DIY Power Candles

Use this simple (and fun!) technique to empower your plain candles with magical *oomph*. You'll need 2 wax pillar or taper candles. (You might want to use one candle first, for practice. For health reasons, choose safe waxes like soy, beeswax, or other non-petroleum-based candles.) You'll also need a small pointy tool (such as a kitchen skewer), fine point permanent markers of the desired color, and paper towels.

Have a purpose in mind: perhaps you'll inscribe the candle with symbols, sacred numbers, words for a spell, magical correspondences, or something else. Know this before beginning.

Use the sharp tool to "write on" or inscribe the candle, creating marks wide and deep enough for the pens to penetrate. Once done, use the pens to fill the carved areas with ink, wiping away any excess with the paper towel. Dry for an hour before using.

Enjoy the process, and enjoy using your empowered candles for spells and rituals!

Susan Pesznecker

November 17
Monday

4th ♎
☽ v/c 6:51 am
☽ → ♏ 4:44 pm

Color of the day: White
Incense of the day: Narcissus

Incense for Feeding household Guardians

While the guardian spirits of the home can be fed using food and drink offerings, this smoke acts as a very potent source of nourishment on its own. You will need:

- 1 part juniper berries, dried
- 1 part rose petals, dried
- 1 part yarrow flowers, dried
- 1 part frankincense resin
- Incense charcoal and burner
- Mortar and pestle
- Matches or lighter
- A whisk made from an evergreen branch (red cedar, juniper, pine, etc.)

Crush the juniper berries, rose petals, and yarrow flowers in a mortar and pestle, then add in the frankincense resin. When you'd like to feed your household guardians, light the incense charcoal and add a little of the incense mixture. Carry this through all of the rooms in your home, using the whisk to fan the smoke. If you have an altar space, offer some of the smoke here as well. This can be paired with food and drink offerings. I like to do this smoke offering on the new and full moons.

Brandon Weston

NOTES:

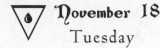

November 18
Tuesday

4th ♏

Color of the day: Red
Incense of the day: Basil

Anahita's Day

Today is the celebration of Anahita, revered in ancient Persia as the goddess of water, fertility, and war (protecting her people).

In her honor, dress a white or gold candle with lotus oil. Set the candleholder in a sturdy, firesafe bowl, and pour some water into the bowl. Place a few branches or twigs of greenery around it.

Light the candle and say:

> Anahita, I honor your fierce protectivity and your generous gifts of fertility. Thank you for your gifts this season. I ask for your help in _____ (name something you wish to grow or protect).

If possible, burn the candle all the way down. Otherwise, extinguish and relight it, speaking the spell, for two more days.

Take action to manifest your request, and perform the gratitude portion of this ritual again once it is achieved.

Cerridwen Iris Shea

November 19
Wednesday

4th ♏

Color of the day: Brown
Incense of the day: Honeysuckle

Bless My Senses Spell

Mercury is the planet that rules Wednesdays. Also called Hermes (in Greek mythology), Mercury, the winged messenger, rules thinking, connections, analysis, discernment, decision-making, clarity, and insight. Let's use the energy of Mercury to consciously invoke clear, concise communication with all of our senses.

While rubbing your hands together vigorously, intone:

*Mercury, help me make conscious
selections. Bless my hands in
creating magical connections.*

Gently cup your ears, saying:

*Mercury, aid me in hearing
perfection. Bless my listening,
understanding, and comprehension.*

Cup your eyes gently, or wipe your glasses, intoning:

*Mercury, enable me to see the light.
Bless my vision, perspective, and sight.*

Touch your fingertips to your lips and say:

*Mercury, help me to always
speak right. Bless my words to be
truthful, gentle, and bright.*

Bring your hands together as if in prayer, and intone:

*Mercury, I greet you with joy and
delight. Bless me and my senses,
bless this day, and bless my life.*

So be it.

Dallas Jennifer Cobb

NOTES:

November 20
Thursday

4th ♏

New Moon 1:47 am

☽ v/c 4:24 am

☽ → ♐ 5:26 am

Color of the day: Green
Incense of the day: Clove

November New Moon

The November new moon is all about creating a sanctuary. In many places, winter is starting and we instinctively want to keep safe and warm. This spell is a fun way to incorporate this idea both physically and spiritually. You will need:

- Incense
- Lighter or matches
- Your favorite music
- A pillar candle (in the color of your choosing)
- A straight pin (for carving)
- Citrus or ylang-ylang essential oil (optional)
- A firesafe dish
- Pillows and blankets

First create your space by lighting the incense and putting on your favorite music. Next, take your pillar candle and carve into it lengthwise from top to bottom (wick to base) something related to home. Examples include protection, comfort, home, cozy, or sanctuary. Once you have carved your candle, anoint it with essential oil if you like, then place it in a firesafe dish and light it. Feel the energy of the candle filling your space as you organize a comfy spot of your pillows and blankets and settle in. Enjoy the safety and warmth of your home as the candle burns. Extinguish your candle before you go to bed, and light it each night until it is gone.

Amanda Lynn

NOTES:

November 21
Friday

1st ♐

☉ → ♐ 8:36 pm

Color of the day: Rose
Incense of the day: Thyme

Zodiacal Fire

Print out or sketch your astrological birth chart. You don't have to include every detail; a circle divided into twelve pie slices, each labeled with a number, is sufficient. Locate houses ruled by fire signs (Aries, Leo, and Sagittarius), look up correspondences for each house, then choose one to focus on. For instance, if you want to ignite creative ideas, and you see that Sagittarius rules your fifth house (associated with creativity), pick this house as your focus.

Set the chart on your altar, away from flammables, and place a tealight candle in a heatproof dish on the chosen house (it's okay if it doesn't completely fit). Visualize the energy of fire, guided by the wisdom of the sign ruling this house, transforming this area of your life in accordance with the highest good. Take note of any intuitive messages indicating how you can support positive change. When done, snuff out the candle.

Melissa Tipton

 November 22
Saturday

1st ♐

☽ v/c 4:48 pm

☽ → ♑ 5:53 pm

Color of the day: Indigo
Incense of the day: Patchouli

Hallowed Wood Bundles

Gathering twigs and bundling them together for your sacred fire is something that can be done all year long, but November is especially nice for this, as autumn's sometimes blustery weather may leave twigs scattered among fallen leaves—making it easier for gathering. Establish your magickal intention and pick your wood accordingly. Gather just a few twigs approximately 4 to 6 inches in length and tie them with twine at each end. A bundle for protection may include the twigs from a rowan, oak, and/or alder tree tied with red twine. Healing bundles may include the wood of willow, apple, and/or birch tied with pink twine.

Here is a short list of some magickal attributes of common trees:

- *Alder:* Spirit communication, protection, strength
- *Apple:* Love, healing, abundance, fertility
- *Birch:* Rebirth, fertility, cleansing, inspiration

- *Cedar:* Protection, purification, clarity, wisdom
- *Elder:* Wisdom, Otherworld communication
- *Hazel:* Psychic powers, wisdom
- *Maple:* Power, protection, strength
- *Oak:* Wisdom, power, truth, protection
- *Rowan:* Protection, faery magick, clarity, psychic powers
- *Willow:* Moon, healing, love, divination

Monica Crosson

NOTES:

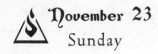

November 23
Sunday

1st ♑

Color of the day: Gold
Incense of the day: Heliotrope

Energy Drink

We all can use a pick-me-up from time to time. Today is Sunday, so we can work on increasing our energetic potential by tapping into the energies of the sun. One way to do that is to infuse a drink with the magical properties of the sun. One fruit that truly contains that type of fire energy is the orange. It not only looks like the sun but also tastes like bottled sunshine.

You will need two oranges or a small bottle of orange juice for this spell. (If you have a citrus allergy, you could substitute another fruit.) Place your hand on the glass of juice you are going to drink and say:

Sunshine in a glass,
a pick-me-up guaranteed to last
and not make me crash.

After reciting that line, you can drink the juice and feel the energy surge within you.

Charlynn Walls

November 24
Monday

1st ♑

Color of the day: Lavender
Incense of the day: Rosemary

Unconditional Self-Love

It is important to remind ourselves of our own self-love, particularly during times of stress. Problems tend to intensify during the holidays. Financial issues, scheduling disputes, and get-togethers, as well as family members, may bring anxiety.

Take a "me" break away from everything and everyone. Sit down in front of a mirror and stare into your own eyes. Appreciate what you see in your reflection. Let the opinions of everyone else pass you by. Rid your mind of any outside impressions. Tell yourself these words:

I love you, unconditionally.

This may be hard to do for some people. Repeat it to yourself several times, allowing time for it to sink in.

When you are down, remind yourself that you are the only you there is, and you are one magical and incredible being!

Kerri Connor

▽ November 25
Tuesday

1st ♑

☽ v/c 4:10 am

☽ → ♒ 5:16 am

Color of the day: Scarlet
Incense of the day: Ginger

To honor Dried Grasses Spell

Now we arrive at the twilight of the year. The skies are gray and the air is brisk. At night the wind may howl. By now, most flowers are just a memory. To capture the essence of summer, observe the regal plumes of dried grasses, both domestic and wild. They may be bleached tan from the frost, but still they stand proud.

For this spell, cut a few stems of grasses. It could be from a meadow or your own yard. Arrange them to dry completely in an empty vase or jar. Display on your altar or elsewhere. Stand before them and honor them with these words:

November's sun dims, the
wild geese are flying,

Flowers bow their heads,
the gardens are dying.

Dusk comes early, frost
sequins the ground,

The leaves turn gold,
then rust to brown.

But you noble grasses, once
green and grand,

You still stand proud and
tall above the land.

Here I'll keep you until spring,

A reminder that birds and
flowers shall return again.

In the spring, if possible lay the
stems gently upon the ground so
they may return to Mother Earth.

James Kambos

NOTES:

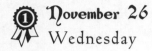

November 26
Wednesday

1st ♒

Color of the day: Topaz
Incense of the day: Lavender

Transformation Spell

If you are a plant lover like me, you
may have a collection of plants
inside and outside of your home.
There comes a time when some
of the leaves on your plants may
wither and turn brown. This spell is
designed for you to think about transformation while you remove the dead
leaves from your plants. Death is part
of the cycle of life. As you gather up
the brown leaves, this chant can help
you stay in the mindset of going with
the flow of transformation, making
space for new things and embracing
new opportunities that will appear:

> As I remove these dead leaves, I know
> they must go, to make space for new
> leaves and opportunities to grow.

You can take this one step further
and place the dead leaves in a metal
cauldron or bowl and safely burn the
leaves (preferably outside) as you
repeat the chant. Always be mindful
of burning things in your magical
practice and use the safest method
possible.

Sapphire Moonbeam

November 27
Thursday

1st ≈

☽ v/c 12:53 pm

☽ → ♓ 2:24 pm

Color of the day: Turquoise
Incense of the day: Nutmeg

Thanksgiving Day

Come in Peace Spell

Use this spell to help improve challenging relationships with loved ones. Draw a circle on the middle of a piece of paper. Within the circle, list the qualities you wish were present in the relationship, be it love, compassion, trust, honesty, accountability, or other traits. Next, draw more circles to represent each person you wish to be affected by the spell, making the circles overlap the middle circle like a Venn diagram. Write each person's name in its own circle. Don't forget to include a circle for yourself as well.

Next, sprinkle lavender flowers or rose petals over the paper. Rub the flowers all over the paper, then gently roll up the paper to make a tube. Secure the loose edge of the paper with tape or string. Keep this roll close at hand when interacting with the people you have included in the magick.

Melanie Marquis

 November 28
Friday

1st ♓

2nd Quarter 1:59 am

Color of the day: Pink
Incense of the day: Yarrow

Potatoes for Prosperity

Plentiful, nutritious, and affordable, potatoes are considered a staple food in many Western households. They represent the basic necessities of life. This spell is designed to bring prosperity and financial stability to someone who is struggling. All you need is a potato, a knife, the name of the person you wish to benefit written on a slip of paper, and about a foot of green or gold thread.

Under the waxing moon, slice a large potato in half. Hold a half in each hand, noticing their heft and weight and considering the potato's earthiness and healthy attributes. These are energies the potato brings to this spell. Place the paper with the name between the two slices of potato. Then wrap the potato with the string and tie it. Visualize the person surrounded and held securely by stabilizing forces, with all their needs met. You can bury the potato if possible, allowing it to sprout and grow, or compost it.

Kate Freuler

November 29
Saturday

2nd ♓

☽ v/c 7:05 pm

☽ → ♈ 8:07 pm

Color of the day: Blue
Incense of the day: Magnolia

Campfire Collage

As autumn winds down and winter approaches, many people think about starting fires—a campfire, a bonfire, a woodstove, a fireplace, and so on. Even lighting candles or incense becomes more appealing. However, not everyone lives where they can enjoy open flames, and some folks find the smoke too irritating. So there are symbolic options instead.

For this magical craft, you need:

- Magazines or catalogs with fire images
- Scissors
- A piece of card stock in red, orange, or yellow
- Craft glue or decoupage medium (such as Mod Podge)
- *Optional*: stickers, glitter glue, metallic markers, glue-on jewels, sequins, or other embellishments

Outdoorsy magazines or catalogs often have fire images, or you can print online images with a color printer. Cut out your fire pictures. Arrange them on the paper until you find a design you like. Glue them down securely. With decoupage medium, you can go over the top to seal it. Add any embellishments. Use this collage to represent the element of fire on your altar, in spells, and so on.

Elizabeth Barrette

NOTES:

November 30
Sunday

NOTES:

2nd ♈

Color of the day: Amber
Incense of the day: Marigold

Cold Water Magic

I grew up fearing cold water. Lately I've come to love and seek it out. Regular cold water immersion has many documented benefits, including boosting immunity, alleviating depression, stimulating hormone regulation, and dumping endorphins into the system. The most powerful shift for me has been the change in self-perception. I feel resilient, strong, and brave.

Do you need a system-wide reset? Cold water can energize and enliven you. If you live near a body of water, immerse yourself in it with a safety buddy. If you don't, enjoy similar benefits from a cold shower or bath at home. Let cold water spray on your face and chest if you're taking a shower. Intone:

Cold water, work your magic in me.

Awaken, enliven, and inspire me.

Begin with a quick dip of thirty seconds. Then towel off, dress warmly, and pay attention to increased energy and activation in your body. Over time, work up to two minutes of immersion.

Dallas Jennifer Cobb

December

December features a palette of cool colors: white snow, silver icicles, evergreen, and, of course, blue—the bright cerulean sky on a clear, cold winter's day, or the deep navy velvet of the darkening nights, culminating on the longest night of the year, the winter solstice. This hue is reflected in December's birthstones: turquoise, zircon, tanzanite, and lapis. The notion of a stone representing each month has been linked to ayurvedic beliefs that suggest correspondences between the planets and crystals. It wasn't until the eighteenth century that associating stones with a birth month became a popular practice in the Western world.

Even if you weren't born in December, you can still tap into the power of this month's special stones. Zircon increases bone stability, which is good for moving over icy terrain. Use turquoise, a rain-making stone, to summon snow. Turquoise also heals and brings peace. Engage tanzanite's powers for psychic visions for the impending new year. Lapis—the mirror of the winter night sky, and a stone that can be found in the breastplate of the high priest—brings wisdom and awareness.

Natalie Zaman

December 1
Monday

2nd ♈

☽ v/c 1:14 pm

☽ → ♉ 10:13 pm

Color of the day: Gray
Incense of the day: Neroli

A Fresh Start

Have you ever wanted to have the opportunity to start over? Today you can use the energy of today's number one to manifest new beginnings in your life. The number one is at the beginning of everything and can symbolize the start of something new.

For this spell you will need a piece of paper and a pencil. In the center of the paper, draw a large numerical one. Around the number one that you drew on your paper, write down all the things you want a fresh start on. You can have as few or as many things as you like. After you make your intention known about everything you want a fresh start on, you can prioritize your word cloud by numbering each item, with the highest-priority item getting a one. When you have all of the items listed, draw a line around the words and say:

Everything within this border
gets a fresh start, a do-over.

Visualize the slate being wiped clean.

Charlynn Walls

December 2
Tuesday

2nd ♉

Color of the day: Maroon
Incense of the day: Bayberry

Peace on Earth Spell

As the holiday season kicks off, this spell will help you prepare for guests. Before guests arrive, say these Words of Power to create a calm, loving atmosphere:

Peace on Earth begins with me.

All who enter my door will
be treated with dignity.

Love lives here, peace lives here,

This is a space without fear.

All are welcome to my hospitality.

And so it must be.

Before guests arrive, as you think of your Words of Power, safely light a green candle to create calm vibrations. No one will know it's magically charged. During your gathering, let it burn in a safe location. When guests leave, extinguish the candle. As your guests arrive, you'll be able to handle any social situation calmly. You'll even be able to tolerate your Aunt Marguerite when she tells you again about that nice young person she's found for you.

James Kambos

December 3
Wednesday

2nd ♉

☽ v/c 8:50 pm

☽ → ♊ 9:48 pm

Color of the day: Brown
Incense of the day: Bay laurel

holly Talisman for Yule

The evergreen leaves of holly, with their festive red berries, are a well-known holiday symbol. During the Yuletide season, real holly is often available at craft stores and florist shops. If you have pets or small children, you might want to remove the berries, which can be toxic if swallowed, or you can place a holly sprig into a plastic sandwich bag. You can also use an artificial sprig of holly, or draw a holly leaf and color it green, with red berries. Or inscribe the ogham letter for holly (≡) using an essential oil. In the ogham alphabet, holly is called Tinne.

Holly represents strength, protection, peace, and comfort. The spiky leaves repel harm and stay green all winter, representing prosperity. Hang your holly talisman above a window in your home. Remove it on Twelfth Night (January 5 or 6) or on Imbolc (February 1–2). Compost it or burn it outdoors.

A.C. Fisher Aldag

 ## December 4
Thursday

2nd ♊

Full Moon 6:14 pm

Color of the day: Purple
Incense of the day: Balsam

Super Cold Moon in Gemini

It's December, the darkest month of the year. Today we have a Super Cold Moon in Gemini, the third and final supermoon of the year. (Just the name evokes thoughts of cuddling into a ball of fluffy fleece blankets.) Inward introspection is at its deepest now. Communication with the self is paramount. The light of the super full moon sheds light on your subconscious. Spend time in deep meditation to find what messages await you.

Before your meditation, drink a cup of mugwort tea to help connect to your spiritual higher self. As you drink your tea, think to yourself:

Full moon above tonight,

Open my mind, open my sight.

Help me to find what I seek.

The voices inside of me shall speak.

Spend as much time as you like in deep meditation and journal about your results.

Kerri Connor

December 5
Friday

3rd ♊

☽ v/c 7:55 pm

☽ → ♋ 8:54 pm

Color of the day: White
Incense of the day: Rose

St. Nicholas Night Spell

St. Nicholas Night was a big deal in my household growing up. We would leave a shoe by our bedroom door before bedtime on December 5 and wake up the next day to find it full of fruit and candy!

In addition to being the patron saint of children, St. Nicholas also helps sailors, merchants, archers, repentant thieves, brewers, pawnbrokers, the unmarried, and students.

For this spell, you will need a bag of chocolate coins (which are available in many stores for the season) and an image of St. Nicholas. In the morning, remove six of the chocolate coins. Place three of them in front of the image of St. Nicholas, saying:

Thank you for spontaneous gifts.

Eat the other three chocolate coins.

As you go about your day, place the rest of the coins from the bag where friends or coworkers will find them, wonder, and enjoy them.

At night, share or eat the coins in front of the image.

Cerridwen Iris Shea

December 6
Saturday

3rd ♋

Color of the day: Black
Incense of the day: Sage

Sculpting the Chakras

When you're in the mood for arts and crafts, obtain air-dry clay, one color for each of the seven primary chakras (rainbow colors are great, or use whichever colors feel best). Hold the clay you've chosen for your root chakra and close your eyes, bringing your awareness to the base of your spine, your root chakra. When you feel a connection to this energy center, open your eyes and sculpt the clay into whatever shape arises intuitively (or sculpt with eyes closed and see what emerges!). You now have a three-dimensional snapshot of your chakra's energetic state. Repeat for all seven chakras.

You can use a toothpick to pierce a hole in each sculpture, which allows you to string them onto a piece of thread or necklace chain once the clay has dried, or you can arrange them on your altar. Use the sculptures as a focal point for chakra work, perhaps placing them in a crystal grid or meditating on healing while holding one in your hand.

Melissa Tipton

December 7
Sunday

3rd ♋

☽ v/c 8:45 pm

☽ → ♌ 9:48 pm

Color of the day: Gold

Incense of the day: Hyacinth

Cut the Gossip Spell

If you're the victim of gossip, try this spell. It's based in old-time Appalachian folk magic. Knives, scissors, and axes were once used to "cut" pain, curses, or gossip. You'll need a pair of scissors and one piece of gray yarn about a foot long. Hold the yarn as you concentrate on the gossip. Then say:

Words dark as night,

Scatter and take flight.

Words that cut like a knife,

Go, so only truth will see the light!

Now cut the yarn in half and throw it in the trash.

James Kambos

December 8
Monday

3rd ♌

Color of the day: Ivory

Incense of the day: Hyssop

Negative Energy Trap

Sometimes when we clean the house, it's not just dirt we're removing but also energy that has built up. It's important to cleanse it away along with the rest of the debris. Here is a simple way to trap that energy and then dispose of it.

After tidying up, fill a small bowl with water. Add a piece of hematite and a tablespoon of lemon juice. Hematite acts as a magnet and lemon juice as a cleanser. Hold your hands above the bowl, close your eyes, and envision the stone acting as a magnet sucking in all negative energy. In your mind, this might look like shadowy figures or moldy spots being drawn into the water and neutralized by the lemon juice. Place the bowl somewhere in the home away from pets and children.

Once a day for three days, repeat the visualization with the water. On the third day, dispose of the water. Keep the hematite for another use.

Kate Freuler

 December 9
Tuesday

3rd ♌

☽ v/c 11:56 pm

Color of the day: Red
Incense of the day: Geranium

Nature Connection Spell

Use this magick to strengthen your connection to the spirit guardians that watch over the land where you live or where you're visiting. You'll need four small quartz crystals and a gallon of water. Look at a map and choose a destination to your north, a destination to the east, a destination to the south, and a destination to the west.

Head to the north first and find a patch of bare ground or a tree or other plant. Kiss one of the crystals and hold it to your heart, pouring your love into the stone. Place the stone on the ground or at the base of a tree or other plant, and pour about a quart of the water in a circle surrounding your feet. Call out to any protective and helpful spirits that dwell there, telling them your name and asking directly for their help and alliance. Then head to your next destinations to the east, south, and west, repeating the process. Your connection to the local spirits will be strengthened.

Melanie Marquis

 December 10
Wednesday

3rd ♌

☽ → ♍ 2:20 am

Color of the day: White
Incense of the day: Lilac

Release Spell

In the last month of the year, before the winter solstice, you can do a spell to release things. First, think about what you want to release. Releasing an attachment to an outcome is a way to regain peace about anything you might feel frustrated about. Find a dead leaf that has fallen from an autumn tree. Make sure it has enough space for you to write on it. If you cannot locate a leaf, use a small piece of biodegradable paper. Find a pencil and write down the things that you want to purge. Once you have the words written down, you can say these words:

> On this list are the things
> that I want to release,
>
> So I may regain inner peace.
>
> There is strength in being
> able to let things go.
>
> I release my attachment
> so peace will flow.

Crush the leaf and rip the tiny paper. Find a place to bury the things you want to release, and be done with it.

Sapphire Moonbeam

December 11
Thursday

3rd ♍

4th Quarter 3:52 pm

Color of the day: Green
Incense of the day: Carnation

Waning Moon herbal Bath Tea

The waning moon phase is a good time to retreat within ourselves to heal, sift through our experiences, and let go of those things that no longer serve us. This is especially important during the winter months, when darker days and inclement weather can wear us down. Holiday stress can also affect us, leaving us feeling frayed and depleted of energy.

This is your reminder that it's okay to take a break, nourish your soul, and ease built-up tension.

For this spell you will need:

- 1 cup dried lavender buds
- 1 cup dried hops
- 1 cup dried rose petals
- A bowl
- 1 quart-size canning jar
- 5 x 7-inch muslin drawstring bags

Mix the herbs together in a bowl. Place the mixture in the canning jar and store in a cool, dry place.

Light some candles and pick out some relaxing music. Place one cup of the herb mixture in a muslin drawstring bag and tie shut. Place in your bath to infuse. Enjoy this quiet time of contemplation. Extinguish the candles when done.

Monica Crosson

NOTES:

December 12
Friday

4th ♍

☽ v/c 9:51 am

☽ → ♎ 11:04 am

Color of the day: Rose
Incense of the day: Orchid

Freya's Delight Spell

Named for Freya, the Norse goddess of love and beauty, Friday is also ruled by Venus, Aphrodite, and Eros. Invoke Freya by doing an attraction spell using a rose quartz, rose oil, or a rose to magnify passion. Whether you choose to attract a mate, lover, or friend, or seek to increase self-love, invoke Freya. She may bring delight to the weekend ahead.

Tuck a rose quartz into your bra or shirt pocket, saying:

Freya delights in heart-centered love.

Dab a little rose oil, diluted with a carrier oil, behind your ears and on the hollow of your throat, saying:

*Freya delights in attraction
and passion.*

Buy a single rose (red for passion, white for purity, pink for admiration, happiness, and friends) and place it in a vase on your desk or altar. Intone:

*Freya delights in beauty. Freya
blesses all of my life with increased
beauty, attraction, love, and light.*

Dallas Jennifer Cobb

 December 13
Saturday

4th ♎

Color of the day: Blue
Incense of the day: Ivy

To Summon Justice

This is a spell to summon justice. You will need:

- A black pen or marker
- A piece of red paper, 4 inches square
- Identifying materials (hair, nail clippings, clothing, etc.) for the person targeted by the spell (optional)
- Charcoal with a heatproof holder/dish/grill
- Matches or lighter
- 1 part frankincense resin
- 1 part pine resin
- 4 garlic cloves

Perform this ritual outside (due to very smelly smoke). Using a black pen or marker, write the full name (First, Middle, Last) of the person you want to summon justice against on the red paper square. Add their birthdate (if known). You can also attach identifying materials for the person targeted by the spell.

Light a bed of charcoal. When hot, hold the paper in your left hand and say:

> Justice, come to my aid. Justice
> be served against (name of
> targeted person) for these crimes:
> _____ (recite their deeds).

Toss the paper onto the coals, followed by three good pinches of the two resins and all four garlic cloves. As it smokes, recite the name of the targeted person until everything has burned up. Dispose of the cold ashes in running water.

Brandon Weston

NOTES:

 # December 14
Sunday

4ℏ ♎
☽ v/c 10:36 pm
☽ → ♏ 10:51 pm

Color of the day: Yellow
Incense of the day: Frankincense

hanukkah begins at sundown

Remembering Resistance

When I was growing up, Hanukkah was one of the bigger holidays that my family celebrated, and it was also one of my favorites. At a basic level, it is a celebration of resistance and persistence, and today, as the first night of Hanukkah, I invite you to utilize that symbolism in your magic by lighting a single candle in a dark room. The light of the flame represents both resistance against the dark and the persistence to shine bright no matter what may come your way. Sit in the room with your candle and reflect on this past year. Were there any instances where you had to stand up for your rights? Or were there times when you had more endurance to face a challenge than you thought you did? Take some time to focus on the flame and connect with the energy of those experiences, and use those as motivation to keep persisting. You can either let the candle burn out completely or burn it a little each day until it's gone.

Amanda Lynn

December 15
Monday

4th ♏

Color of the day: Silver
Incense of the day: Lily

Oils and Balms for Winter healing

We're in cold and flu season. With simple ingredients, you can make your own oils and balms to ease winter maladies and boost your well-being. You'll need:

- 1 or more fresh or dried warming herbs (whole allspice, cardamom pods, cinnamon sticks, thin slices of fresh ginger, rosemary, sage, star anise, or thyme)
- 2 clean 8-ounce glass jars with tight-fitting lids
- A neutral, unscented oil (sunflower, safflower, avocado, etc.)
- A square of cheesecloth
- A small strainer

Pack the herbs into a jar and pour oil over them to cover, making sure air pockets are filled. Tighten lid. Place in a cool indoor location, and shake every few days. After 4 to 6 weeks, strain through a cheesecloth-lined strainer into a clean jar.

Optional: To make a balm, melt an ounce of beeswax in a custard cup and stir in ½ teaspoon of your infused oil.

Use the oil or balm to anoint chakra points, rub into the chest when ill with a cold or flu, or scent a hot bath or shower, each time repeating:

Scent of oil, herbal healing,

Hand of the mothers, anoint me.

May I feel their power.

Susan Pesznecker

NOTES:

December 16
Tuesday

4th ♏

Color of the day: Gray
Incense of the day: Cedar

Boost Your Confidence

Tuesdays are associated with the masculine energy of Mars, the Roman god of war who deals with courage and bravado. We can use that energy to our advantage to boost our confidence when stepping into a situation where we need to project confidence and strength.

Before taking on such a daunting task, prepare yourself for battle. Don clothing that makes you feel invincible. It could be a favorite dress or shirt. Color choices could include reds, burgundies, and blacks in order to align with Mars. You can also put a power stone in your pocket, such as a bloodstone. In your mind's eye, see yourself completing the task or challenge at hand, and say three times:

Power exudes power.

With each repetition, feel yourself becoming taller and more assertive. When you are finished, you can both feel and see yourself having accomplished the task at hand.

Charlynn Walls

 December 17
Wednesday

4th ♏

☽ v/c 10:24 am
☽ → ♐ 11:38 am

Color of the day: Topaz
Incense of the day: Marjoram

National Maple Syrup Day

Today is National Maple Syrup Day. This delicious treat is made by boiling sap from sugar maple trees. You can also take it farther to make maple sugar. These natural sweeteners represent abundance. They form the foundation of many small and sustainable businesses, as people gather maple sap and turn it into various products. They also support a number of seasonal festivals and other events in areas where maple syrup is important. For this ritual, you need a bit of maple syrup or maple sugar and a picture of a sugar maple tree. First, sit in a comfortable position and meditate on the generosity of the maple tree. It cleans the air, houses wildlife, casts shade, and gives us food. Say:

I honor the generosity of the maple tree for its many gifts.

Eat your maple treat. Then say:

Taste the sweetness of abundance.

Meditate on the ways that abundance touches your life, and what you hope to enjoy in the future.

Elizabeth Barrette

December 18
Thursday

4th ♐

Color of the day: Turquoise
Incense of the day: Myrrh

Eponalia Workout

On the old Roman calendar, the Gaulish goddess Epona's feast day, Eponalia, was observed on December 18. She is conflated with the Roman/Italic Rigantona, the Cymri (Welsh) Rhiannon, and sometimes the Irish Macha. Epona rules sports, movement, travel, fertility, and physical fitness. Her symbols are birds, horses, keys, a gate, sheaves of wheat, roses, and a crescent moon.

Eponalia is a beneficial time to begin a new fitness regimen. This can be as easy as stretching your muscles or as elaborate as a full workout. Call upon Epona to help you increase strength and endurance and achieve optimal health. Wear a symbol of Epona to help you expand your physical abilities. Visualize her as a powerful woman riding a white horse as you exercise.

A.C. Fisher Aldag

December 19
Friday

4th ♐

New Moon 8:43 pm
☽ v/c 10:41 pm
☽ → ♑ 11:53 pm

Color of the day: Pink
Incense of the day: Cypress

A New Moon Wishes Ritual

As December thins away, we are about to observe the last new moon of the year. This is the ideal time to plant the seeds for your hopes, wishes, and dreams that you want to carry with you into the new year. Anything you wish to expand should be planned now.

For this ritual, you'll need a piece of paper, a pen, and one white candle in a holder. Place your supplies on your altar. On the paper, write no more than three hopes/wishes you want to achieve in the new year, beginning at this new moon. Next, carefully light the candle and say:

*An old year is about to end, a
new year is about to begin,*

*The Wheel of the Year
continues to spin.*

These are the wishes I want to sow

As the new moon begins to grow.

Meditate on your goals. See yourself completing them. When you're ready, safely snuff out the candle and let it cool. Use it for other moon magic. Keep your wish list for as long as you desire. When you've accomplished your goals, discard it.

James Kambos

NOTES:

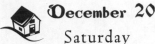

December 20
Saturday

1st ♑

Color of the day: Indigo
Incense of the day: Pine

The Astral Cozy Retreat

We're almost at the longest night of the year, holiday expectations are high, and we need a bit of cozy. Block off two hours for this spell, in a place where you will not be disturbed.

You will need a hot beverage, blankets, pillows, a key, a pen, and a journal. Create a comfortable space where you feel cozy. Write a few paragraphs in your journal depicting YOUR perfect cozy day in the cozy retreat of your dreams.

Then, sipping your beverage, read it over as if you are living it. This is now your astral cozy retreat, to which you can withdraw whenever you want; you can build, change, and decorate however you want. It's a place to rest, to dream, to grow, to reflect. It's a place where you can feel safe, no matter what is going on in the material world.

Keep the key on your nightstand to remind you to visit.

Cerridwen Iris Shea

December 21
Sunday

1st ♍

☉ → ♍ 10:03 am

Color of the day: Orange
Incense of the day: Juniper

Yule – Winter Solstice

Witchy Yuletide Gifts

Giving holiday gifts to your magical friends is fun because you can pack so much meaning and magic into them. These ornaments are inexpensive, personalized, and powerful. You can make each one to match the recipient's desires and needs.

This is the recipe for a protection ornament, but with a little googling you can make one for love, prosperity, health, or anything you can imagine. Gather these materials:

- Chalk
- A 1-inch square of black paper
- 5 inches of black thread
- An empty fillable ball ornament, available at craft stores
- 1 tablespoon rosemary
- 1 tablespoon frankincense
- 1 tablespoon juniper berries
- A small black tourmaline crystal

Using the chalk, draw a picture of a pentagram (or any symbol that is protective to you) on the black paper. Roll it up and secure it with the thread, like a tiny scroll. Place this paper along with the other materials inside the ornament ball. It's ready to be gifted. You might want to include a note explaining the meaning of the ornament.

Years from now, every time the recipient hangs the ornament during the holidays, they'll be reminded of your well wishes.

Kate Freuler

NOTES:

December 22
Monday

1st ♑

☽ v/c 9:44 am

☽ → ♒ 10:52 am

Color of the day: Ivory
Incense of the day: Clary sage

hanukkah ends

Activating Your Tarot Cards

Consecrate a tarot deck using elemental representations, adapting the following pairings to suit your practice: air/swords, water/cups, fire/wands, earth/pentacles. Choose something to represent each of the four elements. Options include a blade, feather, or incense for air; a chalice, shell, or bowl of water for—you guessed it—water; a wand or candle for fire; and a dish of salt or a stone for earth. For spirit, which corresponds to the major arcana (trump cards), a piece of clear quartz or a selenite tower are great options.

Divide your tarot deck into five stacks, one for each suit and the trumps. Arrange the elemental objects on your altar, and place the appropriate tarot stack next to its element. (If using candles, situate them on a heatproof surface and don't leave them unattended.) Allow the elemental objects to awaken your deck, aligning the suits and the trumps with the relevant energies.

Melissa Tipton

December 23
Tuesday

1st ♒

Color of the day: Scarlet
Incense of the day: Ginger

Festivus Transformation Spell

Today is Festivus for the rest of us! Festivus became part of pop culture when it was featured on *Seinfeld*, a popular television sitcom in the 1990s. It is an actual nonreligious holiday that was created by Daniel O'Keefe back in 1966. Although Festivus is a parody type of holiday that has "feats of strength" competitions and the proclaiming of "Festivus miracles," this spell is for the airing of grievances. It is a way to rid yourself of your frustrations privately, rather than airing your grievances in person with others. You can use the power of fire to transform things that irritate you. Fire transforms, and air allows your thoughts and ideas to disperse and flow.

Obtain a black candle to absorb the negativity. Safely light the candle and speak your words of frustration over the flame. The candle flame will help burn it away, transform it, and release it into the air. After you speak your words over the flame, douse the candle.

Sapphire Moonbeam

December 24
Wednesday

1st ♒

☽ v/c 4:42 pm

☽ → ♓ 8:09 pm

Color of the day: Brown
Incense of the day: Lavender

Christmas Eve

Christmas Eve Blessing

With its bright evergreen leaves, holly represents hope in a dreary winter landscape. For the Romans, it was a plant of good fortune. For the Celts, it was a plant of protection that was sometimes planted near their dwellings so the spiky leaves might snag evil spirits before having a chance to enter the home. When brought into the house during the darkest days of winter, the green leaves and bright berries brought cheer to the inhabitants of the home, as they were a reminder that spring would soon come.

Use a holly sprig as an aspergillum to cleanse and bless your home on Christmas Eve. Starting at the main entry of your home, dip your holly sprig into a bowl of fresh water and work your way deosil (clockwise), sprinkling the water around your home. As you do so, say something like this:

> With love and light on
> this darksome night,

> Bless this home and all
> who dwell within.

> Negativity away, bright
> blessings to stay,

> For all who enter, both kith and kin.
>   Monica Crosson

Notes:

December 25
Thursday

1st ♓

Color of the day: Crimson
Incense of the day: Jasmine

Christmas Day

Like Christmas Spell

As a young child, I remember lying under the Christmas tree, smelling the tang of fresh pine and dreaming of what was in the boxes lying next to me. Resting my fingers lightly on them, I would imagine their contents. In this moment, anything was possible.

Whether you celebrate Christmas or not, today you can capitalize on the gift-giving energy of Christmas, using it for magical benefit. Sit quietly for just a moment, and ask yourself:

*What do I delight in? What
is my perfect gift?*

*What do I long for? What
will inspire and uplift?*

*Like a child with a brand-new toy,
I now know what brings me joy.*

*Like Father Christmas bringing
parcels, I give myself only tasty morsels.*

As you socialize today, perhaps celebrating with family and friends, know that the greatest gifts are those that you give to yourself. They are the most delightful gifts of spirit.

Dallas Jennifer Cobb

December 26
Friday

1st ♓

Color of the day: Coral
Incense of the day: Mint

Kwanzaa begins (ends Jan. 1) –
Boxing Day (Canada & UK)

Spiritual Unity

The principle celebrated on the first day of Kwanzaa is Umoja, which means "unity." Today, work on a rededication to your own spiritual unity. Safely light a blue candle. Say and feel these words:

*Today, I do not start anew,
but I do begin again.*

*Each day is a new beginning,
a new step along my path.*

*Today, I begin again with
harmony, peace, and unity in
my heart and in my spirit.*

Spend as much time as you like in meditation and journal about your results. Extinguish the candle.

Kerri Connor

December 27
Saturday

1st ♓

☽ v/c 2:03 am

☽ → ♈ 3:02 am

2nd Quarter 2:10 pm

Color of the day: Gray
Incense of the day: Patchouli

Candle Spell for Balance

Use this spell to bring balance and peace whenever chaos is reigning. You'll need two candles, one to represent the things you want to diminish or banish from your life and one to symbolize the things you wish to increase or attract to your life. Place them both in holders side by side over a fireproof surface in front of you.

First, light the candle representing the things you want to diminish or banish. Name the things you wish to let go of, expressing your thoughts to the candle as you gaze at the flame. Watch the wax melting down as you focus on your desire to have these things you speak of reduced or done away with completely. You can either let the candle burn all the way down as you watch or snuff it out when you have finished this part of the spell.

Next, take some deep breaths and light the candle you've chosen to represent the things you want in your life. Watch the flame burn bright as you express to the candle those things you wish to welcome or increase in your life. Envision what this reality will look like and feel like as you look at the glowing light. Take slow, deep breaths and relax your shoulders and jaw muscles. Let this candle burn all the way down, and stay with it until it extinguishes.

Melanie Marquis

NOTES:

December 28
Sunday

2nd ♈

☽ v/c 9:13 pm

Color of the day: Amber
Incense of the day: Almond

Shedding the Skin

The year is ending, and it's almost time to start anew! This spell is a symbolic shedding of skin using the image of a snake. In many traditions, the snake is a symbol of transformation, ascension, and renewal. By shedding its skin, the snake reveals a more beautiful and brighter self that was waiting to shine.

For this spell, you will need a paper cutout of a snake (large enough to write on), a pen, and your chosen method of magical disposal. Create your sacred space and get focused. As you think about the culmination of the year, focus on all the things you are shedding to reveal what is yet to come. Write those down on the snake cutout. When you have filled up the snake to your liking, review what you have written and give thanks for the lessons. Bless them in your preferred way and "shed" them how you see fit—bury, burn, etc.

Amanda Lynn

NOTES:

December 29
Monday

2nd ♈

☽ → ♉ 6:57 am

Color of the day: White
Incense of the day: Rosemary

New Year Protection for home and Family

This traditional home ward is created by families around the turn of the new year. You will need:

- Dirt from the home or land you wish to bless and protect

- A pint-size glass canning jar with a lid

- A silver item: coin, ring, necklace, chain, etc. (can be plated, but must be real silver)

- A piece of white paper, 4 inches square

- A black pen or marker

Gather together everyone who lives in the home or on the land you're blessing and protecting. This can be your family, roommates, or even just yourself. Fill the glass canning jar with dirt from the land. This can also include rocks, sticks, and plants that are found around the home.

Next, bury your silver item inside the dirt in the jar, making sure it's completely covered. Seal the jar, then have everyone present write their full name (First, Middle, Last) on the paper square. You can also write any blessings you might have for the new year to come. Bury this in the dirt as well.

As this jar is a protective ward, try to hide it inside the home, somewhere where no one will see it. Around the next new year, open the jar, retrieve the silver item, dump out the dirt outside, then repeat the building process.

Brandon Weston

NOTES:

December 30
Tuesday

2nd ♉

Color of the day: Red
Incense of the day: Cinnamon

A Spell for Severing

As the year's end approaches, a round of good magical housekeeping often includes a severance spell. It's a chance to let go, release, undo, and sever any negative energy that's lurking in your personal space and causing problems. You'll need:

- 1 small light-colored pillar candle, representing the light: the "light candle"
- 1 small pillar candle in a color representing the problem: the "problem candle"
- 2 saucers
- 14–18 inches of string
- Matches
- Pair of scissors
- A candle extinguisher

Place each candle on a saucer, and place one end of the string under each saucer. The string symbolizes the connection between you (the light candle) and the person or problem troubling you (the problem candle).

Ignite the light candle. Repeat:

*My light is bright but
sometimes troubled.*

Light the problem candle. Repeat:

May the darkness now be muffled.

Cut the string in the middle, then blow or pinch out the problem candle. Repeat:

Connection gone, my light burns bright.

Free from darkness, aflame with light.

Meditate on the severed cord, then extinguish the light candle.

Susan Pesznecker

NOTES:

December 31
Wednesday

2nd ♉

☽ v/c 7:25 am

☽ → ♊ 8:13 am

Color of the day: Yellow
Incense of the day: Honeysuckle

New Year's Eve

New Year's Eve Divination

It is the end of the old year and the beginning of the new, according to the Gregorian calendar. This is a time when many people conclude projects or recordkeeping with the intent of starting new ones on January 1st. That makes this a powerful time for divination.

This little rite is simply about setting the stage before you begin the divination proper. You will need a quiet place, a cloth or mat, and your favorite divinatory materials. You can use any type of divination tool that you like, such as Tarot cards, Norse runes, or a pendulum. Sit comfortably and quiet your mind. Spread your cloth or mat and set out your divination gear. Then say:

Close of the year,

So bright and clear,

An end is here,

Beginning's near.

Now let me see,

As time swings free,

What was will be

In store for me.

Keep your focus and begin the divination as you usually do.

Elizabeth Barrette

NOTES:

Daily Magical Influences

Each day is ruled by a planet that possesses specific magical influences:

Monday (Moon): peace, healing, caring, psychic awareness, purification

Tuesday (Mars): passion, sex, courage, aggression, protection

Wednesday (Mercury): conscious mind, study, travel, divination, wisdom

Thursday (Jupiter): expansion, money, prosperity, generosity

Friday (Venus): love, friendship, reconciliation, beauty

Saturday (Saturn): longevity, exorcism, endings, homes, houses

Sunday (Sun): healing, spirituality, success, strength, protection

Lunar Phases

The lunar phase is important in determining best times for magic.

The new moon is when the moon and sun are conjunct each other. It corresponds to all new beginnings and is the best time to start a project.

The waxing moon (from the new moon to the full moon) is the ideal time for magic to draw things to you.

The full moon is when the sun and moon are opposite each other. It is the time of greatest power.

The waning moon (from the full moon to the new moon) is a time for study, meditation, and little magical work (except magic designed to banish harmful energies).

Astrological Symbols

The Sun	☉	Aries	♈
The Moon	☽	Taurus	♉
Mercury	☿	Gemini	♊
Venus	♀	Cancer	♋
Mars	♂	Leo	♌
Jupiter	♃	Virgo	♍
Saturn	♄	Libra	♎
Uranus	♅	Scorpio	♏
Neptune	♆	Sagittarius	♐
Pluto	♇	Capricorn	♑
		Aquarius	♒
		Pisces	♓

The Moon's Sign

The moon's sign is a traditional consideration for astrologers. The moon continuously moves through each sign in the zodiac, from Aries to Pisces. The moon influences the sign it inhabits, creating different energies that affect our daily lives.

Aries: Good for starting things but lacks staying power. Things occur rapidly but quickly pass. People tend to be argumentative and assertive.

Taurus: Things begun now do last, tend to increase in value, and become hard to alter. Brings out an appreciation for beauty and sensory experience.

Gemini: Things begun now are easily changed by outside influence. Time for shortcuts, communications, games, and fun.

Cancer: Stimulates emotional rapport between people. Pinpoints need, supports growth and nurturance. Tend to domestic concerns.

Leo: Draws emphasis to the self, to central ideas or institutions, away from connections with others and emotional needs. People tend to be melodramatic.

Virgo: Favors accomplishment of details and commands from higher up. Focus on health, hygiene, and daily schedules.

Libra: Favors cooperation, compromise, social activities, beautification of surroundings, balance, and partnership.

Scorpio: Increases awareness of psychic power. Favors activities requiring intensity and focus. People tend to brood and become secretive under this moon sign.

Sagittarius: Encourages flights of imagination and confidence. This moon sign is adventurous, philosophical, and athletic. Favors expansion and growth.

Capricorn: Develops strong structure. Focus on traditions, responsibilities, and obligations. A good time to set boundaries and rules.

Aquarius: Rebellious energy. Time to break habits and make abrupt change. Personal freedom and individuality are the focus.

Pisces: The focus is on dreaming, nostalgia, intuition, and psychic impressions. A good time for spiritual or philanthropic activities.

2025 New and Full Moons

○ Full Moon, 24 ♋ 00, January 13, 5:27 p.m. EST

◑ New Moon, 9 ♒ 51, January 29, 7:36 a.m. EST

○ Full Moon, 24 ♌ 06, February 12, 8:53 a.m. EST

◑ New Moon, 9 ♓ 41, February 27, 7:45 p.m. EST

○ Full Moon/Lunar Eclipse, 23 ♍ 57, March 14, 2:55 a.m. EDT

◑ New Moon/Solar Eclipse, 9 ♈ 00, March 29, 6:58 a.m. EDT

○ Full Moon, 23 ♎ 20, April 12, 8:22 p.m. EDT

◑ New Moon, 7 ♉ 47, April 27, 3:31 p.m. EDT

○ Full Moon, 22 ♏ 13, May 12, 12:56 p.m. EDT

◑ New Moon, 6 ♊ 06, May 26, 11:02 p.m. EDT

○ Full Moon, 20 ♐ 39, June 11, 3:44 a.m. EDT

◑ New Moon, 4 ♋ 08, June 25, 6:32 a.m. EDT

○ Full Moon, 18 ♑ 50, July 10, 4:37 p.m. EDT

● New Moon, 2 ♌ 08, July 24, 3:11 p.m. EDT

○ Full Moon, 17 ♒ 00, August 9, 3:55 a.m. EDT

◑ New Moon, 0 ♍ 23, August 23, 2:07 a.m. EDT

○ Full Moon/Lunar Eclipse, 15 ♓ 23, September 7, 2:09 p.m. EDT

◑ New Moon/Solar Eclipse, 29 ♍ 05, Sept. 21, 3:54 p.m. EDT

○ Full Moon, 14 ♈ 08, October 6, 11:48 p.m. EDT

◑ New Moon, 28 ♎ 22, October 21, 8:25 a.m. EDT

○ Full Moon, 13 ♉ 23, November 5, 8:19 a.m. EST

◑ New Moon, 28 ♏ 12, November 20, 1:47 a.m. EST

○ Full Moon, 13 ♊ 04, December 4, 6:14 p.m. EST

◑ New Moon, 28 ♐ 25, December 19, 8:43 p.m. EST

Glossary of Magical Terms

altar: A table that holds magical tools as a focus for spell workings.

athame: A ritual knife used to direct personal power during workings or to symbolically draw diagrams in a spell. It is rarely, if ever, used for actual physical cutting.

aura: An invisible energy field surrounding a person. The aura can change color depending on the state of the individual.

balefire: A fire lit for magical purposes, usually outdoors.

casting a circle: The process of drawing a circle around oneself to seal out unfriendly influences and raise magical power. It is the first step in a spell.

censer: An incense burner. Traditionally a censer is a metal container, filled with incense, that is swung on the end of a chain.

censing: The process of burning incense to spiritually cleanse an object.

centering yourself: To prepare for a magical rite by calming and centering all of your personal energy.

chakra: One of the seven centers of spiritual energy in the human body, according to the philosophy of yoga.

charging: To infuse an object with magical power.

circle of protection: A circle cast to protect oneself from unfriendly influences.

crystals: Quartz or other stones that store cleansing or protective energies.

deosil: Clockwise movement, symbolic of life and positive energies.

deva: A divine being according to Hindu beliefs; a devil or evil spirit according to Zoroastrianism.

direct/retrograde: Refers to the motion of a planet when seen from the earth. A planet is "direct" when it appears to be moving forward from the point of view of a person on the earth. It is "retrograde" when it appears to be moving backward.

dowsing: To use a divining rod to search for a thing, usually water or minerals.

dowsing pendulum: A long cord with a coin or gem at one end. The pattern of its swing is used to answer questions.

dryad: A tree spirit or forest guardian.

fey: An archaic term for a magical spirit or a fairylike being.

gris-gris: A small bag containing charms, herbs, stones, and other items to draw energy, luck, love, or prosperity to the wearer.

mantra: A sacred chant used in Hindu tradition to embody the divinity invoked; it is said to possess deep magical power.

needfire: A ceremonial fire kindled at dawn on major Wiccan holidays. It was traditionally used to light all other household fires.

pentagram: A symbolically protective five-pointed star with one point upward.

power hand: The dominant hand; the hand used most often.

scry: To predict the future by gazing at or into an object such as a crystal ball or pool of water.

second sight: The psychic power or ability to foresee the future.

sigil: A personal seal or symbol.

wand: A stick or rod used for casting circles and as a focus for magical power.

widdershins: Counterclockwise movement, symbolic of negative magical purposes, sometimes used to disperse negative energies.

About the Authors

A.C. Fisher Aldag has practiced a folk religion from the British Isles for over 45 years. She is the author of *Common Magick: Origins and Practices of British Folk Magick*, published by Llewellyn in 2019. A.C. lives on a small homestead near beautiful Lake Michigan.

Elizabeth Barrette has been involved with the Pagan community for more than thirty-four years. She served as the managing editor of *PanGaia* for eight years and the dean of studies at the Grey School of Wizardry for four years. She has written columns on beginning and intermediate Pagan practice, Pagan culture, and Pagan leadership. Her book *Composing Magic: How to Create Magical Spells, Rituals, Blessings, Chants, and Prayers* explains how to combine writing and spirituality. She lives in central Illinois, where she has done much networking with Pagans in her area, such as coffee-house meetings and open sabbats. Her other public activities include Pagan picnics and science fiction conventions. Visit her blog, *The Wordsmith's Forge* (https://ysabetwordsmith.dreamwidth.org), or website, *PenUltimate Productions* (http://penultimateproductions.weebly.com). Her coven site, which includes extensive Pagan materials, is *Greenhaven: A Pagan Tradition* (http://greenhaventradition.weebly.com).

Dallas Jennifer Cobb lives in a magical village on Lake Ontario where she enjoys cold dips throughout the winter. A Pagan, mother, feminist, writer, and animal lover, she enjoys a sustainable lifestyle with a balance of time and money. She writes about what she knows: brain injury, magic, herbs, astrology, healing, recovery, and vibrant sustainability. When she isn't car camping or communing with nature, she likes to correspond with like-minded beings. Reach her at jennifer.cobb@live.com.

Kerri Connor is the High Priestess/Minister of the Gathering Grove (a non-profit family-friendly, earth-based spiritual group) and has been practicing her craft since the 1980s. A graduate of the University of Wisconsin, Kerri earned a BA in communications. She is a cancer survivor and lives with her family in northern Illinois. Visit her at KerriConnor.com.

Monica Crosson (Concrete, WA) has been a practicing Witch and educator for over thirty years and is a member of Evergreen Coven. She is the author of *A Year in the Enchanted Garden*, *The Magickal Family*, and *Wild Magical Soul* and is a regular contributor to the Llewellyn annuals as well as magazines such as *Enchanted Living* and *Witchology*.

Kate Freuler is the author of *Magic at the Crossroads: The Devil in Modern Witchcraft* and *Of Blood and Bones: Working with Shadow Magick and the Dark Moon*. She has written articles for *Llewellyn's Magical Almanac*, *Llewellyn's Spell-A-Day Almanac*, and *Llewellyn's Sabbats Almanac*. She lives in Ontario, Canada, and can be found making art, wandering around in libraries, and writing. Visit her at www.katefreuler.com.

James Kambos is a writer and an artist from Ohio. He writes articles and essays about folk magic, occult lore, and living a magical life. He raises many wildflowers and herbs. When not writing, he paints in an American primitive style. He holds a degree in social sciences and geography from Ohio University.

Amanda Lynn has been dedicated to Witchcraft since childhood. For thirteen years she was a priestess in her local community, where she developed a penchant for ritual creation and spellcraft. These days, when she's not taking long walks in cemeteries or circling with one of her covens, she studies aromatherapy, esoterica, and intuitive magic. You can often find her checking out new music and wearing lots of glitter.

Melanie Marquis is an award-winning author, the founder and producer of the Mystical Minds Convention, and a local coordinator for the Pagan Pride Project. She is the author of *Cookbook of Shadows*, *Llewellyn's Little Book of Moon Spells*, *Carl Llewellyn Weschcke: Pioneer and Publisher of Body, Mind & Spirit* (IPPY Award Gold winner for Best Biography), *A Witch's World of Magick*, *The Witch's Bag of Tricks*, *Beltane*, and *Lughnasadh*, as well as the coauthor of *Witchy Mama* (with Emily A. Francis) and the creator of the *Modern Spellcaster's Tarot* (illustrated by Scott Murphy), all from Llewellyn. She is the producer of Stuffed Animal Magick Shop on YouTube and TikTok and is also a folk artist and an avid crafter, creating unique stuffed animals and magickal household products to make everyday life more fun. Learn more at MelanieMarquis.com or connect with her on Instagram @Magickalmelaniemarquis, Facebook @MelanieMarquisauthor, or Tiktok and YouTube @StuffedAnimalMagickShop.

Sapphire Moonbeam is a rainbow energy artist, metaphysical jewelry maker, card reader, author, and nature photographer, and has a bachelor's degree in psychology from the University of Missouri–Kansas City. Sapphire is the artist and author of the Moonbeam Magick oracle card deck. She is a self-taught artist who teaches intuitive abstract art classes in the Kansas City area as well as locations around the world. Sapphire loves to visit ancient sites and temples in far-off lands to connect with the mystical energies there. She is a social media influencer and sends out good vibes to her worldwide following on her Sapphire's Moonbeams page on Facebook. Find her on Instagram, Threads, and Twitter @ssmoonbeam and visit her website at SapphireMoonbeam.com.

Susan Pesznecker is a mother, grandmother, writer, retired nurse, and soon-to-be-retired college English professor living in the beautiful green Pacific Northwest with her poodle, Sarah. An initiated Druid and green magick devoteé, Sue loves reading, writing, cooking, travel, and anything having to do with the outdoors. Previous works include *Crafting Magick with Pen and Ink*, *The Magickal Retreat*, and *Yule: Recipes & Lore for the Winter Solstice*. Follow her on Instagram @Susan Pesznecker.

Cerridwen Iris Shea is a writer, tarot practitioner, and home/hearth witch. She started as an urban witch, became an ocean witch, is now a mountain witch, and is likely to become a bog witch. She is owned by cats who love to knock her crystals off the tables. Visit her at www.cerridwenscottage.com.

Melissa Tipton is a Jungian Witch, Structural Integrator, and founder of the Real Magic Mystery School, where they teach online courses in Jungian Magic, a potent blend of ancient magical techniques and modern psychological insights. They're the author of *Living Reiki: Heal Yourself and Transform Your Life* and *Llewellyn's Complete Book of Reiki*. Learn more and take a free class at www.realmagic.school.

Charlynn Walls is an active member of her local community and coven. A practitioner of the Craft for over twenty-five years, she currently resides in Central Missouri with her family. Charlynn draws on her background in anthropology and archaeology and her own personal experience to help shape her daily practice. She continues to share her knowledge by teaching online and at local festivals.

Brandon Weston (Fayetteville, AR) is a healer, writer, and folklorist who owns and operates Ozark Healing Traditions, an online collective of articles, lectures, and workshops focusing on the Ozark Mountain region. As a practicing folk healer, his work with clients includes everything from spiritual cleanses to house blessings. He comes from a long line of Ozark hillfolk and is also a folk herbalist, yarb doctor, and power doctor. His books include *Ozark Folk Magic*, *Ozark Mountain Spell Book*, and *Granny Thornapple's Book of Charms*. Visit him at ozarkhealing.com or on Instagram @ozarkhealingtraditions.

2024

SEPTEMBER
S	M	T	W	T	F	S
1	2	3	4	5	6	7
8	9	10	11	12	13	14
15	16	17	18	19	20	21
22	23	24	25	26	27	28
29	30					

OCTOBER
S	M	T	W	T	F	S
		1	2	3	4	5
6	7	8	9	10	11	12
13	14	15	16	17	18	19
20	21	22	23	24	25	26
27	28	29	30	31		

NOVEMBER
S	M	T	W	T	F	S
					1	2
3	4	5	6	7	8	9
10	11	12	13	14	15	16
17	18	19	20	21	22	23
24	25	26	27	28	29	30

DECEMBER
S	M	T	W	T	F	S
1	2	3	4	5	6	7
8	9	10	11	12	13	14
15	16	17	18	19	20	21
22	23	24	25	26	27	28
29	30	31				

2025

JANUARY
S	M	T	W	T	F	S
			1	2	3	4
5	6	7	8	9	10	11
12	13	14	15	16	17	18
19	20	21	22	23	24	25
26	27	28	29	30	31	

FEBRUARY
S	M	T	W	T	F	S
						1
2	3	4	5	6	7	8
9	10	11	12	13	14	15
16	17	18	19	20	21	22
23	24	25	26	27	28	

MARCH
S	M	T	W	T	F	S
						1
2	3	4	5	6	7	8
9	10	11	12	13	14	15
16	17	18	19	20	21	22
23	24	25	26	27	28	29
30	31					

APRIL
S	M	T	W	T	F	S
		1	2	3	4	5
6	7	8	9	10	11	12
13	14	15	16	17	18	19
20	21	22	23	24	25	26
27	28	29	30			

MAY
S	M	T	W	T	F	S
				1	2	3
4	5	6	7	8	9	10
11	12	13	14	15	16	17
18	19	20	21	22	23	24
25	26	27	28	29	30	31

JUNE
S	M	T	W	T	F	S
1	2	3	4	5	6	7
8	9	10	11	12	13	14
15	16	17	18	19	20	21
22	23	24	25	26	27	28
29	30					

JULY
S	M	T	W	T	F	S
		1	2	3	4	5
6	7	8	9	10	11	12
13	14	15	16	17	18	19
20	21	22	23	24	25	26
27	28	29	30	31		

AUGUST
S	M	T	W	T	F	S
					1	2
3	4	5	6	7	8	9
10	11	12	13	14	15	16
17	18	19	20	21	22	23
24	25	26	27	28	29	30
31						

SEPTEMBER
S	M	T	W	T	F	S
	1	2	3	4	5	6
7	8	9	10	11	12	13
14	15	16	17	18	19	20
21	22	23	24	25	26	27
28	29	30				

OCTOBER
S	M	T	W	T	F	S
			1	2	3	4
5	6	7	8	9	10	11
12	13	14	15	16	17	18
19	20	21	22	23	24	25
26	27	28	29	30	31	

NOVEMBER
S	M	T	W	T	F	S
						1
2	3	4	5	6	7	8
9	10	11	12	13	14	15
16	17	18	19	20	21	22
23	24	25	26	27	28	29
30						

DECEMBER
S	M	T	W	T	F	S
	1	2	3	4	5	6
7	8	9	10	11	12	13
14	15	16	17	18	19	20
21	22	23	24	25	26	27
28	29	30	31			

2026

JANUARY
S	M	T	W	T	F	S
				1	2	3
4	5	6	7	8	9	10
11	12	13	14	15	16	17
18	19	20	21	22	23	24
25	26	27	28	29	30	31

FEBRUARY
S	M	T	W	T	F	S
1	2	3	4	5	6	7
8	9	10	11	12	13	14
15	16	17	18	19	20	21
22	23	24	25	26	27	28

MARCH
S	M	T	W	T	F	S
1	2	3	4	5	6	7
8	9	10	11	12	13	14
15	16	17	18	19	20	21
22	23	24	25	26	27	28
29	30	31				

APRIL
S	M	T	W	T	F	S
			1	2	3	4
5	6	7	8	9	10	11
12	13	14	15	16	17	18
19	20	21	22	23	24	25
26	27	28	29	30		